SHORTLIST

Paris
2011

WHAT'S NEW | WHAT'S ON | WHAT'S BEST

www.timeout.com/paris

Contents

Paris by Area

Essentials

Published by Time Out Guides Ltd
Universal House
251 Tottenham Court Road
London W1T 7AB
Tel: + 44 (0)20 7813 3000
Fax: + 44 (0)20 7813 6001
Email: guides@timeout.com
www.timeout.com

Managing Director Peter Fiennes
Editorial Director Ruth Jarvis
Business Manager Daniel Allen
Editorial Manager Holly Pick
Assistant Management Accountant Ija Krasnikova

Time Out Guides is a wholly owned subsidiary of Time Out Group Ltd.

© **Time Out Group Ltd**
Director & Founder Tony Elliott
Chief Executive Officer David King
Group Financial Director Paul Rakkar
Group General Manager/Director Nichola Coulthard
Time Out Communications Ltd MD David Pepper
Time Out International Ltd MD Cathy Runciman
Time Out Magazine Ltd Publisher/Managing Director Mark Elliott
Group Commercial Director Graeme Tottle
Production Director Mark Lamond
Group IT Director Simon Chappell

Time Out and the Time Out logo are trademarks of Time Out Group Ltd.

This edition first published in Great Britain in 2010 by Ebury Publishing
A Random House Group Company
Company information can be found on www.randomhouse.co.uk
Random House UK Limited Reg. No. 954009
10 9 8 7 6 5 4 3 2 1

Distributed in the US and Latin America by Publishers Group West (1-510-809-3700)
Distributed in Canada by Publishers Group Canada (1-800-747-8147)

For further distribution details, see www.timeout.com

ISBN: 978-1-84670-191-7

A CIP catalogue record for this book is available from the British Library.

Printed and bound in Germany by Appl.

Paris Shortlist

The **Time Out Paris Shortlist 2011** is one of a new series of annual guides that draws on Time Out's background as a magazine publisher to keep you current with what's going on in town. As well as Paris's key sights and the best of its eating, drinking and leisure options, it picks out the most exciting venues to have opened in the last year and gives a full calendar of events from September 2010 to December 2011. It also includes features on the important news, trends and openings, all compiled by locally based editors and writers. Whether you're visiting for the first time in your life or the first time this year, you'll find the *Time Out Paris Shortlist* contains all you need to know, in a portable and easy-to-use format.

The guide divides central Paris into ten areas, each containing listings for Sights & Museums, Eating & Drinking, Shopping, Nightlife and Arts & Leisure, and maps pinpointing their locations. At the front of the book are chapters rounding up these scenes city-wide, and giving a shortlist of our overall picks. We include itineraries for days out, plus essentials such as transport information and hotels.

Our listings give phone numbers as dialled within France. From abroad, use your country's exit code followed by 33 (the country code for France) and the number given, dropping the initial '0'.

We have noted price categories by using one to four euro signs (€-€€€€), representing budget, moderate, expensive and luxury.

Major credit cards are accepted unless otherwise stated. We also indicate when a venue is NEW, and give Event highlights.

All our listings are double-checked, but places do sometimes close or change their hours or prices, so it's a good idea to call a venue before visiting. While every effort has been made to ensure accuracy, the publishers cannot accept responsibility for any errors that this guide may contain.

Venues are marked on the maps using symbols numbered according to their order within the chapter and colour-coded as follows:

❶ Sights & Museums
❶ Eating & Drinking
❶ Shopping
❶ Nightlife
❶ Arts & Leisure

Map key	
Major sight or landmark	▮
Hospital or college	▮
Railway station	▮
Park	▮
River	▮
Autoroute	═
Main road	
Main road tunnel	
Pedestrian road	▮
Arrondissement boundary	—
Airport	✈
Church	✚
Métro station	Ⓜ
RER station	ⓇⒺⓇ
Area Name	LES HALLES

Time Out **Paris** Shortlist 2011

EDITORIAL
Editor Dominic Earle
Proofreader Marion Moisy

DESIGN
Art Director Scott Moore
Art Editor Pinelope Kourmouzoglou
Senior Designer Kei Ishimaru
Group Commercial Designer Jodi Sher
Picture Editor Jael Marschner
Acting Deputy Picture Editor Liz Leahy
Picture Desk Assistant/Researcher
Ben Rowe

ADVERTISING
New Business & Commercial Director
Mark Phillips

International Advertising Manager
Kasimir Berger
Head of French Advertising Sales
Charlie Sokol

MARKETING
**Sales & Marketing Director, North America
& Latin America** Lisa Levinson
Senior Publishing Brand Manager
Luthfa Begum
Group Commercial Art Director
Anthony Huggins
Marketing Co-ordinator Alana Benton

PRODUCTION
Production Manager Brendan McKeown
Production Controller Katie Mulhern

CONTRIBUTORS
This guide was researched and written by the writers of *Time Out Paris*.
The editor would like to thank Eurostar.

PHOTOGRAPHY
Photography by Oliver Knight; except pages 8, 161 Elan Fleisher; page 21 Dave Bruel;
pages 26, 50, 55, 56, 95, 100, 153 Olivia Rutherford; pages 34, 47, 48, 49,
119, 122, 141 Heloise Bergman; pages 41, 44, 45, 52, 53, 158 Karl Blackwell;
page 51 Jean-Christophe Godet; page 80 Ben Rowe.

The following images were provided by the featured establishemts/artists: pages 37,
38, 93.

Cover Image: Fisheye view of the Paris cityscape from Sacre Coeur. Credit: Photolibrary.com

MAPS
JS Graphics (john@jsgraphics.co.uk).

About **Time Out**

Founded in 1968, Time Out has expanded from humble London beginnings into the
leading resource for those wanting to know what's happening in the world's greatest
cities. As well as our influential what's-on weeklies in London, New York and Chicago,
we publish nearly 30 other listings magazines in cities as varied as Beijing and Mumbai.
The magazines established Time Out's trademark style: sharp writing, informed
reviewing and bang up-to-date inside knowledge of every scene.

Time Out made the natural leap into travel guides in the 1980s with the City Guide
series, which now extends to over 50 destinations around the world. Written and
researched by expert local writers and generously illustrated with original photography,
the full-size guides cover a larger area than our Shortlist guides and include many more
venue reviews, along with additional background features and a full set of maps.

Throughout this rapid growth, the company has remained proudly independent,
still owned by Tony Elliott four decades after he started Time Out London as a single
fold-out sheet of A5 paper. This independence extends to the editorial content of all
our publications, this Shortlist included. No establishment has been featured because
it has advertised, and no payment has influenced any of our reviews. And, for our critics,
there's definitely no such thing as a free lunch: all restaurants and bars are visited
and reviewed anonymously, and Time Out always picks up the bill.
For more about the company, see www.timeout.com.

Don't Miss 2011

Sights & Museums

In April 2009 Sarkozy presented his project for a Grand Paris ('Greater Paris'), with many observers dubbing it the most ambitious plan for the capital since Baron Haussmann reshaped the city with his famed rectilinear boulevards in the mid 19th century. In many ways, the project typifies the kind of brash ambition that has already landed Sarkozy a pop-star wife. French presidents like to leave their mark on Paris.

Pompidou bequeathed a cultural centre bearing his name, Chirac left behind the elegant Musée du Quai Branly, and Mitterrand pushed through a whole gamut of architectural *grands projets*, including the pyramid at the Louvre and the Opéra Bastille. For Sarkozy, though, a mere monument is not quite enough; he wants to transform the city's very fabric. It's an open secret that Sarkozy wants a 'greater Paris' more in line with the London model than the French capital's current set-up, and bringing that aim to fruition will entail vast building projects that would make the *grands projets* of his predecessors – such as the Louvre pyramid (see p74), the Opéra Bastille (see p115) and the Musée du Quai Branly (see p125) – look like a child's Lego set.

The main focus of the projects – more skyscrapers at La Défense, a skyscraper just inside the city ring road (*horreur!*) and the remaking of a great swathe of the east of the city – is economic, not cultural; but Sarkozy's fixation with status is offset by the more fun-loving, arts-oriented agenda of the city's mayor, Bertrand Delanoë. On his watch,

Paris has produced some superb new additions to its line-up of museums and attractions – things like the Cité de l'Architecture et du Patrimoine (see p57) and the 104 multimedia arts centre built in premises previously occupied by the city's undertakers (see p159).

The most long-awaited project, though, is undoubtedly the ultra-ambitious Cité de la Mode et du Design, whose opening date has been continually put back. Notwithstanding further setbacks, it should finally be open in late 2010. As a hub for the Paris fashion crowd, the complex promises to bring trendy designers and nocturnal thrill seekers to a previously lifeless Seine-side area near the Gare d'Austerlitz.

Across the rest of the city, the list of sights worth your time is almost endless – from iconic treasures like the Eiffel Tower (see p122) to lesser-known gems like the Musée Jean-Jacques Henner (see p61). All this, and much more that we haven't yet mentioned, in a city that's a manageable size and boasts one of the best transport networks anywhere in the world.

The lie of the land

Parisians identify parts of their city by two systems: there are the named districts, whose frontiers aren't always clear – the Marais, the Latin Quarter, Montparnasse and so on – and the 20 numbered arrondissements that spiral out, clockwise and in ascending order, from the Louvre. Together they comprise an urban jigsaw that the novelist Julien Green once compared to a model of the human brain. Each piece has a particular connotation or function: the fifth is academic; the sixth is arty and chic; the 16th is wealthy and dull; while the 18th, 19th and 20th

SHORTLIST

Best new
- Cité de la Mode et du Design (see left)

Best revamped
- Arc de Triomphe (see p56)
- Musée National Jean-Jacques Henner (see p61)

Best secret
- La Collection 1900 (see p70)
- Musée Fragonard (see p159)

Best art
- Centre Pompidou (see p100)
- Musée du Louvre (see p74)
- Musée d'Orsay (see p133)
- Musée de l'Orangerie (see p74)

Best dead
- Cimetière du Montparnasse (see p154)
- Cimetière du Père-Lachaise (see p101)

Best outdoors
- Jardin du Luxembourg (see p130)
- Bois de Boulogne (see p160)
- Parc des Buttes-Chaumont (see p96)

Best views
- Arc de Triomphe (see p56)
- Cathédrale Notre-Dame (see p118)
- Eiffel Tower (see p122)
- Institut du Monde Arabe (see p144)
- Sacré-Coeur (see p88)
- Tour Montparnasse (see p155)

Best tours
- Bateaux-Mouches (see p57)
- Canauxrama (see p95)
- Vedettes du Pont-Neuf (see p116)

The Sightseeing cruise of Paris
by Vedettes de Paris ✦

Get the best of Paris in 1 hour

www.vedettesdeparis.com

The magic of Paris by Night

Location:
Right by the Eiffel Tower
Port de Suffren, 7th district + 00 33 (0)1 44 18 19 50
M° Bir-Hakeim & Trocadero; RER Champs de Mars

The Parisian sightseeing cruise has to be at the top of
your list of things to do when in the French capital.
Ideally located right by the Eiffel Tower, its charming
boats enhance the pleasure of a guided cruise on the
River Seine.
Listed by the UNESCO World Heritage, the river banks
offer you some of the most appreciated and well-known
monuments such as the Eiffel Tower, the Louvre and
Notre Dame Cathedral amongst others.
Recorded multilingual commentary and a bar service
on board.

Departures :
Everyday: Departures every 30-45 mins from 11am
to 10pm. Times vary depending on the season.
Check our websitesite for exact times.

Sightseeing or "by Night"cruise: Adult: 11€;
Children 5-12s: 5€; free under 4s

PASTA PARTY

Exclusive : Sparkling cruise
Sightseeing cruise + 1 Glass of Champagne for 16€

✦ Special offer for Time Out Readers *

La Terrasse: **outdoor restaurant**

Discover the **heart of Paris**

arrondissements are riotously multicultural. Residents are frequently assessed, on first meeting at least, by their postcode, and as a consequence often develop a fierce sense of local pride. Indeed, many of them will tell you that Paris isn't so much a city as a jumble of villages, each pungently and defiantly distinctive.

We've divided this book into areas, though not necessarily into shapes that residents would recognise; we've imagined the city as a series of visitor friendly concentrations of shops, sights, restaurants and bars. The Champs-Elysées & Western Paris section has the famous avenue as its spine, lined with high-end shops and showrooms. It also contains fashion's most glamorous thoroughfare, avenue Montaigne, which is almost matched in lustre and allure by rue du Fbg-Saint-Honoré.

Montmartre & Pigalle has, at its northern end, picturesque Montmartre with its vertiginous flights of steps, narrow winding streets and the massive bulk

of Sacré-Coeur (see p88). To the south lies Pigalle, famous for the Moulin Rouge and its strip clubs and scuzzy bars (though it's a good deal more salubrious today than it once was).

Opéra to Les Halles used to be the centre of royal power in Paris, and you can get a sense of this by taking a stroll around the Palais-Royal (see p74). Today, however, it's the city's commercial and cultural powerhouse: it's home to the massive Les Halles shopping complex, the jewellers and fashion houses of place Vendôme, and to the Louvre, Palais Garnier (see p86) and Monet showcase Musée de l'Orangerie (see p74).

North-eastern Paris is the area visitors from the UK are likely to see first: Eurostar trains terminate at the Gare du Nord (see p95) in the tenth arrondissement. The area is on the up, with its main artery, the charming Canal St-Martin, lined with chic boutiques and cafés. Further north and east of here is the magnificently odd Parc des Buttes-Chaumont (see p96), a warren of cliffs and grottoes carved

Musée de l'Orangerie

LE PARIS DES PARISIENS*

© Photos : S.N.T.E. Éclairage de la Tour Eiffel, Illuminations Pierre Bideau, idea stock photos, Cercle de Craie. Photos du monde

*The most parisian journey

Sightseeing Cruise
Lunch Cruise
Dinner Cruise
Private Cruise

Bateaux Parisiens

At the foot of the Eiffel Tower

Port de la Bourdonnais - 75007 Paris

Tel. : +33(0)1 76 64 14 45

www.bateauxparisiens.com

out of a former quarry. Marais, Bastille & Eastern Paris is barfly territory, especially along rue Oberkampf, rue Jean-Pierre Timbaud and rue St-Maur. The ever-trendy Marais is chock-full of independent galleries and quirky shops, and is also the centre of gay life in Paris.

The Islands – the Ile de la Cité, the oldest part of the city and home to Notre-Dame cathedral (see p118), and the more elegant Ile St-Louis, with its shops and restaurants – are highly distinctive and essential ports of call.

Undeniably, the main attraction of the affluent (and sometimes stuffily institutional) 7th & Western Paris area is the Eiffel Tower, the universal emblem of the French capital. Its elegant ironwork is most alluring at night, when it is lit up by tens of thousands of shimmering lightbulbs. This is also the best time to climb it, because the queues are at their shortest.

For many years, St-Germain-des-Prés was the intellectual heartland of the city, home to Sartre and de Beauvoir. But these days it's more about fashion than philosophy, and the expensive cafés are no place for starving writers. The city's most beautiful park, the Jardin du Luxembourg (see p130), won't cost you a sou, however; and the Musée d'Orsay (see p133), currently undergoing major renovations, is still excellent value. Due east, the Latin Quarter is home to several of Paris's most august academic institutions, including the Sorbonne. And to the south, Montparnasse, although no longer the artistic stronghold it was in the 1920s, still boasts a number of excellent cafés and restaurants, and the resting place of some of France's most illustrious dead, the Cimetière du Montparnasse (see p154).

The only missing piece in Paris's cultural jigsaw at the moment is the Musée Picasso, which has been closed since 2009 for extensive renovation work, designed to upgrade facilities and increase exhibition space for a reopening in 2012. But Picasso fans need not despair: Paris still provides opportunities aplenty to view the works of its famed former resident, from the Pompidou Centre to the Musée de l'Orangerie. Besides its Monet waterlilies, the museum is home to the collection of Paul Guillaume, which includes a dozen mostly early Picassos.

Getting around

Vélib', the municipal bike hire scheme that puts some 20,000 bicycles at the disposal of residents and visitors, continues to flourish, and in 2009 the scheme moved beyond the Périphérique. If you don't feel confident about your chances in Paris traffic, the métro is extensive and reliable, and buses are clean, frequent and cheap. Some of the bus routes are worth riding just for the sightseeing opportunities they offer; no.24 takes you through St-Germain-des-Prés and the Latin Quarter; no.69 runs all the way from Gambetta in the east, via the Louvre, to the Champ de Mars in the west; and no.73 connects the Champs-Elysées to the futuristic concrete jungle of La Défense.

But when all is said and done, you can't beat walking. Paris is compact enough to be navigated on foot, and this is the best way to hear the heartbeat of the city. This way you'll discover that far from being a 'museum city' suffocating under the weight of its 'heritage', Paris is a thriving capital that looks to the future without ever forgetting its past.

Granterroirs p62

Eating & Drinking

Despite the recent economic gloom, restaurants continue to thrive in Paris. Wander through the streets of St-Germain, the Marais, Canal St-Martin or Pigalle any night of the week and you'll be hard-pressed to find a table, while the most popular restaurants fill up weeks or months ahead.

The ongoing health of restaurants is good news for visitors, who will find that in most cases prices have remained stable or gone down while chefs make a greater effort to provide good value. Contributing to that is the lowering of the TVA (VAT) for restaurants from 19.6 per cent to 5.5 per cent. In return for this tax break, restaurant owners agreed to reduce their prices on at least seven of ten key menu items, such as the *plat du jour*, children's menu, dessert and coffee. If many

restaurateurs seem to have forgotten this part of the bargain, others have co-operated – in this case, the old and new prices are clearly marked.

New arrivals

A notable new arrival is Frenchie (see p76), a brick-walled bistro run by a young French chef who previously worked with Jamie Oliver. His limited-choice set menu, which often surprises with unexpected flavour combinations, keeps the locals coming back for two dinner sittings every night. The past year has also seen the opening of the city's first raw food restaurant, Cru (see p109), which has a stunning courtyard terrace. For the fashion-minded, the apartment-restaurant Derrière (see p109) is the latest place to be seen digging into a help-yourself terrine of chocolate mousse.

Since the smoking ban came into effect, Parisians have gradually been growing more health-conscious. This shows in the popularity of cafés such as Rose Bakery (see p92) and the new Cantine Merci (see p109), where a plate of crunchy salads topped with sprouts and served with carrot juice might replace the traditional steak-frites washed down with red wine. For guilt-free organic grub, you can't beat Le Ruban Vert (42 rue des Jeûneurs, 2nd, 01.40.28.97.41, www.lerubanvert.com) with a daily-changing menu of home-made soups (mushroom, carrot and orange, sweet potato and pea), salads and *tartines*.

Bistro boom

Thankfully, the French continue to love their classic grub, which can be found in slightly updated form (think snails in puff pastry with oyster mushrooms and romaine lettuce) at the latest neo-bistros such as Le Miroir (see p91), as well as along more traditional lines – where locals go to be greeted with a handshake and a smile, where wine comes in carafes and the dishes make you feel warm inside. L'Ambassade d'Auvergne (see p107), for example, deliberately serves only time-honoured (often regional) dishes. Though a full bistro meal rarely comes in at less than €30 without drinks, it's often better value than a mediocre café.

Brasseries still have their appeal, even if most now belong to chains such as the Flo group, the Frères Blanc or the Costes. The spectacle of sitting amid art nouveau extravagance, as waiters in black and white rush between tables serving platters of oysters and choucroute, comes at a price, but is cheaper at lunchtime or late at night. Bofinger (see p107) and

SHORTLIST

Best new
- Cantine Merci (see p109)
- Derrière (see p109)
- Frenchie (see p76)
- Thaïm (see p78)

Best value
- Le Hangar (see p110)
- A la Bière (see p96)
- L'Encrier (see p109)
- Rouge Passion (see p92)

Most glamorous
- Alain Ducasse
  au Plaza Athénée (see p62)
- L'Arpège (see p126)
- Café de la Paix (see p76)
- Jules Verne (see p128)
- Lapérouse (see p147)
- Le Meurice (see p78)

Bars with character
- Café Charbon (see p109)
- Chez Jeanette (see p99)
- La Fourmi (see p91)
- La Palette (see p134)
- La Perle (see p110)

Cocktail classics
- Café Marly (see p75)
- Le Crocodile (see p146)
- Le Fumoir (see p76)
- Lizard Lounge (see p110)

Best for nighthawks
- Le Brébant (see p88)
- Harry's New York Bar
  (see p76)
- Le Sancerre (see p92)
- Le Tambour (see p78)

Regional stars
- L'Ambassade
  d'Auvergne (see p107)
- L'Ami Jean (see p126)
- Le Chateaubriand
  (see p109)
- Le Ch'ti Catalan (see p91)
- Granterroirs (see p62)

Located in the heart of the Latin Quarter,
the Bouillon Racine combines art nouveau charm and
exceptionally tasty food.

Open daily noon-11pm
Live jazz 1st & 3rd Tuesdays of the month
3 rue Racine, 6th. M° Odéon.
Tel: 01.44.32.15.60
Email.bouillon.racine@wanadoo.fr
www.bouillonracine.com

La Coupole (see p157), both part of the Flo chain, pull in a crowd of locals and tourists. The Costes brothers set the standard for the modern brasserie experience in Paris with stylish restaurants like Le Georges (6th floor, Centre Pompidou, 19 rue Beaubourg, 4th, 01.44.78.47.99); they have also taken over a few vintage bistros, such as Chez Julien (1 rue du Pont Louis-Philippe, 4th, 01.42.78.31.64).

Top tables

To crank it up a notch, you could opt for a spot of all-out luxury in one of the city's haute cuisine restaurants. And it doesn't come much more haute than Jules Verne (see p128), Alain Ducasse's classy venue perched in its eyrie on the second floor of the Eiffel Tower. For once, the food is as good as the views, with dishes such as turbot with champagne zabaglione. Other sumptuous dining experiences are to be had at Le Meurice (see p78), Stella Maris (see p64) and Alain Passard's L'Arpège (see p126).

Restaurants where you can easily spend €200 or more a head often have lunch menus for €75-€80 – still a lot of money, but for this you are treated to a full-blown experience from *amuse-bouches* to *mignardises*. Ordering the lunch menu often means having a more limited choice of dishes, but they are likely to draw on the freshest ingredients from the market. A notch down from haute cuisine, restaurants such as Le Restaurant (see p134) and Pétrelle (see p91) offer sumptuous dining experiences for less than €100 per person.

Café culture

A growing trend is the Anglo-style snack shop. Cojean (17 bd Haussmann, 9th, 01.47.70.22.65),

La Ferme (55 rue St-Roch, 1st, 01.40.20.12.12), Bioboa (3 rue Danielle-Casanova, 1st, 01.42.61.17.67) and Bob's Juice Bar (15 rue Lucien Sampaix, 10th, 06.82.63.72.74) all serve healthy sandwiches, soups, salads and juices to eat in or take out. The Anglo theme continues at boho-chic Rose Bakery (see p91) and Rose Bakery II (30 rue Debelleyme, 3rd, 01.49.96.54.01), where organic soups, quiches and inventive salads have shown Parisians that the British know a thing or two about nosh. Bread & Roses (see p133) is a mostly organic bakery run by a French couple that is passionate about British food, especially cakes.

The ubiquitous Parisian café, where wine is cheaper than water, is still present, although the iconic, scruffy neighbourhood haunt with its peeling paintwork is fortunately becoming a thing of the past. Many cafés have upgraded their interiors and prices accordingly, but you can

Café de la Paix p19

O'Sullivans
Irish pubs , clubs & restaurants – Paris

O'Sullivans by the mill 92 Boulevard de Clichy 75018 Paris M°2 Blanche

O'Sullivans café bar 1 Boulevard Montmartre 75002 Paris M° 8/9 Grands Boulevards

O'Sullivans rebel bar 10 Rue des Lombards 75004 Paris M° 1 Hotel de ville

Music , madness , fresh sports , live bartenders , early mornings , late nights
w w w . o s u l l i v a n s - p u b s . c o m

still find affordable snacks such as omelettes and croques monsieur. Just a handful of addresses cling to their shabby-chic image – generally in the artsy north-east. A perfect example is Chez Jeanette (see p99), which despite the new owner's decision to preserve the 1970s decor, grease 'n' all, has never been busier. If grime gets you down, you still can't beat a chic café experience in the famous Left Bank institutions Les Deux Magots (see p134) and Café de Flore (see p133), or at Café de la Paix (see p76), whose millefeuilles are unrivalled.

If you're after something stronger, the tenth and 11th, especially around rue Oberkampf, continue to be the most happening areas for bars. Café Charbon (see p109), which acts as both a restaurant and pre-club cocktail bar, and L'Alimentation Générale (see p106), whose excellent concerts give stage space to up-and-coming musicians, are the places to be seen. Other trendy locals gravitate to grungy all-nighters like Le Sancerre (see p92) or La Fourmi (see p91). Also worth a trip is the area of St-Blaise, in the 20th, where a handful of buzzing venues have turned the area into a hub of city subculture. Pick of the bunch include the Piston Pélican (15 rue de Bagnolet, 20th, 01.43.71.15.76) and the Flèche d'Or (102bis rue de Bagnolet, 20th, 01.44.64.01.02).

For those with money to burn, the city's other party central is the area around Champs-Elysées. Abandoned by all but a 'wannabe' crowd a few years ago, the area has regained favour with the smart set and now boasts some very posh addresses indeed.

In the know

Except for the very simplest restaurants, it's wise to book ahead. This can usually be done on the same day as your intended visit, although really top-notch establishments require bookings weeks or even months in advance and confirmation the day before. Many venues close for their annual break in August, and some also close at Christmas. All bills include a service charge, but an additional tip of a few euros (for the whole table) is polite unless you're unhappy with the service.

As a general rule, the closer the tourist site and the better the view, the worse the food – although there are exceptions, such as bistro Au Bon Accueil (14 rue de Monttessuy, 7th, 01.47.05.46.11), which serves sophisticated fare with a view of the Eiffel Tower from its terrace.

If you are looking for a snack, bear in mind that the hundreds of Chinese 'traiteurs' in Paris are almost uniformly mediocre, reheating dishes in a microwave while you wait. You are much better off finding a bakery or packing a picnic and saving your cash for a special dinner. There are a number of decent crêperies around Montparnasse, where the Bretons originally settled, or you could try gourmet crêperie Breizh Café (109 rue Vieille-du-Temple, 3rd, 01.42.72.13.77) in the Marais.

Apart from fast-food outlets, non-French food is increasingly popular. The streets around Belleville (20th) and the southern end of the 13th are crammed with decent Chinese, Vietnamese and Laotian restaurants; the second, around rue Ste Anne, is flourishing with Japanese eateries, including the excellent Kaï (see p78). Rue des Rosiers in the Marais is a centre for Jewish cooking, and Italian, Indian, Moroccan and Lebanese cuisine can be found across the city.

Finally, try to avoid anywhere with a menu labelled 'menu touristique' or 'we speak English'.

L'Eclaireur p22

WHAT'S BEST
Shopping

With the looming prospect of relaxed Sunday trading laws, Paris shopping has never been in better shape. Where else in the world can you find so many independent boutiques and specialist shops, in the middle of some of the most picturesque areas of the city? Whether it's tasting cheeses for a dinner party, getting measured up for a bra or selecting handmade gloves or a one-off piece of vintage clothing, shopping in Paris is a sensual pleasure based around quality, not quantity. Although chain stores have made their mark, it's a long way removed from the uniformity of so many provincial high streets.

Different areas of the city have different specialities. There are clusters of antiques shops in the seventh arrondissement, and second-hand and rare book outlets in the fifth; crystal and porcelain manufacturers still dot rue de Paradis in the tenth; furniture craftsmen as well as children's clothes shops inhabit rue du Fbg-St-Antoine; bikes and cameras are clustered on boulevard Beaumarchais; and the world's top jewellers can be found on place Vendôme. The historic covered passages in the second and ninth are also fun places in which to shop, with chic stores mixed in with philatelists and booksellers.

Family-run food shops have thankfully not been eroded by supermarket culture, and tend to cluster in 'market streets' such as rue des Martyrs and rue Mouffetard, as well as around the many covered and open-air food markets. Here everything from a vintage bottle of armagnac to a single praline chocolate is lovingly presented, served and wrapped. Informed discussion is still very much part of the purchasing process, and beautiful, old-style shops, unchanged for decades, add to the pleasure.

Green, organic and ethical have also suddenly become sexy concepts to the French. Even luxury brands have embraced them, seen at the first sustainable luxury trade fair, called 1.618, at the Palais de Tokyo in May 2009. The not-for-profit concept store Merci (see p112) offers guilt-free clothes shopping, and Designpack Gallery (see p79) recycles packaging into funky and ingenious objects for the home.

Cool concept

The concept shop trend is a central feature of the shopping scene, crossing the boundaries between clothes, music and product design. The capital's concept kings have very different personalities. There's cosmopolitan, metropolitan, glamorous but down-with-the-kids Colette (see p79); bobo I-probably-care-more-about-my-home-than-my-wardrobe Merci; sophisticated, avant-garde L'Eclaireur (see p112). And then the smaller ones: tomboyish Spree (16 rue de La Vieuville, 18th, 01.42.23.41.40, www.spree.fr), full of music and film industry cool; and new girl on the block Hotel Particulier (15 rue Léopold Bellan, 2nd, 01.40.39.90.00, www.hotelparticulier-paris.com). But what they all have in common is a product range that is both entertainingly diverse and seductively scarce.

At Colette, you can find Zippo lighters a few feet away from Smythson diaries, a few feet away from Ladurée macaroons, all one

Le Bon Marché

flight of stairs away from Alexander Wang and Valentino. At Merci, perfume and porcelain sit happily alongside each other on the main floor. And in Spree, antique furniture at the entrance gives way to a corridor with Dr Hauschka cleansers and toners, which in turn opens on to a room with racks of cute designer clothes. On the high-tech front, Sony has opened its first European concept store, Sony Style, on avenue George V (see p67).

Boutique chic

The stretch of rue St-Honoré and rue du Fbg-St-Honoré from the Hôtel Costes to the Hôtel Bristol is wall-to-wall fashion boutiques, with Givenchy (see p65), Lanvin (see p82) and Jimmy Choo (376 rue St-Honoré, 8th, 01.58.62.50.40) the three major highlights.

Rue Boissy d'Anglas has a branch of L'Eclaireur with its Fornassetti café (10 rue Boissy d'Anglas, 8th, 01.53.43.03.70, www.leclaireur.com) and Paris's other famous fashion picker Maria Luisa (7 rue Rouget de Lisle, 1st, 01.47.03.96.15) is just a step away.

Avenue Montaigne's headliners include Fendi at no.22, the Roberto Cavalli flagship at no.50 and, next door at no.52, Ralph Lauren's three-floor womenswear store in the former home of couturier Madeleine Vionnet. Agnès B has joined the more casual crowd infiltrating the Golden Triangle (38 av George V, 01.40.73.81.10). The small streets criss-crossing the Golden Triangle also have a few surprises, such as Lola.J (15 rue Clément Marot, 8th, 01.47.23.87.40), a boutique that brings together luxury clothes with attitude for men and women, including Ni-Search Swarovski-studded jeans.

Palais-Royal & around

If you're visiting Colette, don't miss a detour to the Marché St-Honoré. This former food market, rebuilt in glass by Ricardo Bofill, combines bistros and boutiques, with Marc by Marc Jacobs (see p83) the big attraction.

Easily reached on foot from here, the Palais-Royal just gets better and better. On the eastern side, galerie du Valois has Stella McCartney (see p84), cult Swedish brand Acne Jeans at no.124, the covetable and racy gloves of Maison Fabre at no.128, and Paris star Robert Normand (see p83). Opposite, with the idyllic gardens in between, is galerie de Montpensier containing Marc Jacobs (see p83) and vintage wear from Didier Ludot (see p81), as well as Martin Margiela in the road behind (see p83). Also in the area is Kitsuné (52 rue de Richelieu, 1st, 01.42.60.34.28), the record label now selling its own-brand clothing.

SHORTLIST

Best new
- Designpack Gallery (see p79)
- Merci (see p112)
- Purple Ice (see p83)

Best concept stores
- Colette (see p79)
- L'Eclaireur (see p112)
- LE66 (see p65)
- Merci (see p112)

Best hand-picked fashion
- L'Eclaireur (see p112)
- Kokon To Zai (see p82)

Best for accessories
- Colette (see p79)
- Marc by Marc Jacobs (see p83)

Best for eveningwear
- Lanvin (see p82)
- Yves Saint Laurent (see p140)

Best souvenirs
- Arty Dandy (see p136)
- Diptyque (see p149)

Best food and wine
- Alléosse (see p64)
- Christian Constant (see p136)
- Lavinia (see p82)
- Du Pain et des Idées (see p111)
- Pierre Hermé (see p139)
- Première Pression Provence (see p114)

Literary life
- La Hune (see p137)
- I Love My Blender (see p112)
- Shakespeare & Company (see p149)

The classics
- Le Bon Marché (see p136)
- Galeries Lafayette (see p81)
- Printemps (see p83)

DON'T MISS: 2011

Offset your flight with **Trees for Cities** and make your trip mean something for years to come

www.treesforcities.org/offset

Trees for Cities
Charity registration number 1032154

Further east, the Etienne-Marcel area is the centre for club and streetwear with All Saints (49 rue Etienne-Marcel, 1st, 01.44.88.91.30), Kiliwatch (see p82), and the good-looking Purple Ice (see p83) with jeans by Real Real Genuine next to designer bags by JC de Castelbajac.

Marais mode

The northern part of the Marais, dubbed NoMa, has sealed its identity as the essential district for hot and hip fashion. Here, you'll find multi-label boutique Shine (see p114), and young French label Swildens (22 rue de Poitou, 3rd, 01.42.71.19.12) which boasts Carla Sarkozy as a client. Stylish menswear is also strong here, with Frenchtrotters Homme (116 rue Vieille-du-Temple, 3rd, 01.44.61. 00.14. www.frenchtrotters.fr), and Christophe Lemaire's lounge lizard separates (28 rue de Poitou, 3rd, 01.44.78.00.09).

Going Gauche

St-Germain tends to be more conservative, but is increasingly offering a mirror image of the Right Bank with brands insisting on a presence on both sides of the Seine. These include Paul & Joe (see p139) and Vanessa Bruno (see p140). Shoe heaven is found along rue de Grenelle with all the top brands. Other highlights include bobo bags in colourful fabrics and denim from the former prêt-à-porter designer Jérome Dreyfuss (1 rue Jacob, 6th, 01.43.54.70.93), Hélène Lamey's French-made nightwear and childrenswear at Bluet (18 rue du Pré-aux-Clercs, 7th, 01.45.44.00.26), and multi-brand shop Kyrie Eleison (15 carrefour de l'Odéon, 6th, 01.46.34.26.91) with lush creations by Orla Kiely, Eros-Erotokritos, Velvet and La Fée Parisienne.

On the luxury scene, opium-coloured walls and lacquered ceilings provide a showcase for Stephane Pilati's creations at Yves Saint Laurent (see p140), while at Sonia Rykiel's St-Germain flagship (see p140) black mosaics, smoked glass and multiple mirrors evoke a '70s nightclub. And if you're in the market for some jewellery, don't miss out on a trip to Marie Hélène de Taillac's Left Bank store (see p139), a Tom Dixon-designed space.

Foodie heaven

The new layout of Fauchon (28 & 30 pl de la Madeleine, 8th, 01.70.39.38.00), with different areas (pâtisserie, bakery, fruit and vegetables, etc) and chefs on hand at each to offer advice and recipes, provides an excuse to indulge at this luxury store. Food markets are found in all arrondissements – two of the most popular are the historic Marché d'Aligre in the 12th, and the Marché des Enfants Rouges in the 3rd, which focuses on organic produce. Near the Marché d'Aligre, pop into Première Pression Provence (see p114), an olive oil paradise created by L'Occitan founder Olivier Baussan. Foodie streets include rue de Buci (6th), rue des Martyrs (9th) and rue Mouffetard (5th).

Practicalities

Shops are generally open from 10am to 7pm Monday to Saturday. Some are closed on Monday mornings. Sunday opening is found in the Marais, on the Champs-Elysées, at Bercy Village and in the Carrousel du Louvre, although President Sarkozy is trying to extend Sunday trading. Many shops on the Champs-Elysées stay open until midnight, and Thursday is late closing at department stores.

Point Ephémère p28

Nightlife

When it comes to hardcore clubbing, the French capital is no longer a global challenger – serious nighthawks migrated long ago to more happening cities such as London, New York and Berlin, and the best Paris party experiences tend to be reserved for those connected enough to be in the know or on the guestlist. In addition, the ban on all-you-can-drink events in 'open bars', which was introduced in early 2009 in an effort to prevent binge drinking, has dealt a further blow to the city's late night revellers. However, all is not lost after dark: the city is fighting back with a string of great new venues aimed at a more laid-back crowd.

Music-wise, jazz is enjoying a mini revival, talented new rock bands are emerging, as are venues to accommodate them, and *chanson* is managing to reinvent itself for a 21st-century audience.

Nightclubs

Ritzy places such as VIP Room (188 rue de Rivoli, 1st, 01.58.36.46.00) and Le Baron (see p67) are still the talk of the town, but more low-key indie venues such as Panic Room (see p115) are pulling in a diverse crowd – with the emphasis more about having fun than posing.

For big-room clubbing, Queen (see p69) is a gay-friendly club known for its wild disco nights, while Rex (see p85) offers up mainstream and experimental electro on one of the best sound systems in Europe.

For standard house try Le Folie's Pigalle (see p94) or Red Light (see p157), but don't ignore the city's smaller venues, which frequently feature leading DJs. It is not unusual to find Berlin's DJ M.A.N.D.Y at Elysée Montmartre (see p94), Jarvis Cocker at the Nouveau Casino (see p115) or Birdy Nam Nam at the Social Club (142 rue Montmartre, 2nd, 01.40.28.05.55). These intimate gigs are also where you'll discover most of Paris's 'after' parties too, with almost as many early Sunday morning events as there are Saturday nighters. Worth checking out are the floating Batofar (see p152) and, in summer, the Bateau Concorde Atlantique (23 quai Anatole-France, 7th, 01.47.05.71.03).

If you like your clubbing cosy, plenty of bars around Bastille, Oberkampf and the Grands Boulevards are willing to oblige. Panic Room is one of the hippest around, with a stream of French electro nights. Traditionalists can choose their poison too; a host of school disco-type nights where the DJ is no superstar take place at the twice-monthly Bal at Elysée Montmartre, and salsa and world music get a good hammering at Le Divan du Monde (see p94).

Another new nightlife twist is the recent wave of designer-led hotel cocktail bars, which are attracting some big-name DJs. Mama Shelter (see p173) may be famous for its great design by Philippe Starck, but it's also picking up style points for its music selection; the Hôtel Ritz (see p171) boasts some of the finest resident DJs in the bar at weekends; the Murano Urban Resort (see p175) hosts Lucky Star on Thursday nights, when a famous French actor and/or singer takes over the decks; and the Kube Hotel (see p173) has daily DJ sets.

August is traditionally the time when most Paris clubs shut down. But one beacon of summer light is

SHORTLIST

Best new/revamped
- Baxo (see p99)
- Le Régine (see p69)

Best bands
- Le Bataclan (see p114)
- La Cigale (see p94)
- Point Ephémère (see p99)

Best sound systems
- Panic Room (see p115)
- Rex (see p85)

All night long
- Batofar (see p152)
- Red Light (see p157)

Sunday sessions
- La Bellevilloise (see p29)

Perfect for posing
- L'Arc (see p67)
- Le Baron (see p67)

Best for star DJs
- Les Bains Douches (see p114)
- Rex (see p85)

Best for party snacks
- Chacha Club (see p84)
- Le Showcase (see p69)

Best gay club
- Queen (see p69)

Best for jazz
- Caveau de la Huchette (see p149)
- Au Duc des Lombards (see p84)
- Le Sunset/Le Sunside (see p85)

Killer cocktails
- L'Arc (see p67)

Life is a cabaret
- Le Lido (see p67)
- Moulin Rouge (see p94)

Le Showcase p69

Ed Banger Records, which has been throwing amazing parties instead.

Because Paris clubs don't really get going until 2am, people usually hit a DJ bar before, and diehards finish their evening at an 'after' on Sunday morning. Free passes can be found on various flyers; flyer information is available at www. flyersweb.com. Other good sites are www.radiofg.com, www.nova planet.com and www.lemonsound. com. Also look out for big, one-off events in venues such as Rex and Point Ephémère (see p99).

The last métro leaves at around 12.45am (1.45am on Friday and Saturday), and the first gets rolling at 5.45am; in between you'll have to use a night bus, Vélib or taxi.

Rock, roots & jazz

Paris's music scene is bubbling with talent, and the recent emergence of some great new bands speaks volumes about the creativity of today's up-and-coming artists. The capital is overflowing with authentic concert venues, from monster stadiums to intimate bars and jazz clubs, and venues like Nouveau Casino (see p115) and L'International (5-7 rue Moret, 11th, 01.49.29.76.45) give precious stage space to those on the way up the ladder. Much-loved indie and electro venue La Flèche d'Or (102bis rue de Bagnolet, 20th, 01.44.64.01.02), which closed its doors in April 2009, has now reopened under new management.

Chanson française is still going strong, helped by the revival of Les Trois Baudets (see p94), a government-subsidised *chanson* hall in the heart of Pigalle – French law dictates that 40 per cent of music broadcast in France must be in the French language.

Jazz is having a mini revival too: after the disappearance of old flames like Le Slow Club (once one of the most famous jazz joints in Europe), Le Bilboquet and Les 7 Lézards, a handful of new joints have opened up, while flagship clubs Au Duc des Lombards (see p84), New Morning (see p99) and Le Sunset/Le Sunside (see p85) continue to book top-notch acts from around the globe.

Paris is also a European leader for world music, particularly African and Arab acts. And don't forget that every 21 June, the city turns into one giant music venue for the Fête de la Musique, when a party in the street is guaranteed.

Website www.gogoparis.com selects regular concert highlights and also features a decent gig list for the coming months; www.infoconcert.com is also well worth a look. The weekly magazine *Les Inrockuptibles* is a valuable resource. Alternatively, try reliable, bi-monthly gig bible *Lylo*, free in bars and branches of Fnac. The Fnac (see p65) and Virgin Megastore ticket offices (see p67) also display details of up-and-coming concerts. For reduced-price tickets try www.billetreduc.com.

Venue box offices are usually closed in the daytime, and most venues take a break in August. Prices for gigs vary according to a group or artist's pulling power, but several excellent venues, like La Bellevilloise (19-21 rue Boyer, 20th, 01.46.36.07.07), host regular free nights – ideal if you're feeling adventurous and/or are on a budget. For concerts, it's best to turn up at the time stated on the ticket: strict noise curfews mean that start times are adhered to pretty closely.

Cabaret & comedy

The promise of busty babes slinking across stage in frilly knickers has turned glamour cabarets into some of the hottest spots around. The Moulin Rouge (see p94) popularised the skirt-raising concept during the 19th century, and since then venues such as Le Lido (see p67) have institutionalised garter-pinging.

These days, a cabaret is an all-evening, smart-dress affair, with a pre-show meal and champers. The Moulin Rouge is the most traditional revue and the only place with cancan. Toulouse-Lautrec posters, glittery lamp-posts and fake trees lend tacky charm, while 60 Doriss dancers cover the stage with faultless synchronisation. Sadly, elbow room is nil, with tables packed in like sardines.

For space go to Le Lido. With 1,000 seats, this classy venue is the largest, priciest cabaret of the lot: the art nouveau hall's high-tech touches optimise visibility and star chef Paul Bocuse has revolutionised the menu. The slightly tame show, with 60 Bluebell Girls, has boob-shaking, wacky costumes and numerous oddities.

For a more risqué performance, try the Crazy Horse (12 av George V, 8th, 01.47.23.32.32) whose neo-Dadaist 'l'art du nu' (the art of nudity) concept was invented by Alain Bernadin in 1951.

Perhaps the biggest change on Paris's entertainment circuit is the success of *le stand-up*. It hit town in a big way in 2008 thanks to comedian Jamel Debbouze, who opened Le Comedy Club (42 bd de la Bonne Nouvelle, 10th, 08.11.94.09.40) – a launch pad for new French stand-up comics and a spinoff from his TV show *Le Jamel Comedy Club*, and the trend looks set to stay. If French isn't your forte, though, fear not: veteran Anglo venue Laughing Matters (105 rue du Fbg-du-Temple, 10th, 01.53.19.98.88, www.anything matters.com) still provides belly laughs in English with comedy acts from across the Channel, the US and Australia.

Forum des Images p31

Arts & Leisure

A number of cultural developments and innovations, and several new sites, have given a significant lift to Paris's cultural scene in the last couple of years. The Maison des Métallos (see p115), a former trade union centre, reopened as a cutting-edge showcase for up-and-coming artists; and an old funeral parlour was transformed into 104 (see p159), a centre for contemporary art. The Théâtre de la Gaîté Lyrique, meanwhile, is set to reopen as a hub for digital arts and contemporary music in 2010.

Construction has also begun on the Cité Européenne du Cinéma in the northern suburb of St-Denis. Backed by maverick French film director Luc Besson, the massive complex will house nine studios and promises to give the national film industry a massive boost when it opens in 2012. Even so, the French film industry remains in extremely good health, with more tickets per head bought here than anywhere else in Europe.

Another major building project is the much-vaunted Philharmonie, which is rising near the Cité de la Musique. Architect Jean Nouvel's 2,400-seat concert hall will give the city a major venue for the classical repertoire.

What's especially good about the arts here is the accessibility: there are any number of festivals and discount promotions on offer throughout the year, many organised by the city council, that bring what the Brits often consider to be 'elitist' art forms within the reach and appreciation of the general public.

Film

Cinema-going is a serious pastime in Paris. In any given week there's a choice of some 350 movies – not including the numerous festivals (see p34), many of which offer free or discounted entry. The city houses nearly 90 cinemas and around 400 screens, almost a quarter of which show nothing but arthouse. Even the multiplexes regularly screen documentaries and films from Eastern Europe, Asia and South America. This vibrant scene is constantly evolving, with new multi-screen complexes under construction and classic picture houses constantly under renovation.

Visiting one of the city's many picture palaces is an experience in itself – from the glorious faux-oriental Pagode (see p128) and kitsch excesses of the Grand Rex (see p86) to the innovative Forum des Images (see p86), which reopened at the end of 2008.

New releases hit the screens on Wednesdays – when certain cinemas offer reduced rates.

Opera & classical

It's all change at the Opéra National de Paris (see p86). After years under controversial modernist director Gérard Mortier, the Paris opera company has entered a new era under Nicolas Joel, who comes to the capital after 18 years at Toulouse Opera. With a reputation for traditional values, Joel is likely to favour a more classical repertoire, while talented new music director Philippe Jordan will offer some youthful energy. The Opéra Comique (see p86), meanwhile, continues to capitalise on new financial security following its promotion to National Theatre status by offering a crowd-pleasing season of revivals and classics.

SHORTLIST

Wonderful settings
- La Pagode (see p128)
- Palais Garnier (see p86)
- Théâtre Marigny (see p69)

Most innovative
- International opera at the Festival d'Automne (see p34)

Most romantic
- Candlelit recitals for the Festival Chopin (see p38)
- Lovers' seats at MK2 Bilbliothèque (see p152)

Best bargains
- €3.50 film tickets, Printemps du Cinéma (see p36)
- Free concerts at Paris Jazz Festival (see p38)
- Free museum entry, Printemps des Musées (see p36)

Best alfresco
- Cinéma en Plein Air (see p38)
- Festival Classique au Vert (see p34)
- Fête de la Musique (see p38)

Best film venues
- Le Grand Rex (see p86)
- La Pagode (see p128)

Best opera venues
- Opéra Comique (see p86)
- Palais Garnier (see p86)

Original creations
- 104 (see p159)
- Maison des Métallos (see p115)
- Quinzaine des Réalisateurs, Forum des Images (see p37)

Culture after dark
- Midnight closing at Palais de Tokyo (see p61)
- Nuit Blanche (see p35)
- Nuit des Musées (see p37)

MOULIN ROUGE®

DISCOVER "*FÉERIE*",
THE SHOW OF THE MOST FAMOUS CABARET IN THE WORLD !

DINNER & SHOW AT 7PM FROM 150€ • SHOW AT 9PM 102 €, AT 11PM 92 €
Montmartre - 82, Boulevard de Clichy - 75018 Paris
Reservations : +33(0)1 53 09 82 82 • www.moulin-rouge.com

Elsewhere, there's disappointment at the Châtelet (see p86), where director Jean-Luc Choplin's populist programming is faltering – this season's *The Sound of Music* may please retro musical lovers, but is indicative of a general lack of musical beef.

Contemporary composition remains a strong suit, thanks to the work of IRCAM, the Ensemble Intercontemporain and the active involvement of Pierre Boulez. Another Parisian forte is Early Music, led by William Christie's Les Arts Florissants, which has become an international benchmark for the Baroque repertoire.

Many venues offer cut-rate tickets to students (under 26) an hour before curtain-up. On the Fête de la Musique (21 June) all events are free, and year-round freebies crop up at the Maison de Radio France and the Conservatoire de Paris.

Dance

Paris is home to a thriving dance scene. Although the sumptuous ballet productions at the Palais Garnier and international companies at Châtelet will always delight audiences, it's in the sphere of contemporary dance that Paris currently shines brightest. The prestigious Centre National de la Danse (1 rue Victor-Hugo, 93507 Pantin, 01.41.83.27.27), just outside the city centre, is an impressive HQ for France's 600-plus regional dance companies. Every season sees some kind of contemporary dance festival in or near Paris; the Festival d'Automne (see p34) is one of the best.

Theatre

French-speaking theatre buffs can choose from some 450 productions every week: from offbeat shows in small, independent venues to high-brow classics in grandiose auditoriums like the Comédie Française (2 rue Richelieu, 1st, 08.25.10.16.80), whose staples include Molière and Racine.

Fortunately for Anglophones, the Paris theatre scene is becoming ever more international. The restored and re-baptised Odéon Théâtre de l'Europe (pl de l'Odéon, 6th, 01.44.85.44.00) offers plays in a number of languages, including at least one per season in English. Anglophone performances are occasionally programmed at the Théâtre des Bouffes du Nord (37bis bd de la Chapelle, 10th, 01.46.07.34.50), which remains under the direction of maverick Brit-born director Peter Brook until 2011, while the cutting edge MC93 Bobigny (1 bd Lénine, 93000 Bobigny, 01.41.60.72.72) regularly hosts international companies performing in their mother tongue. Meanwhile, the Improfessionals (www.improfessionals.com) stage regular improv performances in English, and Shakespeare in English is performed every summer at the Bois de Boulogne's Théâtre de Verdure du Jardin Shakespeare (01.40.19.95.33) by London's Tower Theatre Company (www.towertheatre.org.uk).

What's on

For listings, see weekly magazines *L'Officiel des Spectacles* or *Pariscope*. When it comes to films, take note of the two letters printed near the title: VO (*version originale*) means a screening in the original language with French subtitles; VF (*version française*) means that it's dubbed into French. Cinema seats can be reserved at www.allocine.fr. For new blockbuster releases, it pays to buy tickets at least one screening in advance.

Calendar

Tour de France p39

This is the pick of events that I had been announced as we went to press. On public holidays, or *jours feriés*, banks, many museums, most businesses and a number of restaurants close. New Year's Day, May Day, Bastille Day and Christmas Day are the most piously observed holidays. Dates highlighted in **bold** indicate public holidays.

September 2010

To 6 Mar 2011 **In the Wake of the Sharks**
Aquarium de la Porte Dorée
www.aquarium-portedoree.fr
Children will love this exhibition, which features zebra sharks, bamboo sharks, blacktip reef sharks, and several species of Amazonian rays, as well as skeletons, teeth and fossilised jawbones galore.

1-12 **Jazz à la Villette**
Parc de la Villette
www.jazzalavillette.com

One of the capital's best jazz festivals, including the new series of Jazz for Kids concerts.

Early Sept
Festival Classique au Vert
Parc Floral de Paris
www.paris.fr
A series of free classical recitals held in a park setting.

Early Sept-mid Oct **Festival Paris Ile-de-France**
Various venues
www.festival-ile-de-france.com
Classical, contemporary and world music festival set in various venues.

Mid Sept **Techno Parade**
www.technopol.net
This parade (finishing up at Bastille) marks the start of the electronic music festival Rendez-vous Electroniques.

Mid Sept-end Dec
Festival d'Automne
Various venues
www.festival-automne.com

This major annual arts festival focuses on bringing challenging theatre, dance and modern opera to Paris.

18-19 Journées du Patrimoine
Various venues
www.journeesdupatrimoine.culture.fr
Embassies, ministries, scientific establishments and corporate headquarters open their doors to the public.

22 Sept 2010 24 Jan 2011 Monet
Grand Palais
www.grandpalais.fr
Paris's first big Monet show for 30 years includes hundreds of works from the Musée d'Orsay, plus foreign loans.

October 2010

Ongoing Festival d'Automne (see Sept); Festival Paris Ile-de-France (see Sept); In the Wake of the Sharks (see Sept); Monet (see Sept)

Early Oct Nuit Blanche
Various venues
www.nuitblanche.paris.fr
Galleries, museums, swimming pools, bars and clubs stay open till very late for one night only.

2, 3 Oct Prix de l'Arc de Triomphe
Hippodrome de Longchamp
www.prixarcdetriomphe.com
France's richest flat race attracts the elite of horse racing.

6-10 Fête des Vendanges de Montmartre
Various venues
www.fetedesvendangesde
montmartre.com
The modest 1,000-bottle harvest of the Clos Montmartre vineyard is the pretext for a weekend of street parties.

21-24 FIAC
Various venues
www.fiac.com
The Louvre and Grand Palais are the two venues for this week-long contemporary art fair.

November 2010

Ongoing Festival d'Automne (see Sept); In the Wake of the Sharks (see Sept); Monet (see Sept)

1 Toussaint (All Saints' Day)

Early Nov Festival des Inrockuptibles
Various venues
www.lesinrocks.com
This rock, pop and trance festival, curated by popular rock magazine *Les Inrockuptibles*, attracts top international indie, rock, techno and trip hop acts. Bill-toppers in 2009 included La Roux, Passion Pit and Bat for Lashes.

11 L'Armistice (Armistice Day)
Arc de Triomphe
The President lays wreaths to honour French combatants who died in the World Wars.

18 Fête du Beaujolais Nouveau
Various venues
www.beaujolaisgourmand.com
The new vintage is launched to packed cafés and wine bars.

Nov-Dec Africolor
Various venues in St-Denis
www.africolor.com
African music festival with a spirited wrap party.

December 2010

Ongoing Africolor (see Nov); Festival d'Automne (see Sept); In the Wake of the Sharks (see Sept); Monet (see Sept)

Dec-Mar Paris sur Glace
Various venues
www.paris.fr
Three free outdoor ice rinks.

24-25 Noël (Christmas)

31 New Year's Eve
Jubilant crowds swarm along the Champs-Elysées, and restaurants hold expensive soirées.

January 2011

Ongoing **In the Wake of the Sharks** (see Sept); Monet (see Sept); Paris sur Glace (see Dec)

1 Jour de l'An (New Year's Day)
The Grande Parade de Paris brings floats, bands and dancers.

6 Fête des Rois (Epiphany)
Pâtisseries all sell *galettes des rois*, frangipane-filled cakes in which a *fève*, or tiny charm, is hidden.

Mid Jan **Mass for Louis XVI**
Chapelle Expiatoire
Royalists and right-wing crackpots mourn the end of the monarchy.

February 2011

Ongoing **In the Wake of the Sharks** (see Sept); Paris sur Glace (see Dec)

3 Nouvel An Chinois
Various venues
Lion and dragon dances, and lively martial arts demonstrations to celebrate the Chinese new year.

Early Feb-mid Mar **Six Nations**
Stade de France
www.rbs6nations.com
Paris is invaded by Brits and Celts for big weekends of rugby.

March 2011

Ongoing **In the Wake of the Sharks** (see Sept); Paris sur Glace (see Dec); Six Nations (see Feb)

Early Mar-Apr **Banlieues Bleues**
Various venues in Seine St-Denis
www.banlieuesbleues.org
Five weeks of top-quality French and international jazz, blues, R&B and soul.

End Mar **Printemps du Cinéma**
Various venues
www.printempsducinema.com
Film tickets across the city are cut to a bargain €3.50 for this popular three-day film bonanza.

April 2011

Ongoing **Banlieues Bleues** (see Mar)

Early Apr-end May **Foire du Trône**
Pelouse de Reuilly
www.foiredutrone.com
France's biggest funfair runs for nearly nine weeks, noon to midnight daily.

10 Marathon de Paris
Av des Champs-Elysées to av Foch
www.parismarathon.com
More than 35,000 runners take part, cheered on by 200,000 spectators.

22 Le Chemin de la Croix (Way of the Cross)
Square Willette
Good Friday pilgrimage as crowds follow the Archbishop of Paris from the bottom of Montmartre to Sacré-Coeur.

24 Pâques (Easter Sunday)

End Apr-mid May **Foire de Paris**
Paris-Expo
www.foiredeparis.fr
Enormous lifestyle fair, full of craft and food stores, plus health exhibits.

End Apr-early May **Grand Marché d'Art Contemporain**
Place de la Bastille
www.joel-garcia-organisation.fr
Contemporary artists display and sell their work at this annual arts fair.

May 2011

Ongoing **Foire du Trône** (see Apr); Foire de Paris (see Apr); Grand Marché d'Art Contemporain (see Apr)

1 Fête du Travail (May Day)
Key sights close; unions march in eastern Paris via Bastille.

Early May **Printemps des Musées**
Various venues
www.printempsdesmusees.culture.fr
For one Sunday in May, selected museums open for free.

FIAC p35

8 **Victoire 1945 (VE Day)**

Mid May **La Nuit des Musées**
Various venues
www.nuitdesmusees.culture.fr
For one night, landmark museums
across Paris stay open late and put on
special events.

Mid May **Art St-Germain-des-Prés**
Various venues
www.artsaintgermaindespres.com
Nicknamed the 'block party': almost 50
galleries get together to showcase their
top artists.

Mid May **Festival Jazz à Saint-
Germain-des-Prés**
St-Germain-des-Prés,
various venues
www.espritjazz.com
A ten-day celebration of jazz and blues
on the Left Bank.

Mid May-early June **Quinzaine
des Réalisateurs**
Forum des Images
www.quinzaine-realisateurs.com
The Cannes Directors' Fortnight programme comes to Paris; 2009 was the
30th anniversary of this festival.

24 **Lundi de Pentecôte
(Whit Monday)**

End May **Le Printemps des Rues**
Various venues
www.leprintempsdesrues.com
Annual street-theatre festival.

End May-mid July
Foire St-Germain
Various venues
www.foiresaintgermain.org
St-Germain lets its hair down with con-
certs, theatre and workshops.

End May-early June
French Tennis Open
Stade Roland Garros
www.rolandgarros.com
Glitzy Grand Slam tennis tournament,
whose tricky clay courts have been the
downfall of many a champion.

June 2011

Ongoing Quinzaine des
Réalisateurs (see May);
French Tennis Open (see May);
Foire St-Germain (see May)

2 **Jour de l'Ascension**

Early June **Fête du Vélo**
Across Paris
www.tousavelo.com
Cycling tours and activities as Paris's
two-wheelers take to the streets.

Techno Parade p34

Early June-July **Paris Jazz Festival**
Parc Floral de Paris
www.parcfloraldeparis.com
Two months of free jazz weekends at
the lovely Parc Floral.

Early June-early July **Festival
de St-Denis**
Various venues in St-Denis
www.festival-saint-denis.com
Four weeks of concerts showcasing
top-quality classical music.

June-July **Festival Chopin à Paris**
Orangerie de Bagatelle
www.frederic-chopin.com
Romantic candlelit piano recitals in the
Bois de Boulogne.

Late June **Fête de la Musique**
Various venues
www.fetedelamusique.fr
Free gigs take place across the city.

Late June **Gay Pride March**
www.inter-lgbt.org
Outrageous floats and costumes parade
towards Bastille, followed by an official
party and various club events.

July 2011

Ongoing Foire St-Germain
(see May); Paris Jazz Festival
(see June); Festival de St-Denis
(see June); Festival Chopin à Paris
(see June)

Early July **Paris Cinéma**
Various venues
www.pariscinema.org
Premieres, tributes and restored films
at the city's excellent summer film-
going initiative.

Early July **Solidays**
Hippodrome de Longchamp
www.solidays.com
A three-day music bash for AIDS
charities, featuring French, world and
new talent.

Early-late July **Etés de la Danse**
Théâtre du Châtelet
www.lesetesdeladanse.com
International classical and contemporary dance festival.

July-Aug **Cinéma en Plein Air**
Parc de la Villette
www.villette.com
A summer fixture on the city calendar:
a themed season of free films screened
under the stars.

14 Quatorze Juillet
(Bastille Day)
Various venues

France's national holiday commemorates 1789. On the 13th, Parisians dance at place de la Bastille. At 10am on the 14th, crowds line the Champs-Elysées as the President reviews a military parade. By night, the Champ de Mars fills for a huge firework display.

Mid July-mid Aug
Paris, Quartier d'Eté
Various venues
www.quartierdete.com
Classical and jazz concerts, plus dance and theatre, in outdoor venues.

Mid July-mid Aug **Paris-Plage**
Pont des Arts to Pont de Sully
www.paris.fr
Palm trees, huts, hammocks and around 2,000 tonnes of fine sand on both banks of the Seine bring a seaside vibe to the city. Not only this, there's a floating pool and a lending library too.

Late July **Tour de France**
Av des Champs-Elysées
www.letour.fr
The ultimate cycle endurance test climaxes on the Champs-Elysées.

August 2011

Ongoing Cinéma en Plein Air (see July); Paris, Quartier d'Eté (see July), Paris-Plage (see July)

15 Fête de l'Assomption (Assumption Day)
Cathédrale Notre-Dame de Paris
Notre-Dame again becomes a place of religious pilgrimage.

Late Aug **Rock en Seine**
Domaine National de St-Cloud
www.rockenseine.com
Three days, three stages, one world-class line-up of rock and indie groups.

September 2011

Early Sept **Jazz à la Villette**
Parc de la Villette
www.jazzalavillette.com
This is one of the best jazz festivals in the city.

The new revolution

Celebrate Paris's bike boom with festivals galore.

Thanks to Mayor Delanoë's eco-friendly policies, the bike has enjoyed a major boom in Paris – and it's now the focus of several annual festivals in the city. The **Fête du Vélo** (see p37) in June is a celebration of urban riding with thousands of cyclists invited to meet up at various points in the suburbs and pedal to Paris en masse. The result is what the organisation calls 'la convergence', with a procession of two-wheelers meeting up for a huge picnic in the city centre.

Launched in 2009, **Paris Bike Days** (www.parisbikedays.com) is all about getting people on bikes – of every type. This spring festival, based in the Bois de Vincennes, allows visitors to try out racers on closed roads and mountain bikes on specially designed forest trails, as well as on a bump-filled 'pump track'. There's also a range of BMX, trial and electric bikes available for test spins. Once you've found the right bike, you can buy it onsite.

The ultimate spectacle in cycling is reserved for the end of July when the world's biggest bike race, the **Tour de France** (see left), arrives in Paris. After three weeks of hard racing, the battle for the leader's famed yellow jersey is all but over, and the final stage usually climaxes in a mass sprint with everyone finishing together. It's an incredible spectacle, so make sure you turn up early for a front-row spot.

Sept **Festival Classique au Vert**
Parc Floral du Paris
www.paris.fr
Free classical recitals in a park setting.

Early Sept-mid Oct **Festival Paris
Ile-de-France**
Various venues
www.festival-ile-de-france.com
Classical, contemporary and world
music festival in venues around Paris.

Mid Sept **Techno Parade**
Various venues
www.technopol.net
This parade (finishing up at Bastille)
marks the start of electronic music
festival Rendez-vous Electroniques.

Mid Sept-late Dec **Festival
d'Automne**
Various venues
www.festival-automne.com
Major annual festival for theatre, dance
and modern opera performances.

Mid Sept **Journées du Patrimoine**
Various venues
www.journeesdupatrimoine.culture.fr
Embassies, ministries, scientific establishments and corporate headquarters
open their doors to the public.

October 2011

Ongoing Festival d'Automne
(see Sept)

Early Oct **Prix de l'Arc de Triomphe**
Hippodrome de Longchamp
www.prixarcdetriomphe.com
France's richest flat race.

Early Oct **Nuit Blanche**
Various venues
www.paris.fr
For one night, a selection of galleries,
museums, swimming pools, bars and
clubs stay open until very late.

Mid Oct **Fête des Vendanges
à Montmartre**
Various venues
www.fetedesvendangesde
montmartre.com

The modest 1,000-bottle harvest is the
pretext for a weekend of street parties.

Mid Oct **FIAC**
Various venues
www.fiac.com
Respected international art fair.

End Oct **Grand Marché
d'Art Contemporain**
Place de la Bastille
www.organisation-joel-garcia.fr
Annual arts fair.

November 2011

Ongoing Festival d'Automne
(see Sept)

1 Toussaint (All Saints' Day)

Early Nov **Festival Inrockuptibles**
Various venues
www.lesinrocks.com
Rock, pop and trance festival curated
by rock magazine *Les Inrockuptibles*.

11 L'Armistice (Armistice Day)
Arc de Triomphe
The President lays wreaths to honour
French dead of both World Wars.

Late Nov **Fête du
Beaujolais Nouveau**
Various venues
www.beaujolaisgourmand.com
The new vintage is launched.

Nov-Dec **Africolor**
Various venues in St-Denis
www.africolor.com
African music festival.

December 2011

Ongoing Festival d'Automne
(see Sept)

Dec-Mar **Paris sur Glace**
Various venues
www.paris.fr

24-25 **Noël (Christmas)**

31 **New Year's Eve**

Itineraries

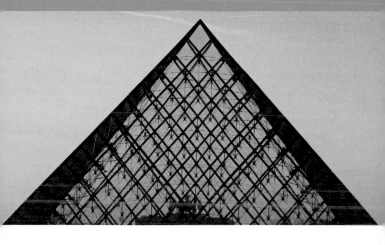

Bibliothèque Nationale – Richelieu p43

ITINERARIES

Dead Famous

The French capital has some of history's most influential characters buried on its soil; the Montparnasse cemetery alone shelters hundreds of writers and artists within its confines, including the likes of Baudelaire, Beckett and Man Ray. But these are the lucky ones. Other historical figures did not always get to their final resting place in one piece – their bones, hair or innards led to great traffic back in the day. This trip around central Paris gives you the chance to get up close and personal with some of the city's more macabre relics.

Start on place du Palais-Royal, 1st (M° Palais Royal Musée du Louvre). Turn your back on the Louvre and walk into the **Comédie Française** (2 rue de Richelieu, 1st). Founded in 1640 by Louis XIV with Molière as its lead playwright, 'La Comédie' is still the only state theatre with a permanent troupe of actors. In the foyer, look out for an old armchair inside a glass cage. It is believed to be the one from which Molière delivered his last lines at a performance of *Le Malade Imaginaire* in 1673. He died shortly after the curtain fell. As a tribute to the playwright, the seat is put back on stage every 15 January, the anniversary of his birth.

In the same room, the statue of an old man regards theatregoers with a sarcastic smile. You may have recognised Voltaire, the French Enlightenment philosopher, immortalised here by sculptor Jean-Antoine Houdon. But it is a lesser known fact that the statue serves as reliquary for the philosopher's brain, sealed inside its pedestal.

After Voltaire's death in 1778, the apothecary who performed the autopsy removed his brain and heart and put them in boiling alcohol to solidify them. Voltaire's brain then passed through many hands before finally ending up at the Comédie in 1924.

As for his heart, it remained on display for a long time at the Château de Ferney, where Voltaire died. It was only when the philosopher's body was declared 'property of the state' in 1791 that the heart was given to Napoléon III, who decided to keep it at the Imperial Library, now the **Bibliothèque Nationale – Richelieu**. Walk to the entrance at 58 rue de Richelieu, around the corner from the Comédie, and ask to see the *salon d'honneur*, a stunning oak veneered room presided over by a statue of Voltaire identical to the one at the Comédie. The heart is enclosed in its wooden pedestal.

The next destination is on the Left Bank, a perfect opportunity to test out Vélib, Paris's hugely popular municipal bike scheme. There is a *borne* opposite the library, at 71 rue de Richelieu.

Head south and turn left into rue des Petits Champs. Cycle across place des Victoires and turn right into rue du Louvre. Follow the traffic all the way down to the river, and turn left on to quai du Louvre, a section of riverbank lined with *bouquinistes*. Carry on to Pont au Change, where you can use the bus lane to cycle across the bridge. Once on the island, keep going south, passing the impressive gates of the Palais de Justice, and turn left on to quai du Marché Neuf. Go straight ahead until you're facing Notre Dame cathedral. You can drop your bike at the *borne* on the side of the square, on rue d'Arcole.

Head south across Pont au Double. On quai de Montebello, walk around the small park in front of you and take rue de la Bûcherie. If you're feeling peckish after all that cultural dissection, you can indulge yourself with a dish of gently sautéed brains at offal specialist **Ribouldingue** (see p147) around the corner.

With rested feet and a full stomach, you're ready for more

Comédie Française p42

ITINERARIES

Les Invalides p45

relic-hunting. Find rue St-Jacques
at the end of rue de la Bûcherie
and walk down to rue Soufflot.
The columns of the **Panthéon**
(see p146) should be clear to see
on your left. As the last home of
many French *grands hommes*, the
Panthéon could be seen as the
ultimate reliquary, even though
there's not much to peep at in terms
of old bones. The crypt gathers the
shrines of over 70 illustrious
Frenchmen, including Victor Hugo,
Alexandre Dumas and our old
friend Voltaire, whose carcass –
or what remains of it – can finally
rest in peace here.

A somewhat more sensational
relic can be found in the **Eglise
St-Etienne-du-Mont** (see p142),
just around the corner from
the Panthéon. The church, a
masterpiece of Flamboyant Gothic
architecture, displays a finger bone

belonging to Sainte Geneviève,
the patron saint of Paris, in a glass
reliquary next to her sarcophagus.

Next, retrace your steps towards
boulevard St-Michel and brace
yourself for a particularly creepy
rendezvous. You can pick up a
Vélib from the *borne* at 174 rue
St-Jacques or cross through the
Jardin du Luxembourg for some
much-needed greenery.

From boulevard St-Michel, take
rue de Médicis, followed by rue de
Vaugirard which hugs the north
side of the Jardin du Luxembourg.
After passing the Sénat, turn right
into rue Garancière, then left into
rue St-Sulpice. Carry on along rue
du Vieux Colombier until you reach
rue de Sèvres. Look out for Vaneau
métro station and the Vélib *borne*
around the corner.

Find the Chapelle des Lazaristes,
identifiable by its tall green doors

next to no.95 rue de Sèvres, and climb up the stairs to the side of the altar. Here lies the surprisingly fresh-looking corpse of Saint Vincent de Paul, patron saint of the poor. While his skeleton was preserved in its entirety, his face and hands were covered in wax and moulded to resemble the deceased, giving the disturbing impression that he passed away only minutes ago. The people of Paris, very attached to Saint Vincent de Paul, clubbed together to pay for the sumptuous silver and gold coffin in which the body lies.

Pick up a Vélib on rue Vaneau and head north. Turn left into rue de Babylone and then right into boulevard des Invalides. Keep cycling towards the Seine, with the golden dome of **Les Invalides** (see p125) on your left, the last resting place of Napoléon. The emperor could easily win the title of most scattered cadaver in history. While his heart and innards are in Austria, you will need to travel to New York to get

near his penis, bought at auction by a urologist for $3,800.

After such intense reflections, you should arrive on quai d'Orsay, by the Seine. Cross the Pont Alexandre III and turn left on to cours Albert I. At place de l'Alma, where other pilgrims are gathered by the Princess Diana memorial, take avenue du Président Wilson on your right. Carry on until you reach place du Trocadéro. A Vélib *borne* on avenue d'Eylau, third right on the roundabout, will allow you to dispose of your bike.

The **Musée de l'Homme** (17 place du Trocadéro, 16th, currently closed for refurbishment) is home to philosopher René Descartes' skull. The rest of his body is buried on the Left Bank, which makes the perfect start to another trek. But by now you will probably have had your share of gravestones for the day. Time to take a seat in the Café de l'Homme, order a coffee and enjoy one of the best views there is of the city. Chances are you've never felt more alive.

ITINERARIES

Musée de l'Homme

LIDO
CHAMPS-ELYSEES
PARIS

100 ans
Bluebell Girl
Lido de Paris

1910
2010

Bonheur

SPECIAL OFFER*
for Time Out Short List readers
€20 OFF

DINNER & SHOW from €140
CHAMPAGNE & SHOW from €90
Discover the Revue "Bonheur":
70 artistes, 600 costumes, an amazing show !

Informations / reservation : www.lido.fr - Tel. : + 33 (0)1 40 76 56 95
116 bis avenue des Champs-Élysées - 75008 PARIS

Beyond the Mona Lisa

The world's largest museum is a city within the city, a vast multi-level maze of galleries, staircases and escalators. It's famous for the artistic glories it contains within, but the very fabric of the museum is a masterpiece in itself. You can be systematic and do a trail through the greatest hits, by department, by wing or by theme, or you can follow the route mapped out here and let yourself be sidetracked and beguiled by Flemish landscapes, Byzantine icons, Ancient Egyptian funerary chapels, and France's earliest portrait.

Part of the fascination of the Louvre is that it is not just a museum, but was a royal and later imperial palace and seat of government. The building's history is entwined with that of Paris and France. Behind the 35,000 works of art and 8.5 million annual visitors, you'll also find the giant staircases, sumptuous ceilings and carved panelling of the original palace.

Start on rue du Louvre with its pedimented classical façade and go through the central doorway into the Cour Carrée. Although the main entrance is now via the glass pyramid, this courtyard, with its richly sculpted western façade by Pierre Lescot and Jean Goujon, marked the introduction of Renaissance taste to Paris by François 1er as he established his court in the capital. Head through the arch to the Cour Napoléon, where the two wings added under Napoléon III are set off by I M Pei's glass pyramid in the centre — main entrance since 1993, exactly 200 years after part of the Louvre first became a museum. Pick up a plan of the museum at the welcome desk: the eight collections are colour-coded on it, and signs point to the most popular exhibits.

Start by the Richelieu wing, going up to the Cours Puget glazed sculpture court, on the lower ground floor. Here four vast green

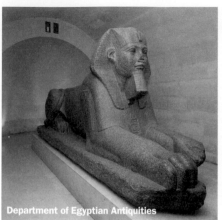

Department of Egyptian Antiquities

bronze captives by Martin van den Bogaert, which originally stood at the foot of a statue in place des Victoires, represent Spain, Brandenburg, Empire and Holland, territories conquered by France. Next go through to the Cours Marly with its pairs of equestrian sculptures by Guillaume Coustou and Antoine Coysevox, and other statues commissioned by Louis XIV for the park of his favourite château at Marly-le-Roi.

Up the stairs to the side, the French Renaissance sculpture galleries are full of caryatids, monuments and fireplaces. Here, you'll find treasures such as the Fontaine de Diane from Anet, a whimsical confection of stag and nude huntress sitting on an urn, plus nymphs, sea beasts and swirling waves by Jean Goujon from the Fontaine des Innocents.

Next, take the Escalier Lefuel to the first floor decorative arts department. Sidetrack through the OTT apartments of Napoléon III, a feast of 19th-century bad taste, to admire the sheer excess of the dining room with its carved,

sculpted and gilded ceiling, and the *grande salle* where the padded circular sofa evokes palmy days of official functions.

Head to the medieval gallery (rooms 1-4) for Byzantine icons and ivories, the medieval treasure of St-Denis (golden eagle wings around an antique porphyry vase) and Limoges enamel reliquaries and caskets, before taking the escalators up to the second floor, which is home to the departments of French and northern European painting.

Here, your first stop should be the Galerie Médicis (room 18), one of the places where the history of France and the museum coincide in 24 virtuoso canvases by Rubens depicting episodes in the life of Marie de Médici – including Henri IV receiving her portrait, her arrival by boat in Marseille accompanied by thrashing sea monsters, her accession as regent and the marriage of Louis XIII.

There's more Rubens just around the corner (room 21) with his two sensitive portraits of his second wife Hélène Fourment. Continue through Flemish landscapes and

Dutch paintings, with Rembrandt in all his registers, from the tenderness of *Bathsheba at her Bath* to the raw meat and thick brushstrokes of *The Flayed Ox* (room 31), Vermeer's *Lacemaker* and Franz Post's Brazilian landscapes (room 38).

Back out on the landing, follow signs for French painting, said to start (room 1) with the 14th-century *Portrait of Jean II the Good*, deemed to be France's earliest independent portrait. There's a much more Gothic verve to Enguerrand Quarton's extraordinary *Pietà*, while Jean Clouet's *François 1er* is a stripy-sleeved incarnation of the dashing Renaissance monarch, a precursor to the wispy figures of the École de Fontainebleau and Antoine Caron's paintings of court festivities.

Against the colour and bravura of 17th-century official Baroque painting for church and state, there is a more ascetic edge in Lubin Baugin's pared-back *Still Life with Wafers* (room 27), while Georges de la Tour's paintings (room 28) still inspire awe with their incredible stillness and calm, simplification of forms, moulding by candlelight and shadow in *Mary Magdelene* or the more worldy moral theme of *The Card Cheat*.

Cross the Salle Alexandre (room 32), a vision of grandiose official history painting in Charles Le Brun's massive battle scenes full of thrashing horses and muscled bodies. This is followed by the 18th-century lightness and frivolity of Watteau's *Gilles*, the dreamy portraits and still lifes of Chardon, and paintings by Fragonard, at his best in his wonderfully free 'fantasy portraits' (room 48).

You've already done Neo-Classicism and Romanticism at its best so exit by the spiral staircase down to Ancient Egypt on the ground floor. Pop into the Mastaba of Akhethetep (room 4), a circa 2400 BC funerary chapel of a royal dignitary from Saqqara with an interior chamber covered in painted reliefs. End your walk where it all began – the underground remains of the sturdy defensive walls, moats and conical towers of the medieval Louvre – before the glass pyramid brings you back to earth.

Bread & Roses p53

Left Bank Picnic

St-Germain-des-Prés may be rather more Louis Vuitton than Boris Vian these days, but there are still enough small galleries and bookshops in the neighbourhood to ensure that it retains a whiff of its bohemian past. Aside from art and books, the 6th arrondissement (and its neighbour the 7th) is also a great place to shop for food, since it boasts some of the finest artisanal bakeries and traiteurs in Paris.

And thanks to **Vélib** (www. velib.paris.fr), it's easier than ever to get around the *quartier* in order to stock up. What's more, the standard-issue bike is equipped with a fairly capacious basket that should accommodate everything you'll need for a sumptuous picnic – which we recommend taking in the elegant surroundings of the Jardin du Luxembourg.

Since you'll be deliberating over your purchases each time you stop, this itinerary will probably take

you the best part of two hours. And remember, after the first half hour on Vélib, which is free, there's a sliding scale of charges. Don't bother searching for a station each time you need to stop; just use the chain provided to lock your bike.

START: Station Vélib, 1 rue Jacques Callot, 6th (M° Mabillon).

Detach your bike from the *borne* and cycle down rue Mazarine as far as the carrefour de Buci. Turn left into rue de Buci and carry on until the junction with rue de Seine. The stretch of rue de Seine between here and boulevard St-Germain is lined with butchers and greengrocers. Ignore the smell of roasting chickens (you'll be getting cooked meat elsewhere), and just buy salad leaves and fruit. Then head back down rue de Seine (it's one way, like many of the narrow streets round here) towards the river. About halfway down, turn left into rue Jacob, a typically well-heeled slice of Left Bank real estate –

all furniture shops, galleries, boutiques and elegantly turned-out *femmes d'un certain age*.

Cross rue Bonaparte and take the next left into rue St-Benoît. Pause for a moment to look in the window of the **Librairie Saint Benoît des Prés** (2 rue St-Benoît, 6th, 01.46.33.16.16), which specialises in rare books and letters.

Continue down rue Saint-Benoît as far as place St-Germain-des-Prés, where you'll find three venerable St-Germain institutions: **Café de Flore** (see p133), **Les Deux Magots** (see p134) and **La Hune** bookshop (see p137). The Flore and the Deux Magots throng more with tourists than writers these days, though the former is still a favoured haunt of ageing enfant terrible Bernard-Henri Lévy. If you spot a man with a mane of black hair and a white shirt open to the navel poring over a notebook, it's probably 'BHL'. Next door, La Hune, which opened in 1949, is a kind of holy shrine for that nearly extinct species, the Left Bank Intellectual.

But it's not books we're after, it's bread; so pick your way across boulevard St-Germain and follow rue Gozlin round into the rue de Rennes. This is a broad, thunderously busy main road lined with chain stores. There's not a great deal to distract as you bowl south for half a kilometre or so, until you reach rue du Vieux Colombier on the right. You'll have to do battle with buses and taxis in this narrow cut-through which leads to the altogether more charming rue du Cherche-Midi. On the left-hand side of the street, wedged in among the usual expensive boutiques, jewellers and galleries, stands **Poilâne** (see p140), the renowned family bakers. You can expect to have to queue here for the famous Poilâne loaf – but it's worth waiting for: dark, firm and distinctively flavoured. The tarts and the biscuits are wonderful too.

Having loaded the bread into your basket, carry on down rue du Cherche-Midi. Go straight across boulevard Raspail. Take the first

Fromagerie Quatrehomme p53

right into rue Dupin (there's a coffee merchant's on one corner, a fishmonger on the other). Running down one side of this quiet street is a fine, if forbidding, example of 1930s art deco municipal housing.

You'll eventually reach rue de Sèvres. Lock your bike up against the railings here and cross the road on foot to La Grande Epicérie, the food hall in Paris's oldest department store, **Le Bon Marché** (see p136). This is a gastronome's paradise, a super-abundant temple to food. Make your way to the traiteurs in the centre of the hall and choose from a staggering array of cooked meats – succulent

hams and pungent garlic sausages in dizzying profusion. While you're here, you can also pick up some dressing for the salad and a bottle of wine (and a corkscrew if you need one).

It just remains to buy some cheese, and for this you'll need to get back on your bike and cycle a little further south down rue de Sèvres, deeper into a residential corner of the 7th arrondissement. You'll pass on the right the wonderful art deco entrance to the Vaneau metro station, with its green iron lattices and globe lanterns. A little further along on the same side of the street, on the

Le Bon Marché

corner of rue Pierre Leroux, stands **Fromagerie Quatrehomme** (see p128). Run by the eponymous Marie, this place is famous across Paris for its comté fruité, beaufort and oozy st-marcellin – all dispensed with winning bonhomie.

Your basket will now be near to overflowing and the smell of the cheese will be making you hungry. It's time to head back into the 6th arrondissement and make for a picnic spot in the Jardin du Luxembourg. Turn round and cycle north back up rue de Sèvres, as far as rue St-Placide on the right, just before you reach Le Bon Marché. Shortly after you pass St-Placide

métro station, turn left into rue de Fleurus. You'll pass the men's and women's branches of the unbearably cool clothing store **APC** (see p136), which stand opposite each other. And if you think you need more biscuits or another tart, pop into **Bread & Roses** (see p133).

The **Jardin du Luxembourg** (see p130) is ahead of you, on the far side of rue Guynemer. There's a Vélib station at 26 rue Guynemer, next to the park entrance. As is usual in Paris, the grass here is not for sitting on, let alone picnicking on. Instead, find a bench in the shade and indulge.

River-boat shuttle service
BATOBUS
PARIS

 **Tour Eiffel**

 **Musée d'Orsay**

 **St-Germain des-Prés**

1 Pass
8 Stops
To discover Paris

Notre Dame

Jardin des Plantes

Hôtel de Ville

Louvre

Champs-Elysées

Information:

▶ N° Indigo 0,15 € TTC / MN
0 825 05 01 01
www.batobus.com

Photo : D. Milherou

Paris by Area

Galeries Nationales du Grand Palais p57

Champs-Elysées & Western Paris

PARIS BY AREA

In truth, *'la plus belle avenue du monde'* is not especially beautiful and it heaves with cars and crowds at pretty much any time of the day. The hordes aren't here for beauty, though. They're here for the shops, which the avenue, after years in the retail doldrums, now supplies in upmarket abundance. Fortunately, in the midst of all this rampant consumerism and airy affluence are a good number of museums covering such cerebral topics as architecture, human evolution and life on the ocean waves.

The western end of the Champs-Elysées is dominated by the renovated **Arc de Triomphe** towering above place Charles-de-Gaulle, also known as L'Etoile. Built by Napoleon, the arch was modified to celebrate the Revolutionary armies. From the top, visitors can gaze over the square (commissioned later by Haussmann), with 12 avenues radiating out in all directions.

South of the arch, avenue Kléber leads to the monumental buildings of the panoramic Trocadéro.

Sights & museums

Arc de Triomphe
Pl Charles-de-Gaulle, 8th (01.55.37.73.77). Mº Charles de Gaulle Etoile.
Open *Oct-Mar* 10am-10.30pm daily. *Apr-Sept* 10am-11pm daily.
Admission €9; free-€5.50 reductions.
Map p58 B2 ❶
The Arc de Triomphe has long been one of the capital's quintessential landmarks, drawing in 1.5 million visitors a year. But until recently, the interior was unimpressive, having changed little since the 1930s. So in 2008, after a revamp by architect Christophe Girault and artist Maurice Benayouna, a new museum opened with interactive screens and multimedia displays allowing

visitors to look at other famous arches around Europe and the world, as well as screens exploring the Arc's tumultuous 200-year history.

Bateaux-Mouches

Pont de l'Alma, 8th (01.42.25.96.10, www.bateaux-mouches.fr). M° Alma-Marceau. **Tickets** €10; free-€5 reductions. **Map** p58 C4 **②**
If you're after a whirlwind tour of the sights and don't mind tourists and schoolchildren, this, the oldest cruise operation on the Seine, is a good option.

Cinéaqua

2 av des Nations Unies, 16th (01.40.69.23.23, www.cineaqua.com). M° Trocadéro. **Open** 10am-8pm daily. **Admission** €19.50; free-€15 reductions. **Map** p58 B5 **③**
This aquarium and three-screen cinema is a wonderful attraction and a key element in the renaissance of the once moribund Trocadéro.

Cité de l'Architecture et du Patrimoine

Palais de Chaillot, 1 pl du Trocadéro, 16th (01.58.51.52.00, www.citechaillot. fr). M° Trocadéro. **Open** 11am-7pm Mon, Wed, Fri-Sun; 11am-9pm Thur. **Admission** €8; free-€5 reductions. **Map** p58 A4 **④**
Opened in 2007 in the east wing of the Palais de Chaillot, this architecture and heritage museum impresses by its scale. The expansive ground floor is filled with life-size mock-ups of cathedral façades and heritage buildings, and interactive screens place the models in context. Upstairs, darkened rooms house full-scale copies of medieval and Renaissance murals and stained-glass windows. The highlight of the modern architecture section is the walk-in replica of an apartment from Le Corbusier's Cité Radieuse in Marseille. Temporary exhibitions are housed in the large basement area.
Event highlights Archi & BD: La Ville Dessinée (until 28 Nov 2010)

Galerie-Musée Baccarat

11 pl des Etats-Unis, 16th (01.40.22.11.00, www.baccarat.fr). M° Boissière or Iéna. **Open** 10am-6pm Mon, Wed-Sat. **Admission** €5; free-€3.50 reductions. **Map** p58 B3 **⑤**
Philippe Starck has created a neo-rococo wonderland in the former mansion of the Vicomtesse de Noailles. See items by Georges Chevalier and Ettore Sottsass, services made for princes and maharajahs, and show-off items made for the great exhibitions of the 1800s.

Galeries Nationales du Grand Palais

3 av du Général-Eisenhower, 8th (01.44.13.17.17, reservations 08.92.68.46.94, www.grandpalais.fr). M° Champs-Elysées Clemenceau. **Open** 10am-10pm Mon, Wed, Fri-Sun; 10am-8pm Thur; pre-booking compulsory before 1pm. **Admission** *Before 1pm with reservation* €12. *After 1pm without reservation* €10; free-€9 reductions. **Map** p59 E4 **⑥**
Built for the 1900 Exposition Universelle, the Grand Palais was the work of three different architects. During World War II it accommodated Nazi tanks. In 1994 the glass-roofed central hall was closed when bits of metal started falling off. After major restoration, the Palais reopened in 2005 and now hosts major exhibitions.
Event highlights Monet retrospective (22 Sept 2010-24 Jan 2011).

Musée d'Art Moderne de la Ville de Paris

11 av du Président-Wilson, 16th (01.53.67.40.00, www.mam.paris.fr) M° Alma Marceau or Iéna. **Open** 10am-6pm Tue-Sun. **Admission** *Temporary exhibitions* €4.50-€9; free-€4.50 reductions. No credit cards. **Map** p58 B4 **⑦**
This monumental 1930s building houses the city's modern art collection. The museum is strong on the Cubists, Fauves, the Delaunays, Rouault, Soutine, Modigliani and van Dongen.

A

Porte Maillot

RUE DU DÉB ARCADÈRE

BOULEVARD PÉREIRE

BLVD PÉREIRE

RUE PIERRE DEMOURS

RUE SAINT

AVENUE DES TERNES

RUE DE COURCELLES

RUE DU COL. MOLL

FERDINAND

RUE DU TILLSART

DES

RUE DE JOYBUSE

RUE BRUNEL

ARGENTINE

TERNES

AVENUE CARNOT

AVENUE DE LA GRANDE ARMÉE

RUE PERGOLÈSE

RUE DURET

RUE LE SUEUR

RUE CHALGRIN

ACACIAS

RUE DE L'ÉTOILE

AV. MAC MAHON

RUE DE L'ARC DE TRIOMPHE

R. D. ÉTANG DES

R. ANATOLE DE LA FORGE

Argentine

PLACE CHARLES

Arc de Triomphe

DE GAULLE

Charles de Gaulle-Étoile

B

RUE PONCELET

R. T RISSO

RUE PONCELET

RUE LAUGIER

25

16

Ternes

17

RUE BREY

RUE DE L'ÉTOILE

AVENUE DE WAGRAM

RUE DARU

RUE DU FAUBOURG

ST HONORÉ

AV. B. ALBRECHT

R. BALZAC

AVENUE HOCHE

22

29

44

BEAUJON

R. LORD BYRON

BALZAC

C

BOULEVARD DE COURCELLES

AVENUE DE FRIEDLAND

24

Chambre de Commerce

WASHINGTON

AVENUE DE

40

41

GALILÉE

33

VERNET

George V

RUE LINCOLN

RUE DE BERRI

DES

30

CHAMPS

RUE DE PONTHIEU

RUE DE LINCOLN

AVENUE FOCH

AVENUE VICTOR HUGO

RUE LÉONARD DE VINCI

RUE LAURISTON

PAUL

AVENUE KLÉBER

Kléber

RUE LA PÉROUSE

RUE DUMONT D'URVILLE

AVENUE D'IÉNA

AVE MARCEAU

RUE EULER

RUE KEPPLER

BASSANO

RUE MAGELLAN

RUE QUENTIN

GEORGE V

AVENUE MARCEAU

RUE PIERRE CHARRON

RUE MARBEUF

RUE LA BOÉTIE

FRANÇOIS TER

27

RUE DE LA TRÉMOILLE

RUE DE BASSANO

Victor Hugo

PLACE VICTOR HUGO

RUE COPERNIC

RUE BOISSIÈRE

RUE LAURISTON

RUE CIMAROSA

VALÉRY

CHAILLOT

RUE GALILÉE

JEAN GIRAUDOUX

PLACE DES ÉTATS-UNIS

RUE G.

CHAILLOT

RUE DE BIZET

AVENUE GEORGE V

American Cathedral

36

RUE FRANÇOIS TER

RUE PIERRE TER

26

46

AVENUE

34

3

PLACE VICTOR HUGO

Boissière

RUE LÉO DELIBES

R. ST DIDIER

AVENUE KLÉBER

RUE DU BOUQUET DE LONGCHAMP

RUE HAMELIN

RUE DE L'AMIRAL D'ESTAING

LUBECK

RUE DE LONGCHAMP

RUE DE MAGDEBOURG

AV. D'IÉNA

Musée Guimet

9

Iéna

AV. PIERRE TER

Palais Galliera

RUE DE SERBIE

RUE GOETHE

PRÉSIDENT

39

Alma Marceau

DE L'ALMA

4

AV. RAYMOND POINCARÉ

16

PL DU TROCADÉRO ET DU 11 NOVEMBRE

Trocadéro

Cimetière de Passy

RUE FRANKLIN

AVENUE DU PRÉSIDENT WILSON

4

Palais de Chaillot

3

AVENUE ALBERT DE MUN

AVENUE DE NEW YORK

RUE FRESNEL

RUE DE LA MANUTENTION

7

12

Palais de Tokyo

15

2

PONT DE L'ALMA

Pont de l'Alma

QUAI D'ORSAY

Seine

QUAI BRANLY

Musée du Quai Branly

RUE DE L'UNIVERSITÉ

R. COGNACQ JAY

AVENUE RAPP

RUE DE MONTTESSUY

R. ED. VALENTIN

AVENUE BOSQUET

5

PONT

Tour Eiffel

AV. S. DU CAMOU

Legend:
- 1 Sights & museums
- 1 Eating & drinking
- 1 Shopping
- 1 Nightlife
- 1 Arts & leisure

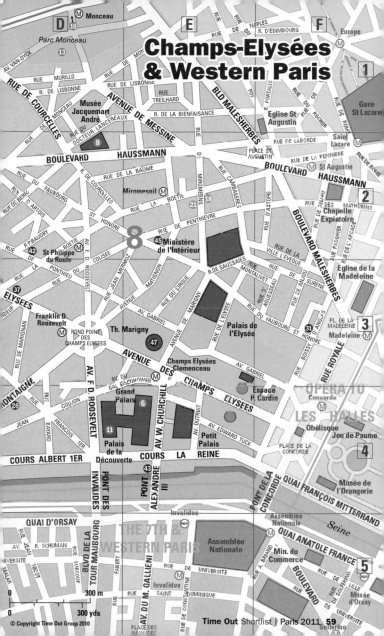

Champs-Elysées
& Western Paris

© Copyright Time Out Group 2010

mondays
2 for 1 moosehead beer
all night

sundays
american style brunch
11:30am-3:30pm

tuesdays
ladies' night
happy hour for ladies

everyday
happy hour
4pm-8:00pm

the moose
canadian sports bar & grill

NATIONS

www.mooseparis.com
16 rue des quatre vents 75006 paris metro odeon tel 01 46 33 77 00

Musée Jacquemart-André

158 bd Haussmann, 8th (01.45.62. 11.59, www.musee-jacquemart-andre.com). M° Miromesnil or St-Philippe-du-Roule. **Open** 10am-6pm daily. **Admission** €10; free-€7.50 reductions. **Map** p59 D2 **8**

Long terrace steps and a stern pair of stone lions usher visitors into this grand 19th-century mansion, home to a collection of equally stately *objets d'art* and fine paintings. The collection was assembled by Edouard André and his artist wife Nélie Jacquemart, using money inherited from his rich banking family. The mansion was built to order to house their art hoard, which includes Rembrandts, Tiepolo frescoes and paintings by Italian masters Uccello, Mantegna and Carpaccio.

Musée National des Arts Asiatiques – Guimet

6 pl d'Iéna, 16th (01.56.52.53.00, www.museeguimet.fr). M° Iéna. **Open** 10am 5.45pm Mon, Wed-Sun (last entry 5.15pm). **Admission** €6.50; free-€4.50 reductions. **Map** p58 B4 **9**

The museum houses 45,000 objects from Neolithic times onwards, in a voyage across Asian religions and civilisations. Lower galleries focus on India and South-east Asia, centred on Hindu and Buddhist Khmer sculpture from Cambodia. Don't miss the Giant's Way, part of the entrance to a temple complex at Angkor Wat. Upstairs, Chinese antiquities include mysterious jade discs. Afghan glassware, Tibetan mandalas and Moghul jewellery also feature.

Musée National Jean-Jacques Henner

NEW *43 av de Villiers, 17th (01.47. 63.42.73). M° Malesherbes.* **Open** 11am-6pm Mon, Wed-Sun. **Admission** €5; €3 reductions. Map p59 D1 **10**

Reopened in 2009 after four years of renovation work, the Musée National Jean-Jacques Henner traces the life of one of France's most respected artists, from his humble beginnings in Alsace

in 1829 to his rise as one of the most sought-after painters in Paris. On the first floor, Alsatian landscapes and family portraits are a reminder of the artist's lifelong attachment to his native region. What brought the artist most acclaim (and criticism), however, was his trademark nymph paintings.

Palais de la Découverte

Av Franklin-D.-Roosevelt, 8th (01.56. 43.20.21, www.palais-decouverte.fr). M° Champs-Elysées Clemenceau or Franklin D. Roosevelt. **Open** 9.30am-6pm Tue-Sat; 10am-7pm Sun (last entry 30mins before closing). **Admission** €7; free-€4.50 reductions. *Planetarium* €3.50. **Map** p59 D4 **11**

This science museum houses designs dating from Leonardo da Vinci's time to the present day. Models, real apparatus and audio-visual material bring the displays to life, and exhibits cover astrophysics, astronomy, biology, chemistry, physics and earth sciences. There are shows at the Planetarium, and 'live' experiments take place at weekends and during school holidays.

Palais de Tokyo: Site de Création Contemporaine

13 av du Président-Wilson, 16th (01.47. 23.54.01, www.palaisdetokyo.com). M° Alma Marceau or Iéna. **Open** noon-midnight Tue-Sun. **Admission** €6; free-€4.50 reductions. **Map** p58 C4 **12**

When it opened in 2002, many thought the Palais' stripped-back interior was a design statement. In fact, it was a practical answer to tight finances. The 1937 building has now come into its own as an open-plan space, hosting exhibitions, shows and performances. Extended hours and a funky café have succeeded in drawing a younger audience, and the roll-call of artists is impressive.

Parc Monceau

Bd de Courcelles, av Hoche, rue Monceau, 8th. M° Monceau. **Open** *Nov-Mar* 7am-8pm daily. *Apr-Oct* 7am-10pm daily. **Admission** free. **Map** p59 D1 **13**

PARIS BY AREA

Monceau is a favourite with well-dressed children and their nannies. It was laid out in the 18th century for the Duc de Chartres in the English style, with a lake, lawns and follies: an Egyptian pyramid, a Corinthian colonnade, Venetian bridge and sarcophagi.

Eating & drinking

Alain Ducasse au Plaza Athénée
Hôtel Plaza Athénée, 25 av Montaigne, 8th (01.53.67.65.00, www.alain-ducasse.com). M° Alma Marceau. **Open** 7.45-10.15pm Mon-Wed; 12.45-2.15pm, 7.45-10.15pm Thur, Fri. Closed mid July-mid Aug & 2wks Dec. €€€€.
Haute cuisine. Map p58 C4 ⑭
The sheer glamour factor would be enough to recommend this restaurant, Alain Ducasse's most lofty Paris undertaking. The dining room ceiling drips with 10,000 crystals. An *amuse-bouche* of a single langoustine in a lemon cream with a touch of Iranian caviar starts the meal off beautifully, but other dishes can be inconsistent. Cheese is delicious, as is the *rum baba comme à Monte-Carlo*.

Antoine
10 av de New York, 16th (01.40.70. 19.28, www.antoine-paris.fr). M° Alma-Marceau or Trocadéro. **Open** noon-2.45pm, 7.30-10.45pm daily. €€€.
Seafood. Map p58 C4 ⑮
Antoine is Paris's newest shrine to the sea. Chic, moneyed crowds gather to sample chef Mickaël Feval's perfect oysters and extravagant dishes like whole roasted lobster with winter vegetables *en cocotte*, plump St-Jacques scallops with creamy purée, and wonderful vanilla millefeuille. The fixed-price lunch menu is excellent value.

Le Dada
12 av des Ternes, 17th (01.43.80. 60.12). M° Ternes. **Open** 7am-2am Mon-Sat; 7am-10pm Sun. €€. **Café**. Map p58 B1 ⑯

Perhaps the hippest café in this stuffy part of town, Le Dada is best known for its well-placed, sunny terrace. Inside, the wood-block carved tables and red walls provide a warm atmosphere for a crowd that tends towards the well-heeled, well-spoken and, well, loaded. That said, the atmosphere is friendly; if terracing is your thing, you could happily spend a summer's day here.

Flute l'Etoile
19 rue de l'Etoile, 17th (01.45.72.10.14, www.flutebar.com). M° Ternes. **Open** 5pm-2am Tue-Sat; 6am-10pm Sun.
Champagne bar. Map p58 B1 ⑰
With a menu of some 23 different champagnes and designer decor (slick wooden panelling, blue walls and red velvet), Paris's first champagne lounge certainly looks the part. For drinkers wishing to sample different vintages without buying a whole glass (from €9), the small tasting glasses (from €5) are a nice touch. And for anyone 'bored' by plain bubbly, cocktails such as champagne sangria make for a sophisticated alternative.

Granterroirs
30 rue de Miromesnil, 8th (01.47.42. 18.18, www.granterroirs.com). M° Miromesnil. **Open** 9am-8pm Mon-Fri. *Food served* noon-3pm Mon-Fri. Closed 3wks Aug. €€.
Bistro. Map p59 E2 ⑲
The walls of this *épicerie* heave with more than 600 enticing specialities from southern France, including Périgord foie gras, charcuterie from Aubrac and a fine selection of wines. Great gifts – but why not sample some of the goodies by enjoying the midday *table d'hôte* feast? Come in early to ensure that you can choose from the five succulent *plats du jour* (such as marinated salmon with dill on a bed of warm potatoes).

Le Hide
10 rue du Général-Lanrezac, 17th (01.45.74.15.81, www.lehide.fr). M° Charles de Gaulle Etoile. **Open**

Galerie-Musée Baccarat p57

noon-3pm, 7.30-10.30pm Mon-Fri; 7.30-10.30pm Sat. €€. **Bistro**. Map p58 B1 ⑲
This bistro is packed with a happy crowd who appreciate Japanese-born chef Hide Kobayashi's superb cooking. Expect dishes such as duck foie gras terrine with pear-and-thyme compôte to start, followed by tender faux-filet steak in a light foie gras sauce. Desserts are excellent: perfect tarte tatin comes with crème fraîche from Normandy.

Ladurée

75 av des Champs-Elysées, 8th (01.40.75.08.75, www.laduree.fr). M° Franklin D. Roosevelt or George V. **Open** 9am-11.30pm Mon-Thur; 9am-12.30am Fri; 10am-12.30am Sat; 10am-11.30pm Sun. €€. **Café**. Map p58 C3 ⑳
Decadence permeates this elegant tearoom. While you bask in the warm glow of bygone wealth, indulge in tea, pastries and, above all, the hot chocolate. It's a rich, velvety tar that will leave you in the requisite stupor for a lazy afternoon.

Maxan

37 rue de Miromesnil, 8th (01.42.65.78.60, www.rest-maxan.com). M° Miromesnil. **Open** noon-2.30pm Mon; noon-2.30pm, 7.30-10.30pm Tue-Fri; 7.30-10.30pm Sat. Closed Aug. €€. **Bistro**. Map p59 E2 ㉑
This is a welcome new-wave bistro. Owner-chef Laurent Zajac uses quality seasonal ingredients, giving them a personal spin in dishes such as scallops with curry spices and artichoke hearts, classic veal sweetbreads with wild asparagus, and an exotic take on *île flottante*. Popular with ministry of interior types at lunch, quieter by night.

Stella Maris

4 rue Arsène-Houssaye, 8th (01.42.89.16.22). M° Charles de Gaulle Etoile. **Open** noon-2.30pm, 7.30-10.30pm Mon-Fri; 7.30-10.30pm Sat. Closed 2wks Aug. €€€€. **Haute cuisine**. Map p58 B2 ㉒

Trained by Robuchon and Troisgros, Tateru Yoshino turns out food that is resolutely French. The service is at times faltering, but charmingly so. You might float your way through foie gras with carrots, truffles and pistachio oil, pan-fried sea bass with saffron risotto, and perfectly lopsided Grand Marnier soufflé. Expensive but wonderful.

La Table Lauriston

129 rue de Lauriston, 16th (01.47.27.00.07, www.restaurantlatablelauriston.com). M° Trocadéro. **Open** noon-2.30pm, 7-10.30pm Mon-Fri; 7-10.30pm Sat. Closed 3wks Aug & 1wk Dec. €€€. **Bistro**. Map p58 A4 ㉓
In spring, stalks of asparagus from the Landes are trimmed to avoid any stringiness and served with the simplest *vinaigrette d'herbes*. More extravagant is *foie gras cuit au torchon*, in which the duck liver is wrapped in a cloth and poached in a bouillon. Skip the crème brûlée and order a dessert with attitude: the giant *baba au rhum*.

Taillevent

15 rue Lamennais, 8th (01.44.95.15.01, www.taillevent.com). M° George V. **Open** 12.15-1.30pm, 7.15-9.30pm Mon-Fri. Closed Aug. €€€€. **Haute cuisine**. Map p58 C2 ㉔
Rémoulade de coquilles St-Jacques is a technical feat, with slices of raw, marinated scallop wrapped in a tube shape around a diced apple filling, encircled by a *rémoulade* sauce. An earthier and lip-smacking dish is the trademark *épeautre* – an ancient wheat – cooked 'like a risotto' with bone marrow, black truffle, whipped cream and parmesan, and topped with sautéed frog's legs.

Shopping

Alléosse

13 rue Poncelet, 17th (01.46.22.50.45, www.fromage-alleosse.com). M° Ternes. **Open** 9am-1pm, 4-7pm Tue-Thur; 9am-1pm, 4.30-7pm Fri, Sat. Map p58 B1 ㉕

People cross town for these cheeses – wonderful farmhouse camemberts, delicate st-marcellins, a choice of *chèvres* and several rarities.

Balenciaga

10 av George V, 8th (01.47.20.21.11, www.balenciaga.com). M° Alma Marceau or George V. **Open** 10am-7pm Mon-Sat. **Map** p58 C4 ㉖

The Spanish fashion house is ahead of Japanese and Belgian designers in the hip stakes. Floating fabrics contrast with dramatic cuts, producing a sophisticated style that the fashion *haut monde* can't wait to slip into.

Balmain

44 rue François 1er, 8th (01.47.20.57.58, www.balmain.com). M° George V. **Open** 10.30am-7pm Mon-Sat. **Map** p58 C3 ㉗

A portrait of the late Pierre Balmain surveys the scene at his eponymous shop. What would he have made of the clothes around him? Long gone are the afternoon dresses with perfectly positioned waists, full skirts and trapezoidal necklines. The racks are these days lined with bondage trousers, studded jackets and animal print drainpipes. There hasn't been such a good display of grungy, punk glamour since Kensington Market closed its doors.

Dior

26-30 av Montaigne, 8th (01.40.73.73.73, www.dior.com). M° Franklin D. Roosevelt. **Open** 10am-7pm Mon-Sat. **Map** p59 D4 ㉘

The Dior universe is here on avenue Montaigne, from the main prêt-à-porter store and jewellery, menswear and eyewear to Baby Dior, where rich infants are coochy-cooed by drooling assistants.

Drugstore Publicis

133 av des Champs-Elysées, 8th (01.44.43.79.00, www.publicisdrugstore.com). M° Charles de Gaulle Etoile. **Open** 8am-2am Mon-Fri; 10am-2am Sat, Sun. **Map** p58 B2 ㉙

On the ground floor there's a newsagent, pharmacy, bookshop and upmarket deli full of quality olive oils and elegant biscuits. The basement is a macho take on Colette, keeping selected design items and lifestyle mags, and replacing high fashion with wines and a cigar cellar.

Fnac

74 av des Champs-Elysées, 8th (08.25.02.00.20, www.fnac.com). M° George V. **Open** 10am-midnight Mon-Sat; noon-midnight Sun. **Map** p58 C3 ㉚

Fnac is a supermarket of culture: books, DVDs, CDs, audio kit, computers and photo equipment. Most branches stock everything; others specialise. All branches operate as a concert box office.

Givenchy

28 rue du Fbg-St-Honoré, 8th (01.42.68.31.00, www.givenchy.com). M° Madeleine or Concorde. **Open** 10am-7pm Mon-Sat. **Map** p59 F3 ㉛

This flagship Fbg-St-Honoré store for men's and women's prêt-à-porter and accessories incorporates surreal rooms within rooms – cut-out boxes filled with white, black or mahogany panelling – providing a contemporary art gallery setting for Givenchy's designs.

LE66

66 av des Champs-Elysées, 8th (01.53.53.33.80). M° George V. **Open** 11am-8pm Mon-Fri; 11.30am-8.30pm Sat; 2-8pm Sun. **Map** p59 D3 ㉜

This fashion concept store is youthful and accessible, with an ever-changing selection of hip brands. Assistants, who are also the buyers and designers, make for a motivated team. The store takes the form of three transparent modules, the first a book store run by Black Book of the Palais de Tokyo, and the second two devoted to fashion.

Louis Vuitton

101 av des Champs-Elysées, 8th (08.10.81.00.10, www.vuitton.com). M° George V. **Open** 10am-8pm Mon-Sat; 11am-7pm Sun. **Map** p58 C2 ㉝

Spreading the word

Sweet honey in the heart of the city.

Paris is buzzing with more than just tourists these days thanks to avid apiarists like Nicolas Géant, founder of bee breeding company Nicomiel (www.nicomiel.com), who has just installed two new beehives in the middle of the Champs-Elysées on the roof of the Grand Palais. Géant expects his 100,000 bees to harvest some 100kg of Miel du Grand Palais per year (on sale in the Grand Palais shop). He follows in the footsteps of Jean Paucton, beekeeper at the Opéra Garnier, whose rooftop hives have been producing Miel des Toits de l'Opéra since 1983 (on sale for €12.50 in Fauchon).

According to Géant, placing beehives on prominent Paris monuments isn't just a money-spinning gimmick. It draws attention to a more serious problem: that bees can no longer thrive in the countryside. 'Like numerous other pollinating insects, bees are being killed by pesticides and intensive farming,' says Géant. 'Around 400,000 French hives have disappeared every year between 1995 and 2007. Paris, on the other hand, is pesticide free, drips in bee-friendly acacia, chestnut and linden trees, and actively encourages apiculture in its parks. In fact, the Ile de France has more bee colonies than anywhere else in the country – around 300.'

But if bees are thriving in the cities, where's the problem? 'Because,' Géant adds, 'we need bees in the countryside where we grow our food. If they keep dying, we may see a worldwide food shortage.'

We can all support the cause by spreading the word – and Paris's honey on our toast. And, for budding beekeepers, the Société Centrale d'Apiculture (www.la-sca.net, 01.45.42.29.08) offers beekeeping lessons in the Jardin du Luxembourg (6th) and Parc Georges Brassens (15th) for €185 a year.

The 'Promenade' flagship sets the tone for Vuitton's global image, from the 'bag bar', bookstore and new jewellery department to the women's and men's ready-to-wear.

Prada

10 av Montaigne, 8th (01.53.23.99.40, www.prada.com). M° Alma Marceau. **Open** 11am-7pm Mon; 10am-7pm Tue-Sat. **Map** p58 C4 ㉞

The high priestess of European chic, Miuccia Prada's elegant stores pull in fashion followers of all ages. Handbags of choice are complemented by the coveted ready-to-wear range.

Sephora

70 av des Champs-Elysées, 8th (01.53.93.22.50, www.sephora.fr). M° Franklin D. Roosevelt. **Open** *Sept-June* 10am-midnight Mon-Thur, Sun, 10am-1am Fri, Sat. *July, Aug* 10am-1.30am daily. **Map** p58 C3 ㉟

The flagship of the cosmetic supermarket chain houses around 12,000 brands of scent and slap. Sephora Blanc (14 cour St-Emilion, 12th, 01.40.02.97.79) features beauty products in a minimalist interior.

Sony Style

39 av George V, 8th (www.boutiquegeorge5.fr). M° George V. **Open** 10.30am-7.30pm Mon-Sat. **Map** p58 C3 ㊱

Sony's first European concept store brings high-tech gadgets and zen decor together in an *hôtel particulier*. Phones, cameras, computers and Playstations are all here, and the latest innovations from Japan are beamed in on big screens. The store also offers a range of services including free IT coaching in a swanky training suite.

Virgin Megastore

52-60 av des Champs-Elysées, 8th (01.49.53.50.00, www.virginmega.fr). M° Franklin D. Roosevelt. **Open** 10am-midnight Mon-Sat; noon-midnight Sun. **Map** p59 D3 ㊲

The luxury of perusing CDs and DVDs till midnight makes this a choice spot, and the listening posts let you sample any CD. Tickets for concerts and sports events are available here too. This main branch has the best book selection.

Nightlife

L'Arc

NEW *12 rue de Presbourg, 16th (01.45.00.78.70, www.larcparis.com). M° Charles de Gaulle Etoile.* **Open** *Restaurant* noon-2.30pm, 7-11pm Mon-Fri; 7-11pm Sat; 11am-4pm Sun. *Club* midnight-5am Fri, Sat. **Admission** free. **Map** p58 B2 ㊳

Paris's jet set darlings have finally found a new haunt in which to strut their stuff. L'Arc boldly steers away from the 'resto-lounge-club' formula that has taken Paris by storm over the last decade, instead focusing on design, discretion and a decent meal. On Fridays and Saturdays, once the posh plates are cleared away, it's party time in the cool but dark, 1960s-style club, awash with black leather sofas and pink and blue lighting.

Le Baron

6 av Marceau, 8th (01.47.20.04.01, www.clublebaron.com). M° Alma Marceau. **Open** times vary. **Admission** free. **Map** p58 C4 ㊴

This small but supremely exclusive hangout for the international jet set only holds 150, most of whom are regulars you'll need to befriend in order to get past the door. But if you manage to get in, you'll be rubbing shoulders with celebrities and super-glossy people.

Le Lido

116bis av des Champs-Elysées, 8th (01.40.76.56.10, www.lido.fr). M° Franklin D. Roosevelt or George V. **Lunch** 1pm. **Matinée** 3pm Tue, Sun (once a mth, dates vary). **Dinner** 7pm. **Shows** 9.30pm, 11.30pm daily. **Admission** *Matinée show* (incl champagne) €80. *Lunch & matinée*

SEE MORE. BE MORE.

This is NEW YORK CITY

Book Now. Get More.

Book your trip to NYC today with Travelocity on **nycgo.com**. Get the most out of your stay with special offers on hotels, dining, shopping, museums, arts, entertainment and more.

✱ travelocity

NYC
nycgo.com

show (incl champagne) €115 Tue; €125
Sun. *9.30pm show* (incl champagne)
€100; €20 reductions. *11.30pm show*
(incl champagne) €90; free under-12s.
Dinner & show €140-€280; €30
reductions. **Map** p58 C2 ④
This is the largest cabaret of all: high-
tech touches optimise visibility, and
chef Philippe Lacroix provides fabulous gourmet nosh. On stage, 60
Bluebell Girls slink around, shaking
their boobs with panache.

Queen

*102 av des Champs-Elysées, 8th (01.53.
89.08.90, www.queen.fr).* M° George V.
Open 11pm-5am Mon; midnight-6am
Tue-Thur, Sun; midnight-8am Fri, Sat.
Admission €15 Mon-Thur, Sun; €20
Fri, Sat. **Map** p58 C2 ④
Once the city's most fêted gay club and
the only venue that could hold a torch
to the Rex, with a roster of top local DJs
holding court, Queen's star faded in the
early noughties but is now starting to
shine more brightly again.

Le Régine

NEW *49 rue de Ponthieu, 8th (01.43.
59.21.13, www.leregine.com)* M° St-
Philippe-du-Roule.* **Open** 11pm-6am
Tue-Sat. **Admission** free-€10.
Map p59 D2 ④
Régine was once a key figure on the
Paris nightlife scene, and the club she
created is now experiencing a rejuve-
nation. The revamped club fits right
into the burlesque cabaret trend, with
crazy performers, a musical mish-mash
and lines of cool kids at the door.

Le Showcase

*Underneath Pont Alexandre III, 8th
(01.45.61.25.43, www.showcase.fr).*
M° Champs-Elysées Clemenceau.* **Open**
10pm-dawn Fri, Sat; 11am-3pm Sun.
Admission free-€15. **Map** p59 E4 ④
A little too flash for some, but there's
no doubting this vaulted club by the
Seine, and its Sous le Pont events – live
performance followed by DJs – have
been a big success story.

Arts & leisure

Le Balzac

*1 rue Balzac, 8th (01.45.61.10.60,
www.cinemabalzac.com).* M° George V.
Admission €9; €5-€7 reductions.
No credit cards. **Map** p58 C2 ④
Built in 1935 and boasting a mock
ocean-liner foyer, the Balzac scores
highly for design and programming.
Manager Jean-Jacques Schpoliansky
often welcomes punters in person.

Salle Pleyel

*252 rue du Fbg-St-Honoré, 8th
(01.42.56.13.13, www.sallepleyel.fr).*
M° Ternes.* **Box office** noon-7pm
Mon-Sat. *By phone* 11am-7pm Mon-
Sat; 11am-5pm Sun. **Admission**
€10-€160. **Map** p59 E2 ④
Home to the Orchestre de Paris, this
restored concert hall has regained its
prestigious status as the only venue
dedicated to large-scale symphonic
concerts in the capital.
Event highlights Patti Smith & Philip
Glass: Hommage à Allen Ginsberg
(21 Jan 2011)

Théâtre des Champs-Elysées

*15 av Montaigne, 8th (01.49.52.50.50,
www.theatrechampselysees.fr).* M° Alma
Marceau.* **Box office** 1-7pm Mon-Sat.
By phone 10am-noon, 2-6pm Mon-Fri
Admission €5-€160 **Map** p58 C4 ④
This beautiful art nouveau theatre
remains the favourite venue for visit-
ing foreign orchestras.

Théâtre Marigny

*Av de Marigny, 8th (01.53.96.70.30,
www.theatremarigny.fr).* M° Champs-
Elysées Clemenceau or Franklin D.
Roosevelt.* **Box office** 11am-6.30pm
Mon-Sat; 11am-3pm Sun. **Admission**
€33-€51. **Map** p59 E3 ④
Théâtre Marigny boasts a location off
the Champs-Elysées, a deluxe interior
conceived by Charles Garnier, high-
profile casts and an illustrious pedigree
stretching back some 150 years.

Musée de l'Orangerie p74

Opéra to Les Halles

In centuries gone by, these two adjoining central districts – bounded by the Grands Boulevards to the north and the river to the south – were the city's commercial and provisioning powerhouses, home to most of the newspapers, banks and major mercantile institutions. Nowadays, although there is still a strong financial slant thanks to the presence of the two stock exchanges and the Banque de France, the focus is on shopping: mass-market stuff in and around **Les Halles**, shading into more exclusive brands the further one moves west, in particular on and just off rue St-Honoré.

Les Halles itself was, famously, the city's wholesale food market until 1969, when the Second Empire iron-framed buildings that housed it were ripped out, and a thousand commentators gnashed their teeth in print. The soulless shopping centre that filled the gap in the 1970s has been one of the city's least liked features, and is itself doomed to destruction in the next few years, to be replaced by a 21st-century glory of gardens, glass and open spaces.

A short distance west of Les Halles is the **Louvre**, no longer the centre of French power though it still exerts considerable influence: first as a grandiose architectural ensemble, a palace within the city; and, second, as a symbol of the capital's cultural pre-eminence. Across rue de Rivoli from the Louvre stands the elegant **Palais-Royal**. After a stroll in its quiet gardens, it's hard to believe this was the starting point of the French Revolution. Today, its arcades house a mix of antiques dealers, philatelists and fashion showcases.

Sights & museums

La Collection 1900

NEW *Maxim's, 3 rue Royale, 8th (01.42.65.30.47, www.maxims-musee-artnouveau.com). Mᵒ Madeleine.* **Open**

Guided tours (reservations essential) 2pm Wed-Sun (English); 3.15pm, 4.30pm (French). **Admission** €15. No credit cards. **Map** p72 A3 **①**

Couturier Pierre Cardin has owned belle époque restaurant Maxim's since 1981, and now he has added a museum of art nouveau, which he has been collecting since the age of 18. There are rooms and rooms of exhibits, arranged so as to evoke a 19th-century courtesan's boudoir. Read Zola's *Nana* before your visit to grasp the full effect of the dreamy lake maidens sculpted in glistening faience, pewter vanity sets in the shape of reclining nudes, and beds inlaid with opium flowers to promote sleep. Dinner settings on display include Gustav Eiffel's own chunky tureens, just crying out for turtle soup.

Eglise de la Madeleine

Pl de la Madeleine, 8th (01.44.51. 69.00, www.eglise-lamadeleine.com). M° Concorde or Madeleine. **Open** 9.30am-7pm daily. **Map** p72 A2 **②**

The building of a church on this site began in 1764, and in 1806 Napoleon sent instructions from Poland for Barthélémy Vignon to design a 'Temple of Glory' dedicated to his Grand Army. After the emperor's fall, construction slowed and the building, by now a church again, was finally consecrated in 1845. The exterior is ringed by huge, fluted Corinthian columns, with a double row at the front, and a frieze of the Last Judgement just above the portico. Inside are giant domes, an organ and pseudo-Grecian side altars in a sea of multicoloured marble.

Forum des Halles

1st. M° Les Halles/RER Châtelet Les Halles. **Map** p73 E4 **③**

The labyrinthine mall and transport interchange extends three levels underground and includes the Ciné Cité multiplex cinema and Forum des Images, as well as clothing chains, a branch of Fnac and the Forum des Créateurs, a section for young designers. Despite an open central courtyard, a sense of gloom prevails. All should change by 2012, with a new landscaping of the whole area.

Jardin des Tuileries

Rue de Rivoli, 1st. M° Concorde or Tuileries. **Open** 7.30am-7pm daily. **Map** p72 B4 **④**

The gravelled alleyways of these gardens have been a chic promenade ever since they opened to the public in the 16th century; and the popular mood persists with the funfair that sets up along the rue de Rivoli side in summer. André Le Nôtre created the prototypical French garden with terraces and central vista running down the *Grand Axe* through circular and hexagonal ponds. As part of Mitterrand's Grand Louvre project, sculptures such as Coysevox's winged horses were transferred to the Louvre and replaced by copies, and the Maillol sculptures were returned to the Jardins du Carrousel; a handful of modern sculptures have been added, including bronzes by Moore, Ernst, Giacometti, and Dubuffet's *Le Bel Costumé*.

Jeu de Paume

1 pl de la Concorde, 8th (01.47.03.12.50, www.jeudepaume.org). M° Concorde. **Open** noon-9pm Tue; noon-7pm Wed-Fri; 10am-7pm Sat, Sun (last admission 30mins before closing). **Admission** €7; €5 reductions. **Map** p72 A3 **⑤**

The Centre National de la Photographie moved into this site in 2005. The building, which once served as a tennis court, has been divided into two white, almost hangar-like galleries. It is not an intimate space, but it works well for showcase retrospectives. A video art and cinema suite in the basement shows new digital installation work.

Event highlights André Kertész (28 Sept 2010-6 Feb 2011)

Musée des Arts Décoratifs

107 rue de Rivoli, 1st (01.44.55.57.50, www.lesartsdecoratifs.fr). M° Palais Royal Musée du Louvre or Pyramides.

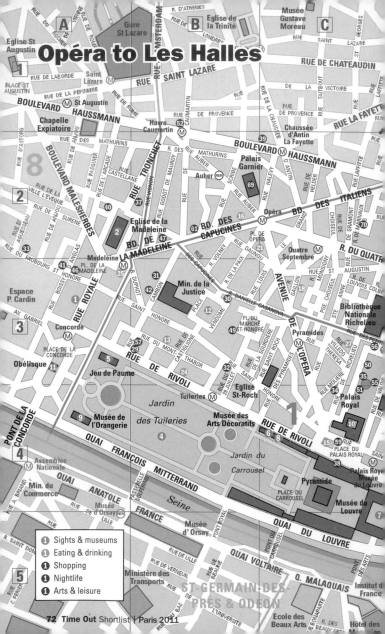

Opéra to Les Halles

A Gare St Lazare
B Église de la Trinité
C Musée Gustave Moreau

Église St Augustin

Chapelle Expiatoire

Église de la Madeleine

Espace P. Cardin

Concorde

Obélisque

Jeu de Paume

Musée de l'Orangerie

Palais Garnier

Min. de la Justice

Bibliothèque Nationale Richelieu

Pyramides

Palais Royal

Tuileries

Jardin des Tuileries

Musée des Arts Décoratifs

Église St-Roch

Jardin du Carrousel

Palais Royal Musée du Louvre

Pyramide

Musée du Louvre

Assemblée Nationale

Min. du Commerce

Musée d'Orsay

Musée d'Orsay

Ministère des Transports

ST-GERMAIN-DES-PRÉS & ODÉON

Ecole des Beaux Arts

Institut de France

Legend:
- ● Sights & museums
- ● Eating & drinking
- ● Shopping
- ● Nightlife
- ● Arts & leisure

Open 11am-6pm Tue, Wed, Fri; 11am-9pm Thur; 10am-6pm Sat, Sun. Closed some hols. **Admission** (with Musée de la Mode & Musée de la Publicité) €8; free-€6.50 reductions. **Map** p72 C4 **6**

Taken as a whole along with the Musée de la Mode et du Textile and Musée de la Publicité, this is one of the world's major collections of design and the decorative arts. The venue reopened in 2006 after a decade-long, €35-million restoration of the building and of 6,000 of the 150,000 items donated mainly by private collectors. The major focus here is French furniture and tableware, from extravagant carpets to delicate crystal and porcelain. Of most obvious attraction to the layman are the reconstructed period rooms, ten in all, showing how the other half lived from the late 1400s to the early 20th century.

Event highlights Mobi-Boom: L'Explosion du Design en France 1945-1975 (23 Sept 2010-2 Jan 2011)

Musée du Louvre

Rue de Rivoli, 1st (01.40.20.50.50, www.louvre.fr). M° Palais Royal Musée du Louvre. **Open** 9am-6pm Mon, Thur, Sat, Sun; 9am-10pm Wed, Fri. **Admission** €9; free-€6 reductions. **Map** p72 C5 **7**

Some 35,000 works of art and artefacts are on show, divided into eight departments and housed in three wings: Denon, Sully and Richelieu. Treasures from the Egyptians, Etruscans, Greeks and Romans each have their own galleries in the Denon and Sully wings, as do Middle Eastern and Islamic works of art. The first floor of Richelieu is taken up with European decorative arts from the Middle Ages up to the 19th century.

The main draw, though, is the painting and sculpture. Two glass-roofed sculpture courts contain the Marly horses on the ground floor of Richelieu, with French sculpture below and Italian Renaissance pieces in the Denon wing. The Grande Galerie and Salle de la Joconde (home to the *Mona Lisa*) run the length of Denon's first floor with French

Romantic painting alongside. Dutch and French painting occupies the second floor of Richelieu and Sully. Laminated panels provide a lively commentary, and the superb website is a technological feat. Work continues on the new Islamic Arts department.

Musée de la Mode et du Textile

107 rue de Rivoli, 1st (01.44.55.57.50, www.lesartsdecoratifs.fr). M° Palais Royal Musée du Louvre or Pyramides. **Open** *Exhibitions* 11am-6pm Tue, Wed, Fri; 11am-9pm Thur; 10am-6pm Sat, Sun. **Admission** (with Musée des Arts Décoratifs & Musée de la Publicité) €8; free-€6.50 reductions. **Map** p72 C4 **8**

This municipal fashion museum holds Elsa Schiaparelli's entire archive and hosts exciting themed exhibitions. Dramatic black-walled rooms make a fine background to the clothes, and video screens and a cinema space show how the clothes move, as well as interviews with the creators.

Musée de l'Orangerie

Jardin des Tuileries, 1st (01.44.77. 80.07, www.musee-orangerie.fr). M° Concorde. **Open** 9am-6pm Wed-Sun. **Admission** €7.50; free-€5.50 reductions. **Map** p72 A4 **9**

The look of this Monet showcase is utilitarian and fuss-free, with the museum's eight, tapestry-sized *Nymphéas* (water lilies) paintings housed in two plain oval rooms. They provide a simple backdrop for the ethereal romanticism of Monet's works, painted late in his life. Downstairs, the Jean Walter and Paul Guillaume collection of Impressionism and the Ecole de Paris is a mixed bag of sweet-toothed Cézanne and Renoir portraits, with works by Modigliani, Rousseau, Matisse, Picasso and Derain.

Palais-Royal

Pl du Palais-Royal, 1st. M° Palais Royal Musée du Louvre. **Open** Gardens 7.30am-8.30pm daily. **Admission** free. **Map** p72 C4 **10**

Built for Cardinal Richelieu by Jacques Lemercier, the building was once known as Palais Cardinal. Richelieu left it to Louis XIII, whose widow Anne d'Autriche preferred it to the Louvre and rechristened it when she moved in with her son, the young Louis XIV. In the 1780s the Duc d'Orléans enclosed the gardens in a three-storey peristyle and filled it with cafés, shops, theatres, sideshows and accommodation to raise money for rebuilding the burned-down opera. Daniel Buren's striped columns grace the main courtyard.

Place de la Concorde

1st/8th. M° Concorde. **Map** p72 A3 ⑪
This is the city's largest square, its grand east-west perspectives stretching from the Louvre to the Arc de Triomphe, and north-south from the Madeleine to the Assemblée Nationale across the Seine. Royal architect Gabriel designed it in the 1750s, along with the two colonnaded mansions astride rue Royale; the west one houses the chic Hôtel de Crillon and the Automobile Club de France, the other is the Naval Ministry. In 1792 the centre statue of Louis XV was replaced with the guillotine for Louis XVI, Marie-Antoinette and many more.

Place Vendôme

1st. M° Opéra or Tuileries.
Map p72 B3 ⑫
Elegant place Vendôme got its name from a *hôtel particulier* built by the Duc de Vendôme that stood on the site. Opened in 1699, the eight-sided square was conceived by Hardouin-Mansart to show off an equestrian statue of the Sun King, torn down in 1792 and replaced in 1806 by the Colonne de la Grande Armée. During the 1871 Commune this symbol of 'brute force and false glory' was pulled down; the present column is a replica. Today the square houses sparkling jewellers, top fashion houses and the justice ministry. At no.12, you can visit the Grand Salon where Chopin died in 1849.

Eating & drinking

L'Ardoise

28 rue du Mont-Thabor, 1st (01.42.96.28.18, www.lardoise-paris.com). M° Concorde or Tuileries. **Open** noon-2.30pm, 6.30-11pm Tue-Sat; 6.30-11pm Sun. Closed 1st 3wks Aug. €€. **Bistro**. **Map** p72 B3 ⑬
One of the city's finest modern bistros, L'Ardoise is regularly packed with gourmets eager to sample Pierre Jay's delicious cooking. A wise choice might be six oysters with warm chipolatas and pungent shallot dressing; equally attractive are a hare pie with an escalope of foie gras nestling in its centre. Unusually, it's open on Sundays.

La Bourse ou la Vie

12 rue Vivienne, 2nd (01.42.60.08.83). M° Bourse. **Open** noon-10pm Mon-Fri. Closed 1wk Aug & 1wk Dec. €€. **Bistro**. **Map** p72 D3 ⑭
After a career as an architect, the round-spectacled owner of La Bourse ou la Vie has a new mission in life: to revive the dying art of the perfect *steak-frites*. The only decision you'll need to make is which cut of beef to order with your chips, unless you pick the cod. Choose between ultra-tender *coeur de filet* or a huge, tender *bavette*. Rich, creamy pepper sauce is the specialty here, but the real surprise is the chips, which gain a distinctly animal flavour from the suet in which they are cooked.

Café Marly

93 rue de Rivoli, cour Napoléon, 1st (01.49.26.06.60). M° Palais Royal Musée du Louvre. **Open** 8am-2am daily. €€. **Café**. **Map** p72 C4 ⑮
A class act, this, as you might expect of a Costes café whose lofty, arcaded terrace overlooks the Louvre's glass pyramid. Reached through the passage Richelieu (the entrance for advance Louvre ticket holders), the prime location comes at a price: it's €6 for a Heineken – so you might as well splash out €12 on a chocolate martini or a

PARIS BY AREA

Shark of vodka, lemonade and grena-dine. Most wines are under €10 a glass, and everything is impeccably served by razor-sharp staff. Brasserie fare and sandwiches are on offer too.

Café de la Paix

12 bd des Capucines, 9th (01.40.07. 36.36, www.cafedelapaix.fr). M° Opéra. **Open** 7am-midnight daily. **€€**. **Café**. **Map** p72 B2 ⑯

Lap up every detail – this is once-in-a-holiday stuff. Whether you're out on the historic terrace or looking up at the ornate stucco ceiling, you'll be sipping in the footsteps of the likes of Oscar Wilde, Josephine Baker, Emile Zola, and Bartholdi and the Franco-American Union (as they sketched out the Statue of Liberty). Let the immaculate staff bring you a kir (€12) or, for an afternoon treat, the vanilla mille-feuille – possibly the best in Paris.

De la Ville Café

34 bd de Bonne-Nouvelle, 10th (01.48.24.48.09, www.delaville cafe.com). M° Bonne Nouvelle. **Open** 11am-2am Mon-Sat; noon-2am Sun. **Bar**. **Map** p73 E2 ⑰

De la Ville has brought good news to Bonne-Nouvelle. A major expansion and refurbishment have upped the ante, bringing the Marais in-crowd to this otherwise ignored quarter. Inside, the distressed walls and industrial-baroque feel remain, but the curvy club section at the back has become very cool. A grand staircase leads to a first-floor lounge and exhibition space. The café was opened by the Café Charbon crew.

Drouant

18 rue Gaillon, 2nd (01.42.65.15.16, www.drouant.com). M° Pyramides or Quatre Septembre. **Open** noon-2.30pm, 7pm-midnight daily. **€€€**. **Brasserie**. **Map** p72 C3 ⑱

Star chef Antoine Westermann has whisked this landmark brasserie into the 21st century with bronze-coloured banquettes and butter-yellow fabrics.

Westermann has dedicated this restaurant to the art of the hors d'oeuvre, in themed sets of four ranging from global (Thai beef salad with brightly coloured vegetables, coriander, and a sweet and spicy sauce) to nostalgic (silky leeks in vinaigrette). The bite-sized surprises continue with the main course accompaniments – four of them for each dish – and multiple mini-desserts.

Frenchie

NEW *5 rue du Nil, 2nd (01.40.39.96.19, www.frenchie-restaurant.com). M° Sentier.* **Open** 8-11pm Tue; noon-2.30pm, 8-11pm Wed-Sat. **€**. **Bistro**. **Map** p73 E3 ⑲

Grégory Lemarchand honed his craft with Jamie Oliver in London before opening this loft-style bistro next to the market street rue Montorgueil. It has been an instant hit thanks to the bold flavours of dishes such as gazpacho with calamari, squash blossoms and plenty of herbs; braised lamb with roasted aubergine and spinach; and coconut tapioca with strawberry sorbet. Book several days ahead.

Le Fumoir

6 rue de l'Amiral-de-Coligny, 1st (01.42.92.00.24, www.lefumoir.fr). M° Louvre Rivoli. **Open** 11am-2am daily. Closed 2wks Aug. **Bar**. **Map** p73 D5 ⑳

This elegant bar facing the Louvre has become a local institution: neo-colonial fans whirr lazily and oil paintings adorn the walls. A sleek crowd sips martinis or reads papers at the mahogany bar (originally from a Chicago speakeasy), giving way to young professionals in the restaurant and pretty things in the library. It can feel a touch try-hard, but expertly mixed cocktails should take the edge off any evening.

Harry's New York Bar

5 rue Daunou, 2nd (01.42.61.71.14, www.harrys-bar.fr). M° Opéra. **Open** 10am-4am daily. **Bar**. **Map** p72 B2 ㉑

The city's most stylish American bar is beloved of expats, visitors and hard-drinking Parisians. The bartenders

Café de la Paix p76

mix some of the most sophisticated cocktails in town, from the trademark bloody mary (invented here, so they say) to the *Pétrifiant*, an elixir of half a dozen spirits splashed into a beer mug. They can also whip up personalised creations that will have you swooning in the piano bar, where Gershwin composed *An American in Paris*.

Kaï

18 rue du Louvre, 1st (01.40.15.01.99). Mº Louvre Rivoli. **Open** noon-2pm, 7-10.30pm Tue-Sat; 7-10.30pm Sun. Closed 1wk Apr & 3wks Aug. **€€**. **Japanese**. Map p73 D4 ㉒
This restaurant has developed a following among fashionable diners. The 'Kaï-style' sushi is a zesty take on a classic: marinated and lightly grilled yellowtail is pressed on to a roll of shiso-scented rice. Not to be outdone, grilled aubergine with miso, seemingly simple, turns out to be a smoky, luscious experience. A main of breaded pork lacks the finesse of the starters, but is still satisfying.

Liza

14 rue de la Banque, 2nd (01.55.35.00.66, www.restaurant-liza.com). Mº Bourse. **Open** 12.30-2pm, 8-10.30pm Mon-Thur; 12.30-2pm, 8-11pm Fri; 8-11pm Sat; noon-4pm Sun. **€€**. **Lebanese**. Map p73 D3 ㉓
Liza Soughayar's eaterie showcases the style and superb food of Beirut. Lentil, fried onion and orange salad is delicious, as are the *kebbe* (minced seasoned raw lamb) and grilled halloumi cheese with home-made apricot preserve. Main courses such as minced lamb with coriander-spiced spinach and rice are light, flavoursome and well presented. Finish with the halva ice-cream with carob molasses.

Le Meurice

Hôtel Meurice, 228 rue de Rivoli, 1st (01.44.58.10.55, www.meuricehotel. com). Mº Tuileries. **Open** 12.30-2pm, 7.30-10pm Mon-Fri. Closed 2wks Feb & Aug. **€€€€**. **Haute cuisine**. Map p72 B3 ㉔

Chef Yannick Alléno produces some glorious, if rather understated, dishes, teasing the flavour out of every leaf, frond, fin or fillet. Turbot is sealed in clay before cooking and then sauced with celery cream and a coulis of flat parsley, and Bresse chicken stuffed with foie gras and served with truffled *sarladais* potatoes is breathtakingly good. A fine cheese tray comes from Quatrehomme, and the pastry chef amazes with his signature millefeuille.

Senderens

9 pl de la Madeleine, 8th (01.42.65. 22.90, www.senderens.fr). Mº Madeleine. **Open** noon-3pm, 7.30-11.30pm daily. Closed 3wks Aug. **€€€€**. **Haute cuisine**. Map p72 A3 ㉕
Alain Senderens reinvented his art nouveau institution (formerly Lucas Carton) a few years ago with a *Star Trek* interior and a mind-boggling fusion menu. You might find dishes such as roast duck foie gras with a warm salad of black figs and liquorice powder. Each dish comes with a suggested wine, whisky, sherry or punch.

Le Tambour

41 rue Montmartre, 2nd (01.42.33. 06.90). Mº Sentier. **Open** 8am-6am daily. **Bar**. Map p73 D3 ㉖
The Tambour is a classic nighthawk's bar decked with vintage public transport paraphernalia, its slatted wooden banquettes and bus stop-sign bar stools occupied by chatty regulars who give the 24-hour clock their best shot. Neither tatty nor threatening, there's a long dining room memorable for its métro map from Stalingrad station.

Thaïm

NEW *46 rue de Richelieu, 1st (01.42.96. 54.67). Mº Bourse or Palais Royal.* **Open** noon-3pm, 7-11.30pm Mon-Fri; 7-11pm Sat. **€**. **Thai**. Map p72 B3 ㉗
Steering well away from Thai clichés, Thaïm has an elegant decor of dark wood and plum fabrics, and a brief menu that changes often, keeping the

regulars coming back. Particularly good value is the three-course lunch menu, which might bring crisp fried parcels filled with spiced vegetables, an aromatic green fish curry (there is a choice of fish, meat or poultry every day), and coconut-pumpkin soup. There is a vast choice of teas, including an iced ginger-coconut version.

Shopping

Agnès b

2, 3, 6 & 19 rue du Jour, 1st (men 01.42.33.04.13, women 01.45.08. 56.56, www.agnesb.com). M° Les Halles. **Open** *Oct-Apr 10am-7pm Mon-Sat. May-Sept 10am-7.30pm Mon-Sat.* **Map** p73 D4 ㉙
Agnès b rarely wavers from her design vision: pure lines in fine quality cotton, merino wool and silk. Best buys are shirts, pullovers and cardigans. Her mini-empire of men's, women's, children's, travel and sportswear shops is compact; see the website for details.

Alice Cadolle

4 rue Cambon, 1st (01.42.60.94.22, www.cadolle.com). M° Concorde or Madeleine. **Open** 11am-7pm Mon-Sat. *Closed Aug.* **Map** p72 B3 ㉙
Five generations of lingerie-makers are behind this boutique, founded by Hermine Cadolle, who claimed to be the inventor of the bra. Great-great-granddaughter Poupie Cadolle continues the tradition in a cosy space devoted to a luxury ready-to-wear line of bras, panties and corsets. For a special treat, Cadolle Couture (255 rue St-Honoré, 1st, 01.42.60.94.94) will create indulgent bespoke lingerie (by appointment only).

Boucheron

26 pl Vendôme, 1st (01.42.61.58.16, www.boucheron.com). M° Opéra. **Open** 10.30am-7pm Mon-Sat. **Map** p72 B3 ㉚
Boucheron was the first to set up shop on place Vendôme, attracting celebrity custom from the nearby Ritz hotel. Owned by Gucci, the grand jeweller

produces stunning pieces, using traditional motifs with new accents: take, for example, its fabulous chocolate-coloured gold watch.

Chanel

31 rue Cambon, 1st (01.42.86.26.00, www.chanel.com). M° Concorde or Madeleine. **Open** 10am-7pm Mon-Sat. **Map** p72 B3 ㉛
Fashion legend Chanel has managed to stay relevant, thanks to Karl Lagerfeld. Coco opened her first boutique in this street, at no.21, in 1910, and the tradition continues in this elegant interior. Lagerfeld has been designing for Chanel since 1983, and keeps on revamping the classics – the little black dress and the Chanel suit – with great success.

Colette

213 rue St-Honoré, 1st (01.55.35. 33.90, www.colette.fr). M° Pyramides or Tuileries. **Open** 11am-7pm Mon-Sat. **Map** p72 B3 ㉜
The renowned and much-imitated one-stop concept and lifestyle store features a highly eclectic selection of accessories, fashion, books, media, gadgets, and hair and beauty brands, all in a swanky space.

Comme des Garçons

54 rue du Fbg-St-Honoré, 8th (01.53.30.27.27). M° Concorde or Madeleine. **Open** 11am-7pm Mon-Sat. **Map** p72 A2 ㉝
Rei Kawakubo's design ideas and revolutionary mix of materials have influenced fashions of the past two decades, and are showcased in this fibreglass store. Comme des Garçons Parfums (23 pl du Marché-St-Honoré, 1st, 01.47.03.15.03) provides a futuristic setting for the brand's fragrances.

Designpack Gallery

NEW *24 rue de Richelieu, 1st (01.44.85.86.00, www.designpack gallery.fr). M° Palais Royal Musée du Louvre.* **Open** 10am-7pm Mon-Fri; 11am-7pm Sat. **Map** p72 C4 ㉞

Shop at the opera

Concept comes to the Palais Garnier.

Like the curtain rising on Clara's dream in *The Nutcracker*, the **Opéra Palais Garnier**'s (see p86) formerly dowdy record shop has been transformed into a magical concept store run by Galeries Lafayette. The first part, where the old record shop used to be, hosts the world's most comprehensive collection of dance and opera books and DVDs, along with a fine collection of CDs. Among the biographies and glossy photography books, there are rarer, limited edition tomes carefully sourced from niche publishers and a large collection of dance magazines. At the back of this space big screens play the latest DVDs and you can request to have a sneak preview of any one that takes your fancy.

Mannequins wearing Repetto tutus lure you into the second space, a long gallery theatrically lit using ceiling mirrors, which stocks an entrancing collection of toys, objets d'art and fashion for balletomanes. The children's section is a little girl's fantasy realm, with deluxe dressing-up costumes, toy theatres, and stories about the Opéra's *petits rats* and growing up to be a dancer. Adults, meanwhile, will be entranced by Sophie Mouton-Perrat's ethereal papier-mâché lights in the form of *demoiselles* inspired by ballet characters. A selection of classic Paris gifts – Baccarat champagne flutes, Mariage Frères teas – have all been subtly branded for the Opéra.

Inspiration for dressing up for the gala performance is found in the form of contemporary fans by Vera Pilo, Murano glass jewellery and silicone necklaces by Tzuri Gueta. Finally, proving you don't have to grow up at all, there are Carrie Bradshaw-style tutus, Bompard *câche-coeurs*, Repetto shoes and a giant Tibetan goat's fleece beanbag that invites you to flump down on it wearing all of the above.

Too much packaging? Not according to Fabrice Peltier, who is passionate about the art of *emballage*, to the extent of opening his own gallery-boutique. Once a Tetrapak designer, he now recycles his own used packaging into desirable objects: red plastic bottles become lighting and clothes hangers, and bottle tops are melted down to become a multi-coloured armchair. African tin trinkets, Austrian vases made from cut-down bottles, and other ingenious recycling is also on sale.

Didier Ludot

20-24 galerie de Montpensier, 1st (01.42. 96.06.56, www.didierludot.com). M° Palais Royal Musée du Louvre. **Open** 10.30am-7pm Mon-Sat. **Map** p72 C3 ③⑤
Didier Ludot's temples to vintage haute couture appear in Printemps, Harrods and New York's Barneys. The pieces are stunning: Dior, Molyneux, Balenciaga, Pucci, Féraud and Chanel, from the 1920s onwards. Ludot also curates exhibitions, using the shop windows around the Palais-Royal as a gallery. La Petite Robe Noire (125 galerie de Valois, 1st, 01.40.15.01.04) stocks Ludot's own line of vintage little black dresses.

Ekivok

39 bd de Sébastopol, 1st (01.42.21. 98.71, www.ekivok.com). M° Les Halles/ RER Châtelet Les Halles. **Open** 11am-7.30pm Mon-Sat. **Map** p73 E4 ③⑥
In Ekivok's graffiti-covered boutique you'll find labels such as Bullrot, Carhartt, Hardcore Session and Juicy Jazz for men, and Golddigga, Punky Fish, Skunk Funk, Emilie the Strange and Hardcore Session for women.

Erès

2 rue Tronchet, 8th (01.47.42.28.82, www.eres.fr). M° Madeleine. **Open** 10am-7pm Mon-Sat. **Map** p72 B2 ③⑦
Erès's beautifully cut swimwear has embraced a sexy '60s look with buttons on low-cut briefs. The top and bottom can be purchased in different sizes, or you can buy one piece of a bikini.

La Galerie du Carrousel du Louvre

99 rue de Rivoli, 1st (01.43.16.47.10, www.lecarrouseldulouvre.com). M° Palais Royal Musée du Louvre. **Open** 10am-10pm daily. **Map** p72 C4 ③⑧
This massive underground centre – open every day of the year – is home to more than 35 shops, mostly big-name chains vying for your attention and cash. The Petit Prince boutique and Réunion des Musées Nationaux shops are great for last-minute gifts.

Galeries Lafayette

40 bd Haussmann, 9th (01.42.82. 34.56, fashion shows 01.42.82.30.25, fashion advice 01.42.82.35.50, www.galerieslafayette.com). M° Chaussée d'Antin/RER Auber. **Open** 9.30am-8pm Mon-Wed, Fri, Sat; 9.30am-9pm Thur. **Map** p72 C2 ③⑨
Espace Luxe on the first floor features luxury prêt-à-porter and accessories and nine avant-garde designers, and a vast new shoe department is home to some 150 brands. The men's fashion space on the third floor, Lafayette Homme, has natty designer corners and a 'Club' area with internet access. On the first floor, Lafayette Gourmet has exotic foods galore, and a wine cellar. Lafayette Maison over the road has five floors of home furnishings and design.

Hédiard

21 pl de la Madeleine, 8th (01.43.12. 88.88, www.hediard.fr). M° Madeleine. **Open** 8.30am-9pm Mon-Sat. **Map** p72 A2 ④⓪
Hédiard's charming shop dates back to 1880, when they were the first to introduce exotic foods to Paris, specialising in rare teas and coffees, spices, jams and candied fruits. Pop upstairs for a cuppa in the shop's posh tearoom.

Hermès

24 rue du Fbg-St-Honoré, 8th (01.40. 17.47.17, www.hermes.com). M° Concorde or Madeleine. **Open** 10.30am-6.30pm Mon-Sat. **Map** p72 A3 ④①

The fifth generation of the family directs the Hermès empire from this 1930s building. Originally – and still – a saddler, it is no also-ran in the fashion stakes, with Jean-Paul Gaultier at the reins. Most of its clients, however, are tourists after a horsey scarf.

Hervé Léger

24 rue Cambon, 1st (01.42.60.02.00, www.herveleger.com). Mº Concorde. **Open** 10am-7pm Mon-Sat. **Map** p72 B3 **42**

A couple of decades ago Hervé Léger's silhouette-cinching bandage dresses were as evocative of the era as supermodels Linda, Christy, Naomi and Cindy. But somewhere in the mid-'90s women lost their love of Lycra. In the past few seasons, however, updated reinterpretations of Léger's style, by the likes of Christopher Kane and Marios Schwab, have been nothing short of a fashion phenomenon. Less modified versions, sold by the Léger label itself (now owned and designed by Max Azria of BCBG fame), have been less critically acclaimed.

Jean-Paul Gaultier

6 rue Vivienne, 2nd (01.42.86.05.05, www.jeanpaulgaultier.com). Mº Bourse. **Open** 10.30am-7pm Mon-Fri; 11am-7pm Sat. **Map** p73 D3 **43**

Having celebrated his 30th year in the fashion business, Gaultier is still going strong. His boudoir boutique stocks men's and women's ready-to-wear and the reasonably priced JPG Jeans lines. The haute couture department (01.72.75.83.00) is by appointment only, and is located above the store.

Kiliwatch

64 rue Tiquetonne, 2nd (01.42.21. 17.37, http://espacekiliwatch.fr). Mº Etienne Marcel. **Open** 2-7pm Mon; 11am-7.30pm Tue-Sat. **Map** p73 E3 **44**

The trailblazer of the rue Etienne-Marcel revival is filled with hoodies, casual shirts and jeans. Brands include Gas, Edwin and Pepe Jeans.

Kokon To Zai

48 rue Tiquetonne, 2nd (01.42.36. 92.41, www.kokontozai.co.uk). Mº Etienne Marcel. **Open** 11.30am-7.30pm Mon-Sat. **Map** p73 E4 **45**

This tiny style emporium is sister to the Kokon To Zai in London. The neon-lit club feel of the mirrored interior matches the dark glamour of the designs. Unique pieces straight off the catwalk share space with creations by Marjan Pejoski, Noki, Raf Simons, Ziad Ghanem and new Norwegian designers.

Lanvin

22 rue du Fbg St-Honoré, 8th (01.44.71. 31.73, www.lanvin.com). Mº Concorde or Madeleine. **Open** 10.30am-7pm daily. **Map** p72 A3 **46**

The couture house that began in the 1920s with Jeanne Lanvin has been reinvented by the indefatigable Albert Elbaz. In October 2007 he unveiled this, the revamped showroom that set new aesthetic standards for luxury fashion retailing. Lanvin has an exhibition room devoted to her in the Musée des Arts Décoratifs, and this apartment-boutique also incorporates original furniture from the Lanvin archive. All this would be nothing, of course, if the clothes themselves were not exquisite.

Lavinia

3 bd de la Madeleine, 1st (01.42.97. 20.20, www.lavinia.fr). Mº Madeleine. **Open** 10am-8pm Mon-Sat. **Map** p72 B2 **47**

Lavinia stocks a broad selection of French and non-French wines; its *cave* has everything from a 1945 Mouton-Rothschild at €22,000 to trendy and 'fragile' wines for under €10. Have fun tasting wine with the *dégustation* machines on the ground floor, which allow customers to taste a sip of up to ten different wines each week for €10.

Legrand Filles et Fils

1 rue de la Banque, 2nd (01.42.60. 07.12, www.caves-legrand.com). Mº Bourse. **Open** 11am-7pm Mon; 10am-

7.30pm Tue-Fri; 10am-7pm Sat. Closed
Mon in July & Aug. **Map** p73 D3 ❹⑧
Fine wines, teas and *bonbons*, and a
showroom for regular wine tastings.

Marc by Marc Jacobs

*19 pl du Marché-Saint-Honoré, 1st
(01.40.20.11.30, www.marcjacobs.com).
M° Tuileries.* **Open** 9am-6pm Mon-Sat.
Map p72 B3 ❹⑨
The new store for Jacobs' casual, punky
line has fashionistas clustering like
bees round a honeypot, not least for the
fabulously inexpensive accessories that
make great gifts or add instant spice to
a tired outfit. A skateboard table and
giant pedalo in the form of a swan are
the centrepieces of the store, which
stocks men's and women's prêt-à-
porter, shoes and special editions.

Marc Jacobs

*56 galerie de Montpensier, 1st (01.55.35.
02.60, www.marcjacobs.com). M° Palais
Royal Musée du Louvre.* **Open** 11am-
8pm Mon-Sat. **Map** p72 C3 ❺⓪
By choosing the Palais-Royal for his
first signature boutique in Europe,
Marc Jacobs brought new life – and
an influx of fashionistas – to these elegant cloisters. Stocking womenswear,
menswear, accessories and shoes, it has
already become a place of pilgrimage
for the designer's legion of admirers,
who are snapping up his downtown
New York style.

Martin Margiela

*23 & 25bis rue de Montpensier,
1st (womenswear 01.40.15.07.55,
menswear 01.40.15.06.44, www.
maisonmartinmargiela.com). M° Palais
Royal Musée du Louvre.* **Open** 11am-
7pm Mon-Sat. **Map** p72 C4 ❺①
This Paris outlet is a pristine, white,
unlabelled space. Martin Margiela's
collection for women (Line 1) has a
blank label but is recognisable by
external white stitching. You'll also
find Line 6 (women's basics) and Line
10 (menswear), plus accessories for
men and women and shoes.

Printemps

*64 bd Haussmann, 9th (01.42.82.
50.00, www.printemps.com). M° Havre
Caumartin/RER Auber.* **Open** 9.35am-
8pm Mon-Wed, Fri, Sat; 9.35am-10pm
Thur. **Map** p72 B1 ❺②
In Printemps you'll find everything
you didn't even know you wanted and
English-speaking assistants to help
you find it. Fashion is where the store
really excels; an entire floor is devoted
to shoes, and the beauty department
stocks more than 200 brands. In
Printemps de la Mode, French designers sit alongside the big international
designers. The Fashion Loft offers a
younger but equally stylish take on
current trends. Printemps de la Maison
stocks everything from everyday tableware to design classics. For refuelling,
Printemps has a tearoom, sushi bar
and Café Be, an Alain Ducasse bakery.

Purple Ice

NEW *15 rue Marie Stuart, 2nd (01.40.
26.87.27, www.purpleiceboutique.com).
M° Etienne Marcel.* **Open** 11.30am-
7.30pm Tue-Sun. **Map** p402 J5 ❺③
You'd be forgiven for assuming
Romain Couapel was obsessed by
Prince. He has, after all, called his shop
Purple Ice, written the sign in the same
'80s rock font as *Purple Rain*, and
painted the walls and floor in the colour
Prince called his own. But he doesn't
seem that bothered by the rock guitar
legend; he's more into the visual qual-
ities than the back story. This attitude
is mirrored in the good-looking, diverse
clothes on sale: streetwear jeans by
Real Real Genuine next to designer
bags by JC de Castelbajac, and
Vêtements de Famille's modern take on
the Breton shirt next to Pearl Diver's
retro Hawaiian shirts made in Japan.

Robert Normand

*149-150 galerie de Valois, 1st
(www.robertnormand.com). M° Palais
Royal Musée du Louvre.* **Open**
1-7pm Mon; 10.30am-7pm Tue-Sat.
Map p72 C3 ❺④

Normand is a new addition to the smart Palais-Royal. The designer, who has collaborated with Lanvin, Pucci and Christophe Lemaire, launched his own label in 2000 – a combination of pop art patterns with gangsta cuts, satin puffballs in peacock colours and blousons made of the kind of fabrics favoured by African potentates.

Salons du Palais-Royal Shiseido

Jardins du Palais-Royal, 142 galerie de Valois, 1st (01.49.27.09.09, www. salons-shiseido.com). M° Palais Royal Musée du Louvre. **Open** 10am-7pm Mon-Sat. **Map** p72 C3 ❺❺
Under the arcades of the Palais-Royal, Shiseido's perfumer Serge Lutens practises his aromatic arts. A former artistic director of make-up at Christian Dior, Lutens is a maestro of rare taste. Bottles of his concoctions – Tubéreuse Criminelle, Rahat Loukoum and Ambre Sultan – can be sampled by visitors. Look out for Fleurs d'Oranger, which the great man defines as the smell of happiness.

Stella McCartney

114-121 galerie du Valois, Jardin du Palais-Royal, 1st (01.47.03.03.80, www.stellamccartney.com). M° Palais Royal Musée du Louvre. **Open** 10.30am-7pm Mon-Sat. **Map** p72 C3 ❺❻
McCartney is crazy about the 'clash of history, fashion and contemporary art' at the Palais-Royal, where she has opened her sumptuous boutique. Thick carpets, maplewood and metal sculptures create a rarified setting for women's prêt-à-porter, bags, shoes, sunglasses, lingerie, perfume and skincare.

Yohji Yamamoto

4 rue Cambon, 1st (01.40.20.00.71, www.yohjiyamamoto.co.jp). M° Concorde. **Open** 10am-7pm Mon-Sat. **Map** p72 B3 ❺❼
Yamamoto has achieved his dream of having a flagship store on rue Cambon, which will forever be synonymous with

Chanel. This temple to the creator is as impressive as those in New York and Antwerp, a pristine white gallery space designed by Sophie Hicks. Behind an origami-screen window mannequins clothed in his showpieces seem to float in the air. A grand staircase leads to womenswear on the first floor, while menswear is on the lower ground.

Nightlife

Au Duc des Lombards

42 rue des Lombards, 1st (01.42.33. 22.88, www.ducdeslombards.com). M° Châtelet. **Open** *Concerts* 8pm Mon-Sat. Closed mid Aug. **Admission** €19-€25. **Map** p73 E5 ❺❽
Some of the capital's venerated jazz spots have lost the fight for survival in recent years. But this one has endured, and attracts a high class of performer and a savvy crowd.

Le Cab

2 pl du Palais-Royal, 1st (01.58.62. 56.25, www.cabaret.fr). M° Palais Royal Musée du Louvre. **Open** 11.30pm-5am Wed-Sat. *Restaurant* 7.30-11.30pm Tue-Sat. **Admission** free Tue, Wed; €20 Thur-Sat. **Map** p72 C4 ❺❾
Le Cab is owned by the management behind Club Mix and Queen, and R&B and commercial house dominate the playlist. The doormen are tough, and if they don't like you, you won't get in (unless you've booked for dinner).

Chacha Club

47 rue Berger, 1st (01.40.13.12.12, www.chachaclub.fr). M° Châtelet. **Open** 8pm-5am Mon-Sat. **Admission** varies. **Map** p73 D4 ❻❶
Paris's fetishistic obsession with the cigarette has produced a new nightlife phenomenon: the fumoir. The Chacha Club was the first high-profile establishment to open one, and it forms just one of the sexy attributes of this hot haunt near Les Halles. It combines restaurant, bar and club in a suite of rooms with 1930s-inspired decor.

Olympia

*28 bd des Capucines, 9th (08.92.68.
33.68, www.olympiahall.com). M°
Opéra.* **Open** *Box office* 10am-9pm
Mon-Sat; 10am-7pm Sun. *Concerts*
times vary. **Map** p72 B2 ⓺❶
The Beatles, Frank Sinatra, Jimi
Hendrix and Edith Piaf have all performed here over the years. Now it's
mostly home to nostalgia and *variété*.

Rex

*5 bd Poissonnière, 2nd (01.42.36.
10.96, www.rexclub.com). M° Bonne
Nouvelle.* **Open** 11.30pm-6am Wed-Sat.
Admission free €15. **Map** p73 E2 ⓺❷
The Rex's sound system puts over 40
different sound configurations at the
DJ's fingertips. Once associated with
iconic techno pioneer Laurent Garnier,
the Rex still occupies an unassailable
position as the city's serious club
music venue.

Le Sunset/Le Sunside

*60 rue des Lombards, 1st (Sunside
01.40.26.21.25, Sunset 01.40.26.46.60,
www.sunset-sunside.com). M° Châtelet.*
Open *Concerts* 9pm, 10pm daily.
Admission €8-€30. **Map** p73 E5 ⓺❸
A split-personality venue, with Sunset
dealing in electric groups and Sunside
hosting acoustic performances. Their
renown pulls in big jazz names from
both sides of the Atlantic.

Théâtre du Châtelet

*1 pl du Châtelet, 1st (01.40.28.28.40,
www.chatelet-theatre.com). M° Châtelet.*
Open times vary. **Admission** €25-
€150. **Map** p73 E5 ⓺❹
This venerable theatre and classic
music hall has another life as a jazz and
chanson venue, with performances by
top-notch international musicians.

Toro

NEW *74 rue Jean-Jacques-Rousseau, 1st
(01.44.76.00.03, www.toroparis.com).
M° Les Halles.* **Open** *DJ sets* 10pm-
2am Thur-Sun. **Admission** free.
Map p73 D4 ⓺❺

Bernhardt backstage

Get behind the scenes.

In 1968, the city of Paris
decided to revamp the **Théâtre
de la Ville** (see p86) – a
seemingly mundane event,
synonymous with France's desire
to modernise. But for lovers of
belle époque architecture and
the 'Divine' Sarah Bernhardt –
the most famous actress of the
19th century and former director
of the theatre, which once bore
her name – it was a veritable
act of heresy.

The sumptuous red and gold
interior was gutted and replaced
with a soulless black and beige
amphitheatre. But worst of all
was the removal of Bernhardt's
Empire-style dressing room,
salon and bathroom; a heinous
crime that her descendants
have been trying to rectify,
with some success.

Nowadays, if you ask when
you book your ticket, you can
organise a free trip backstage
(during the *entr'acte*) to see a
reconstruction of Bernhardt's
dressing room. It makes for a
wholly offbeat alternative to the
interval tipple, plus you might
bump into the actors you've just
seen on stage. Lining the walls
are her original display cabinets
filled with souvenirs: her portrait
by Nadar from 1900, letters
from her son, a note from
Victor Hugo, the cane she
held in *Tosca* and her Legion
d'Honneur medal. There is also
a sumptuous sofa bordered by
wooden sphinxes, along with
her old tin bathtub and mirror.

This no frills tapas bar hides a small but wonderfully wacky dancefloor down in the basement where DJs mix up house music with flamenco tunes.

Arts & leisure

Châtelet – Théâtre Musical de Paris

1 pl du Châtelet, 1st (01.40.28.28.40, www.chatelet-theatre.com). M° Châtelet. **Box office** 11am-7pm Mon-Sat; 1hr before performance Sun. *By phone* 10am-7pm Mon-Sat. Closed July, Aug. **Admission** €10-€122.50. **Map** p73 E5 ⑥⑥
Jean-Luc Choplin has radically changed the programming of this bastion of Paris music making. An attempt to rediscover the theatre's popular roots has been achieved at the expense of traditional fine music subscribers. The general impression is of programming that has been slimmed down for financial reasons.

Forum des Images

2 Grande Galerie, Porte St-Eustache, Forum des Halles, 1st (01.44.76.63.00, www.forumdesimages.net). M° Les Halles. **Open** 1-9pm Tue-Sun. Closed 2wks Aug. **Admission** (per day) €4-€5. **Map** p73 D4 ⑥⑦
The Forum was conceived partly as a screening venue for old and little-known movies, and partly as an archive centre for every kind of moving picture featuring Paris; today the collection numbers over 6,500 documentaries, adverts, newsreels and films, from the work of the Lumière brothers to 21st-century reportage.

Le Grand Rex

1 bd Poissonnière, 2nd (08.92.68. 05.96, www.legrandrex.com). M° Bonne Nouvelle. **Admission** €7.50-€9. *Les Etoiles du Rex tour* €9.80; €8 reductions. **Map** p73 E2 ⑥⑧
With its wedding-cake exterior, fairy-tale interior and the largest auditorium in Europe (2,750 seats), this is one of the few cinemas that manages to upstage whatever it screens: no wonder it's a listed historic monument. Its blockbuster programming is suited to its vast, roll-down screen.

Opéra National de Paris, Palais Garnier

Pl de l'Opéra, 9th (08.92.89.90.90, www.operadeparis.fr). M° Opéra. **Box office** 10.30am-6.30pm Mon-Sat. *By phone* 9am-6pm Mon-Fri; 9am-1pm Sat. **Admission** €7-€172. **Map** p72 B2 ⑥⑨
The Palais Garnier, with its ornate, extravagant decor and ceiling by Marc Chagall, is the jewel in the crown of Paris music-making. The Opéra National often favours the high-tech Bastille for new productions, but the matchless acoustics of the Palais Garnier are superior to the new house. **Event highlights** Mozart's *Così Fan Tutte* (16 June-16 July 2011)

Théâtre National de l'Opéra Comique

Pl Boieldieu, 2nd (01.42.44.45.40, www.opera-comique.com). M° Richelieu Drouot. **Box office** 11am-7pm Mon-Sat; 11am-5pm Sun. *By phone* 11am-7pm Mon-Sat; 11am-5pm Sun. **Admission** €6-€115. **Map** p72 C2 ⑦⑩
Its promotion to national theatre status has brought this jewel box of a theatre back to life and the opening seasons, exploring a specifically French repertoire often ignored by larger houses, have been welcomed with enthusiasm. **Event highlights** Weber's *Le Freischütz* (7-17 April 2011)

Théâtre de la Ville

2 pl du Châtelet, 4th (01.42.74.22.77, www.theatredelaville-paris.com). M° Châtelet. **Box office** 11am-7pm Mon; 11am-8pm Tue-Sat. **Admission** €12-€17. **Map** p73 E5 ⑦①
Programming features hip chamber music outfits such as the Kronos and Takács Quartets, Early Music pioneer Fabio Biondi, and soloists like pianist Aleksandar Madzar.

Sacré-Coeur p88

Montmartre & Pigalle

Perched on a hill (or *butte*), Montmartre is the highest point in Paris, its tightly packed houses spiralling round the mound below the dome of **Sacré-Coeur**. Despite the many tourists, it's surprisingly easy to fall under the spell of this romantic district. Climb stairways, peer down alleys and into ivy-covered houses and quiet squares, and explore streets such as rue des Abbesses, rue des Trois-Frères and rue des Martyrs, with their cafés, boutiques and bohemian residents.

At the bottom of the hill, in once-notorious Pigalle, the seediness of yesteryear's sex clubs and brothels is steadily being replaced by hot music venues and nightspots.

Sights & museums

Cimetière de Montmartre

20 av Rachel, access by staircase from rue Caulaincourt, 18th (01.53.42. 36.30). M° Blanche or Place de Clichy.
Open *6 Nov-15 Mar* 8am-5.30pm Mon-Sat; 9am-5.30pm Sun, public hols. *16 Mar-5 Nov* 8am-6pm Mon-Sat; 9am-6pm Sun, public hols. **Admission** free. **Map** p89 A1 ❶
Truffaut, Nijinsky, Berlioz, Degas, Offenbach and German poet Heine are all buried here. So, too, are La Goulue, the first great cancan star, and con-sumptive heroine Alphonsine Plessis, inspiration for *La Traviata*. Flowers are still left on the grave of diva Dalida.

Musée d'Art Halle St-Pierre

2 rue Ronsard, 18th (01.42.58.72.89, www.hallesaintpierre.org). M° Anvers.
Open *Jan-July, Sept-Dec* 10am-6pm daily. *Aug* noon-6pm Mon-Fri. **Admission** €7.50; free-€6 reductions. **Map** p89 C2 ❷
The former market in the shadow of Sacré-Coeur specialises in *art brut*, *art outsider* and *art singulier* from its own and other collections.
Event highlights Art Brut Japonais (until 2 Jan 2011)

Musée de l'Erotisme

72 bd de Clichy, 18th (01.42.58.28.73, www.musee-erotisme.com). Mº Blanche. **Open** 10am-2am daily. **Admission** €8; €5 reductions. **Map** p89 A2 ❸

Seven floors of erotic art and artefacts amassed by Alain Plumey and Joseph Khalif. The first three run from first-century Peruvian phallic pottery through Etruscan fertility symbols to Yoni sculptures from Nepal; the fourth gives a history of Paris brothels; the top floors host exhibitions of erotic art.

Musée Gustave Moreau

14 rue de La Rochefoucauld, 9th (01.48.74.38.50, www.musee-moreau.fr). Mº Trinité. **Open** 10am-12.45pm, 2-5.15pm Mon, Wed-Sun. **Admission** €5; free-€3 reductions. **Map** p89 A4 ❹

This wonderful museum combines the private apartment of Symbolist painter Gustave Moreau (1825-98) with the vast gallery he built to display his work. Downstairs shows his obsessive collector's nature with family portraits, Grand Tour souvenirs and a boudoir devoted to the object of his unrequited love, Alexandrine Durem. Upstairs is Moreau's fantasy realm, which plunders Greek mythology and biblical scenes for canvases filled with writhing maidens, trance-like visages, mystical beasts and strange plants. Don't miss the trippy masterpiece *Jupiter et Sémélé* on the second floor.

Musée de Montmartre

12 rue Cortot, 18th (01.49.25.89.37, www.museedemontmartre.fr). Mº Abbesses. **Open** 11am-6pm Wed-Sun. **Admission** €7; free-€5.50 reductions. **Map** p89 B1 ❺

At the back of a garden, this 17th-century manor house displays the history of the hilltop, with rooms devoted to composer Gustave Charpentier and a tribute to the Lapin Agile cabaret, with Toulouse-Lautrec posters. There are paintings by Suzanne Valadon, who had a studio above the entrance, as did Renoir, Raoul Dufy and Maurice Utrillo.

Musée de la Vie Romantique

Hôtel Scheffer-Renan, 16 rue Chaptal, 9th (01.55.31.95.67, www.vie-romantique.paris.fr). Mº Blanche or St-Georges. **Open** 10am-6pm Tue-Sun. **Admission** free. *Exhibitions* €7; free-€3.50 reductions. **Map** p89 A3 ❻

When Dutch artist Ary Scheffer lived in this small villa, the area teemed with composers, writers and artists. Aurore Dupin, Baronne Dudevant (George Sand) was a guest at Scheffer's soirées, and many other great names crossed the threshold, including Chopin and Liszt. The museum is devoted to Sand, although the watercolours, lockets, jewels and plastercast of her right arm that she left behind reveal little of her ideas or affairs.

Sacré-Coeur

35 rue du Chevalier-de-la-Barre, 18th (01.53.41.89.00, www.sacre-coeur-montmartre.com). Mº Abbesses or Anvers. **Open** *Basilica* 6am-10.30pm daily. *Crypt & dome* Winter 10am-5.45pm daily. Summer 9am-6.45pm daily. **Admission** free. *Crypt & dome* €5. **Map** p89 C2 ❼

Work on this enormous mock Romano-Byzantine edifice began in 1877. It was commissioned after the nation's defeat by Prussia in 1870, voted for by the Assemblée Nationale and built from public subscription. Finally completed in 1914, it was consecrated in 1919 – by which time a jumble of architects had succeeded Paul Abadie, winner of the original competition. The interior boasts lavish mosaics.

Eating & drinking

Le Brébant

32 bd Poissonnière, 9th (01.47.70.01.02). Mº Grands Boulevards. **Open** 7.30am-6am daily. **Bar**. **Map** p89 C5 ❽

This prominent, round-the-clock bar-bistro has a busy terrace below a colourful, stripy awning, and the split-level interior is all bare bulbs and

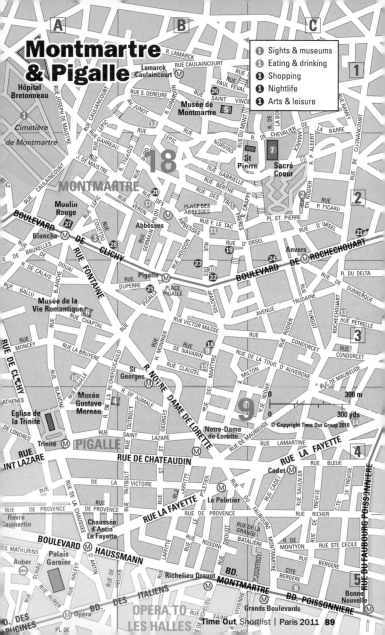

Montmartre & Pigalle

Legend (key):
- 1 Sights & museums
- 1 Eating & drinking
- 1 Shopping
- 1 Nightlife
- 1 Arts & leisure

© Copyright Time Out Group 2010

Le Ch'ti Catalan p91

wrought iron. Prices are steep, so push the boat out and opt for an expertly prepared fruit daiquiri. There are rarer bottled beers too – Monaco, Picon and sundry brews from Brabant.

Le Ch'ti Catalan

4 rue de Navarin, 9th (01.44.63.04.33). Mᵒ Notre-Dame-de-Lorette. **Open** noon-3pm, 7.30-11pm Mon-Fri; 7.30-11pm Sat. **€. Bistro.** Map p89 B3 ❾
It's unconventional, to say the least, to pair ingredients such as endives, bacon and eel, commonly found in the north of France, with the sunny flavours of French Catalan cooking. But that's what two friends have done in this ochre-painted bistro. The amazing thing is, it works. *Anchoïade* – red peppers with tangy anchovies – is fresh and tasty; tender pork cheeks served in a casserole with melting white beans are succulent; and the *gueule noire* (black face) – crushed spice biscuits with crème fraîche and egg – refers to slang for miners in northern France.

La Fourmi

74 rue des Martyrs, 18th (01.42.64. 70.35). Mᵒ Pigalle. **Open** 8am-2am Mon-Thur; 8am-4am Fri, Sat; 10am-2am Sun. **Bar.** Map p89 B3 ❿
La Fourmi is an old bistro that has been converted for today's tastes, with picture windows lighting the spacious interior. The classic zinc bar counter is crowned by industrial lights, and an excellent music policy and cool clientele (although they'd have to go some to beat the bar staff) ensure a pile of flyers.

Le Miroir

NEW *94 rue des Martyrs, 18th (01.46.06.50.73). Mᵒ Abbesses.* **Open** noon-3pm, 7-11pm Tue-Sat; noon-3pm Sun. **€. Bistro.** Map p89 B2 ⓫
This friendly bistro is a welcome addition to the neighbourhood. Big mirrors, red banquettes and a glass ceiling at the back give it character, while the professional food and service reflect the owners' haute cuisine training.

Expect dishes such as salad of whelks with white beans, crisp-skinned duck and chanterelle mushrooms, and a *petit pot de crème vanille.*

Le Moulin de la Galette

83 rue Lepic, 18th (01.46.06.84.77, www.lemoulindelagalette.eu). Mᵒ Abbesses. **Open** noon-2.45pm, 7.30-11pm Tue-Fri. Closed Aug. **€€€. Bistro.** Map p89 B1 ⓬
The Butte Montmartre was once dotted with windmills, and this survivor houses a chic restaurant with a few tables in the cobbled courtyard. It's hard to imagine a more picturesque setting in Montmartre. The kitchen makes an effort with dishes such as foie gras with melting beetroot cooked in lemon balm and juniper or suckling pig alongside potato purée. Desserts, such as figs caramelised with muscovado sugar, look like a painter's *tableau.* If you're on a budget, stick to the set menus and order carefully from the wine list.

Pétrelle

34 rue Pétrelle, 9th (01.42.82.11.02, www.petrelle.fr). Mᵒ Anvers. **Open** 8-10pm Tue-Sat. Closed 4wks July/Aug & 1wk Dec. **€€. Bistro.** Map p89 C3 ⓭
Jean-Luc André is as inspired a decorator as he is a cook, and the quirky charm of his dining room has made it popular with fashion designers and film stars. But behind the style is some serious substance. André seeks out the best ingredients from local producers, and the quality shines through. The €29 no-choice menu is huge value (marinated sardines with tomato relish, rosemary-scented rabbit with roasted vegetables, deep purple poached figs) – or you can splash out with à la carte dishes such as tournedos Rossini.

Poussette Café

6 rue Pierre Sémard, 9th (01.78. 10.49.00, www.lepoussettecafe.com). Mᵒ Poissonnière. **Open** 10.30am-6.30pm Tue-Sat. No credit cards. **€.** **Café.** Map p89 C4 ⓮

Fed up with the impracticalities of pushing her pram (*poussette*) into the local café, mother of two Laurence Constant designed her own parent-friendly establishment. This upmarket *salon de thé* caters for the harassed parent (herbal teas, smoothies, quiches and salads) and demanding baby (purées, solids and cuddly toys). You can sign up for magic shows and parenting workshops via the café's website.

Rose Bakery

46 rue des Martyrs, 9th (01.42.82. 12.80). M° Notre-Dame-de-Lorette. **Open** 9am-7pm Tue-Fri; 10am-5pm Sat, Sun. Closed 2wks Aug & 1wk Dec. **€**. **Café**. Map p89 B3 ⓯
This English-themed café run by a Franco-British couple stands out for the quality of its ingredients – organic or from small producers – as well as the too-good-to-be-true puddings. The DIY salad plate is crunchily satisfying, but the *pizzettes*, daily soups and occasional risottos are equally good.

Rouge Passion

14 rue Jean-Baptiste Pigalle, 9th (www.rouge-passion.fr). M° Pigalle or St Georges. **Open** noon-2.30pm Mon; noon-2.30pm, 7pm-midnight Tue-Sat. **Wine bar**. Map p89 A3 ⓰
Two bright upstarts determined to make their mark on Paris's bar scene are behind this venture. Offering a long list of wines (from just €3), free *assiettes apéros* (peanuts, olives and tapenades on toast) and decor that is satisfyingly vintage (red banquettes and beige walls), the formula is spot on. A small selection of hot dishes, salads, cheese and *saucisson* platters help soak up *le vin* (set lunch menu €20, mains from €15). Look out for wine tasting classes, given by a guest sommelier.

Le Sancerre

35 rue des Abbesses, 18th (01.42.58. 08.20). M° Abbesses. **Open** 7am-2am Mon-Thur; 7am-4am Fri, Sat; 9am-2am Sun. **Bar**. Map p89 B2 ⓱
This popular Montmartre institution is home to a frenzied mix of alcohol-fuelled transvestites, tourists, lovers and bobo (bohemian-bourgeois) locals, who all come for the cheap beer (under €4), trashy music and buzzy terrace. The decor inside is scruffy, the service slow and the food (omelettes, *steak-frites*) nothing special; yet there is something irresistibly refreshing about the no-frills approach that makes this bar stand out from the multitude of try-hard cafés in the area.

Shopping

Arnaud Delmontel

39 rue des Martyrs, 9th (01.48.78. 29.33, www.arnaud-delmontel.com). M° St-Georges. **Open** 7am-8.30pm Mon, Wed-Sun. No credit cards. Map p89 B3 ⓲
With its crisp crust and chewy crumb shot through with irregular holes, Delmontel's Renaissance bread is one of the finest in Paris. He puts the same skill into his almond croissants and *tarte au citron à l'ancienne*.

Base One

47bis rue d'Orsel, 18th (01.73.75. 37.10, www.baseoneshop.com). M° Anvers. **Open** 12.30-8pm Tue-Sat; 3.30-8pm Sun. Closed 2wks Aug. Map p89 B2 ⓳
Clubland duo Princesse Léa and Jean-Louis Favcrole squeeze items from little-known local and international designers, plus small, established brands (Fenchurch, Motel, Consortium) into their boutique.

Le Grenier à Pain

38 rue des Abbesses, 18th (01.46.06. 41.81). M° Abbesses. **Open** 7.30am-8pm Mon, Wed-Sun. Map p89 B2 ⓴
Expect queues at this Montmartre bakery, winner in March 2010 of the 17th Grand Prix de la Baguette de Tradition Française de la Ville de Paris. As well as gaining plenty of new customers, Baker Djibril Bodian also

Cheque in

Rest assured at the new Banke Hotel.

If sleeping in a bank sounds weird, don't worry – there are no carpet tiles or pens screwed to the table at the **Banke Hotel** (see p172). This swish new establishment in the Opéra district occupies the former HQ of the CCF bank, a magnificent early 20th-century building designed by Paul Friesse and Cassien Bernard in the 'Eiffel style' – under the pastiche of its Pompeian red galleries and soaring glass ceiling there is actually an iron frame. The Banke is owned by the Spanish Derby Hotels chain, and Catalan design flair comes through in a just-this-side-of-kitsch approach to dressing up the splendid lobby, with gold leather chesterfields and Swarovski-studded armchairs by Bretz, as well as Starck Perspex bar stools and transparent tables in the circular Lolabar.

Some of the executive rooms seem rather small for the price tag, but all is quality here, with parquet flooring, green Bizazza mosaics in the bathroom and luxurious burgundy taffeta on the bed. The lighting is particularly well done, with huge black pendulum lights either side of the bed, and a walk-in closet that lights up when you approach. The deluxe rooms are significantly bigger, with a jacuzzi bath, and there is also a romantic circular suite on the first floor complete with marble fireplace and gilded mouldings.

The Josefin restaurant serves fine Catalan food with a small choice of excellent Spanish wines. Stand-out dishes include carpaccio of lobster, artichokes with Iberian ham, and line-caught sea bass with broad beans. It's just a shame that they haven't sorted out the music. Tinny pop echoes around the cavernous space when sultry lounge music would be a better match for the designer setting.

Food, design and location are all pretty much spot on, but the ultimate treat here is the sleep you'll have. Perfect black-out curtains, perfect soundproofing and imperceptible air conditioning mean that you can bank on a decent night's slumber.

PARIS BY AREA

picked up a cash prize of €4,000 and a contract to keep President Nicolas Sarkozy in bread for a year.

Tati

4 bd de Rochechouart, 18th (01.55.29. 52.20, www.tati.fr). M° Barbès Rochechouart. **Open** 10am-7pm Mon-Fri; 9.30am-7pm Sat. **Map** p89 C2 ㉑
Expect to find anything from T-shirts to wedding dresses, as well as bargain children's clothes and household goods at this discount heaven.

Nightlife

La Cigale/La Boule Noire

120 bd de Rochechouart, 18th (01.49.25.81.75, www.lacigale.fr). M° Anvers or Pigalle. **Open** times vary. **Map** p89 B3 ㉒
One of Paris's finest venues, the horse-shoe shaped theatre La Cigale is linked to more cosy venue La Boule Noire, good for catching cult-ish visiting acts.

Le Divan du Monde

75 rue des Martyrs, 18th (01.42.52. 02.46, www.divandumonde.com). M° Abbesses or Pigalle. **Open** 8pm-2am Tue-Thur; 7.30pm-5am Fri, Sat. **Admission** €6-€30. **Map** p89 B3 ㉓
After a drink in the Fourmi opposite, pop over to the Divan for one-off parties and regular events. The upstairs specialises in VJ events, and downstairs holds dub, reggae, funk and world music club nights.

Elysée Montmartre

72 bd de Rochechouart, 18th (01.44.92. 45.36, www.elyseemontmartre.com). M° Anvers. **Open** midnight-6am Fri, Sat. **Admission** €10-€15. **Map** p89 C2 ㉔
A gig venue and club, the Elysée hosts big nights by outside promoters, such as Open House, Panik and Nightfever.

Le Folie's Pigalle

11 pl Pigalle, 9th (01.48.78.55.25, www.lefoliespigalle.com). M° Pigalle. **Open** midnight-dawn Mon-Thur;

midnight-noon Fri, Sat; 6pm-midnight Sun. **Admission** €20 (incl 1 drink); €7 Sun eve. **Map** p89 B3 ㉕
The racy Folie's Pigalle's programme includes everything from dancehall and hip hop to techno and electro, go-go dancers, striptease and Paris's only transsexual spectacle.

Au Lapin Agile

22 rue des Saules, 18th (01.46.06. 85.87, www.au-lapin-agile.com). M° Lamarck Caulaincourt. **Shows** 9pm-2am Tue-Sun. **Admission** Show (incl 1 drink) €24; €17 reductions (except Sat & public hols). No credit cards. **Map** p89 B1 ㉖
The prices have gone up, tourists outnumber the locals and they sell their own compilation CDs these days, but that's all that seems to have changed since this quaint, pink bar first opened its doors in 1860.

Moulin Rouge

82 bd de Clichy, 18th (01.53.09.82.82, www.moulin-rouge.com). M° Blanche. **Dinner** 7pm. **Shows** 9pm, 11pm daily. **Admission** *9pm show* (incl champagne) €102. *11pm show* (incl champagne) €92. *Dinner & show* €150-€180. **Map** p89 A2 ㉗
Toulouse-Lautrec posters, glittery lampposts and fake trees lend tacky charm to this revue, while 60 Doriss dancers cavort with faultless synchronisation. Costumes are flamboyant and the *entr'acte* acts funny. The downer is the space, with tables packed in.

Les Trois Baudets

64 bd de Clichy, 18th (01.42.62.33.33, www.lestroisbaudets.com). M° Pigalle. **Open** 6pm-1.30am Tue-Sat; 10.30am-5pm Sun. Closed Aug. **Admission** €5-€20. **Map** p89 A2 ㉘
With a 250-seater theatre, an enviable sound system, two bars and a restaurant, this new concert hall encourages *chanson française* and other musical genres (rock, electro, folk and slam), as long as they're in French.

Canal St-Martin

North-east Paris

In the city's folklore, north-east
Paris is working class Paris –
and although patches of it are
gentrifying and little actual
industry remains, the area still
has a distinctive rough and ready
vibe. Many of the streets here are
somewhat on the tatty side, but
others are artsy and fashionable,
especially those close to the Canal
St-Martin; and large swathes of the
north-east – for example rue du
Fbg-St-Denis and the thoroughfares
leading off it – are excitingly multi-
ethnic, with thriving North African,
Turkish and Caribbean enclaves.

Sights & museums

Canauxrama
*13 quai de la Loire, 19th (01.42.39.
15.00, www.canauxrama.fr).* **Tickets**
€15; free-€8 reductions. **Map** p97 C1 ❶
If the Seine palls, then take a trip up
the city's second waterway, the Canal
St-Martin. The tree-lined canal is a

pretty sight, and the trip even goes
underground, where the tunnel walls
are enlivened by a light show.

Gare du Nord
*Rue de Dunkerque, 10th (08.91.
36.20.20). M° Gare du Nord.*
Map p97 A2 ❷
The grandest of the great 19th-century
train stations (and Eurostar terminal
since 1994) was designed by Hittorff
between 1861 and 1864. The stone
façade, with Ionic capitals and statues
representing towns served by the station, hides a vast iron-and-glass vault.

Musée de la Musique
*Cité de la Musique, 221 av Jean-Jaurès,
19th (01.44.84.45.00, www.cite-
musique.fr). M° Porte de Pantin.*
Open noon-6pm Tue-Sat; 10am-6pm
Sun. **Admission** €8; free-€6.40
reductions. **Map** p97 E1 ❸
This innovative museum houses a
collection of instruments from the old
Conservatoire, interactive computers

Party in the park

Skip the Tuileries and head for the 19th instead.

There are plenty of handsomely ordered opportunities to indulge in a bit of park life in Paris, from the gravelled pathways of the Jardin des Tuileries to the ornamental ponds of the Jardin du Luxembourg. But if you're looking for something a little less formal, one patch of greenery which is definitely worth a stroll is the **Parc des Buttes-Chaumont** (*see right*). Set high up in Belleville and often overlooked by weekenders keen not to stray too far from the tourist loop, this 19th arrondissement gem is one of the city's most magical spots.

When the city's boundaries were expanded in 1860, Belleville – once a village that provided Paris with fruit, wine and weekend escapes – was absorbed and the Buttes-Chaumont was created on the site of a former gypsum and limestone quarry. The park, with its meandering paths, waterfalls, temples and vertical cliffs, was designed by Adolphe Alphand for Haussmann, and was opened as part of the celebrations for the Universal Exhibition in 1867.

After lounging with the locals for a few hours, head for the park's hugely hip hangout, the wonderfully jolly Rosa Bonheur *guinguette* (www.rosabonheur.fr). Open till midnight, it makes the perfect place to sip an *apéro* and take in the stunning views of the city stretching out below.

and scale models of opera houses and concert halls. Visitors are supplied with an audio guide in a choice of languages, and the musical commentary is a joy, playing the appropriate instrument as you approach each exhibit.
Event highlights Steve Coleman: Astronomie/Astrologie (5 May 2011)

Parc des Buttes-Chaumont

Rue Botzaris, rue Manin, rue de Crimée, 19th. Mº Buttes Chaumont. **Open** *Oct-Apr* 7am-8pm daily. *May-Aug* 7am-10pm daily. *Sept* 7am-9pm daily. **Map** p97 E2 ④
See box left.

Eating & drinking

Bar Ourcq

68 quai de la Loire, 19th (01.42.40. 12.26). Mº Laumière. **Open** *Winter* 3pm-midnight Wed, Thur; 3pm-2am Fri, Sat; 3-10pm Sun. *Summer* 5-9.30pm Wed-Fri, Sun; 3pm-2am Sat. No credit cards. **Bar**. **Map** p97 D1 ⑤
This was one of the first hip joints to hit the Canal de l'Ourcq, with an embankment broad enough to accommodate *pétanque* games (ask at the bar) and a cluster of deckchairs. The cabin-like interior is pretty cosy, and drinks are listed in a hit parade of prices, starting with €2.40 for a *demi* or glass of red.

A la Bière

104 av Simon-Bolivar, 19th (01.42.39. 83.25). Mº Colonel Fabien. **Open** noon-3pm, 7pm-1.30am daily. **€**. **Brasserie**. **Map** p97 D2 ⑥
A la Bière looks like one of those nondescript corner brasseries with noisy pop music, but what makes it stand out is an amazingly good-value prix fixe full of fine bistro favourites: home-made rabbit terrine, charcoal-grilled entrecôte with hand-cut chips, juicy Lyonnais sausages with potatoes drenched in olive oil, garlic and parsley. This is one of the few bargains left in Paris.

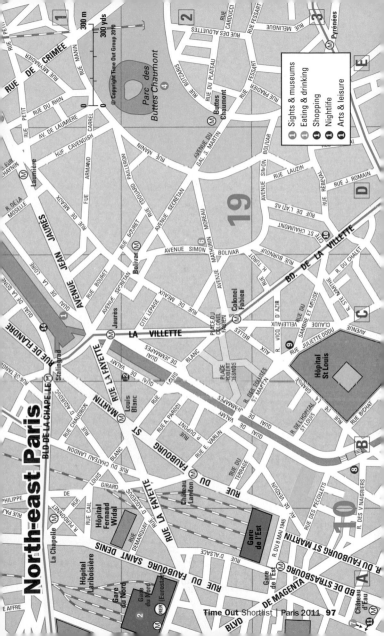

North-east Paris

Legend:
- ➊ Sights & museums
- ➊ Eating & drinking
- ➊ Shopping
- ➊ Nightlife
- ➊ Arts & leisure

300 m
300 yds

© Copyright Time Out Group 2010

RUE DE CRIMEE

Parc des Buttes Chaumont

Buttes Chaumont ➍

AVENUE JEAN JAURÈS

Bolivar Ⓜ

Jaurès Ⓜ

LA VILLETTE

Stalingrad Ⓜ

Louis Blanc

RUE LA FAYETTE

BLVD DE LA CHAPELLE

La Chapelle Ⓜ

Gare du Nord (Eurostar) Ⓜ

Hôpital Lariboisière

Château Landon

Hôpital Fernand Widal

RUE DU FAUBOURG SAINT DENIS

Gare de l'Est Ⓜ

BLVD DE MAGENTA

Château d'Eau Ⓜ

R. DU FAUBOURG ST MARTIN

Gare de l'Est

Colonel Fabien Ⓜ

BD DE LA VILLETTE

Hôpital St Louis

19

10

Pyrénées Ⓜ

Baxo p99

Chez Jeanette

47 rue du Fbg-St Denis, 10th
(01.47.70.30.89). Mº Château d'Eau
or Strasbourg St-Denis. **Open** 8am-
2am daily. **€.** **Café.** Map p97 A3 **7**
When she sold her café back in March
2007, Jeanette handed over to the
young team from Chez Justine. Now the
awful 1940s lights, tobacco-stained
wallpaper depicting the Moulin Rouge
and PVC-covered banquettes have
been rewarded with a Fooding prize for
decor, and the café is fast becoming one
of Paris's hippest spots for an aperitif.

Shopping

Antoine et Lili

95 quai de Valmy, 10th (01.40.37.
41.55, www.antoineetlili.com). Mº
Jacques Bonsergent. **Open** 11am-7pm
Mon, Sun; 11am-8pm Tue-Fri; 10am-
8pm Sat. Map p97 B3 **8**
Antoine et Lili's fuchsia-pink, custard-
yellow and apple-green shopfronts are
a new raver's dream. The designer's
clothes, often in wraparound styles,
adapt to all sizes and shapes. The
Canal St-Martin 'village' comprises
womenswear, a kitsch home decoration
boutique and childrenswear.

Nightlife

Baxo

21 rue Juliette Dodu, 10th
(01.42.02.99.71, www.baxo.fr).
Mº Colonel Fabien. **Open** 9am-3pm,
7pm-2am Mon-Fri; 5pm-2am Sat, Sun.
Admission free. Map p97 C3 **9**
Baxo is a new hybrid venue that triples
as a restaurant, bar and DJ lounge for
a cool clientele. Friday nights are
reserved for resident DJs; Saturdays
feature live bands and guest splicers.

Café Chéri(e)

44 bd de la Villette, 19th (01.42.02.
02.05). Mº Belleville. **Open** 8am-2am
daily. **Admission** free. Map p97 D3 **10**
A popular DJ bar, especially in summer
when people flock to the terrace. Expect

anything from DJ Jet Boy's electro punk
to rock, funk, hip hop, rare groove,
indie, dance, jazz, and '80s classics.

New Morning

7-9 rue des Petites-Ecuries, 10th
(01.45.23.51.41, www.newmorning.
com). **Concerts** 9pm daily. **Admission**
€15-€25. Map p97 A3 **11**
One of the best places for the latest
cutting-edge jazz exponents, with a policy that also embraces *chanson*, blues,
world and sophisticated pop.

Point Ephémère

200 quai de Valmy, 10th (01.40.34.
02.48, www.pointephemere.org).
Mº Jaurès or Louis Blanc. **Open**
noon-2am daily. **Concerts** 8.30pm
daily. Map p97 C2 **12**
This converted warehouse is a classy
affair, bringing together up-and-
coming local rock, jazz and world gigs
with a decent restaurant, dance and
recording studios and exhibitions.

Arts & leisure

Hammam Med Centre

43-45 rue Petit, 19th (01.42.02.31.05,
www.hammammed.com). Mº Ourcq.
Open *Women* 11am-10pm Mon-Fri;
9am-7pm Sun. *Mixed (swimwear*
required) 10am-9pm Sat. Map p97 E1 **13**
This hammam is hard to beat – spotless
mosaic-tiled surroundings, flowered
sarongs and a relaxing pool. The
'Forfait florale' option (€139) will have
you enveloped in rose petals and mas-
saged with *huile d'Argan* from Morocco.

MK2

14 quai de la Seine, 19th (08.92.69.
84.84, www.mk2.fr). Mº Stalingrad.
Open times vary. **Admission** €9.90;
€5.90-€7.20 reductions. Map p97 C1 **14**
MK2's mini multiplex on the quai de la
Loire was seen as a key factor in the
social rise of what had previously been
a scuzzy part of town. Now the chain
has opened another multiplex across the
water, with a boat from one to the other.

Centre Pompidou

The Marais & Eastern Paris

PARIS BY AREA

Whereas historic *quartiers* like Montmartre and St-Germain-des-Prés are well past their heyday, the Marais has been luckier, and for the last two decades has been one of the hippest parts of the city, stuffed with modish hotels, boutiques and restaurants – in no small part due to its popularity with the gay crowd. It's also prime territory for arts lovers, thanks to its generous quotient of museums, and its tightly knit street plan – largely untouched by Haussmann – makes it a charming place in which to get lost. The Marais' neighbour to the west is Beaubourg, whose focal point is the iconic Centre Pompidou, with the city's all-important Hôtel de Ville a stone's throw to the south.

A little further east is the edgy Oberkampf district, home to some of the city's best bars and a nightlife hub for the last decade.

Sights & museums

Atelier Brancusi
Piazza Beaubourg, 4th (01.44.78.12.33, www.centrepompidou.fr). M° Hôtel de Ville or Rambuteau. **Open** 2-6pm Mon, Wed-Sun. **Admission** free. **Map** p102 A2 ❶
When Constantin Brancusi died in 1957, he left his studio and its contents to the state, and it was later moved and rebuilt by the Centre Pompidou. His fragile works in wood and plaster, the endless columns and streamlined bird forms show how Brancusi revolutionised sculpture.

Centre Pompidou (Musée National d'Art Moderne)
Rue St-Martin, 4th (01.44.78.12.33, www.centrepompidou.fr). M° Hôtel de Ville or Rambuteau. **Open** 11am-9pm (last entry 8pm) Mon, Wed, Fri-Sun (until 11pm some exhibitions);

11am-11pm Thur. **Admission** *Museum & exhibitions* €10-€12; free-€8 reductions. **Map** p102 A2 ❷
The Centre Pompidou (or 'Beaubourg') holds the largest collection of modern art in Europe. For the main collection, buy tickets on the ground floor and take the escalators to level four for post-1960s art. Level five spans 1905 to 1960. Masterful ensembles let you see the span of Matisse's career on canvas and in bronze, the variety of Picasso's invention, and the development of cubic orphism by Sonia and Robert Delaunay. Others on the hits list include Braque, Duchamp, Mondrian, Malevich, Kandinsky, Dalí, Giacometti, Ernst, Miró, Calder, Magritte, Rothko and Pollock. Level four houses post-'60s art. Recent acquisitions line the central corridor, and at the far end you can find architecture and design. Video art and installations by the likes of Mathieu Mercier and Dominique Gonzalez-Foerster are in a room given over to *nouvelle création*.

Event highlights Centre Pompidou's new Metz outpost opened in May 2010, just 82 minutes from Paris by TGV.

Cimetière du Père-Lachaise

Bd de Ménilmontant, 20th (01.55. 25.82.10). M° Père-Lachaise. **Open** *6 Nov-15 Mar* 8am-5.30pm Mon-Fri; 8.30am-5.30pm Sat; 9am-5.30pm Sun. *16 Mar-5 Nov* 8am-6pm Mon-Fri; 8.30am-6pm Sat; 9am-6pm Sun & public hols. **Map** p103 F2 ❸
Père-Lachaise is the celebrity cemetery – it has almost anyone French, talented and dead that you care to mention. Not even French, for that matter. Creed and nationality have never prevented entry: you just had to have lived or died in Paris or have an allotted space in a family tomb. Finding a particular grave can be tricky, so buy a €2 map from the hawkers at the Père-Lachaise métro or from shops nearby. Highlights include Chopin's medallion portrait and the muse of Music, plus famous neighbours

La Fontaine and Molière, who knew each other in real life and now share the same fenced-off plot.

Espace Claude Berri

8 rue Rambuteau, 3rd (01.44.54.88.50, www.espace-claudeberri.com). M° Rambuteau. **Open** 11am-7pm Tue-Sat. Closed Aug. **Admission** free. **Map** p102 A2 ❹
Claude Berri, who died in January 2009, was best known as one of France's most successful film directors and producers, but he also made a name for himself in the world of contemporary art. The aim of this space is to alternate exhibitions of works from Berri's private collection with solo shows.

Hôtel de Sully

62 rue St-Antoine, 4th (01.42.74.47.75, www.jeudepaume.org). M° St-Paul. **Open** noon-7pm Tue-Fri; 10am-7pm Sat, Sun. **Admission** €5; €2.50 reductions. **Map** p102 C4 ❺
With the Jeu de Paume, the former Patrimoine Photographique forms part of the two-site home for the Centre National de la Photographie.

Hôtel de Ville

29 rue de Rivoli, 4th (01.42.76.40.40, www.paris.fr). M° Hôtel de Ville. **Open** 10am-7pm Mon-Sat. Tours by appointment only. **Map** p102 A3 ❻
The palatial, multi-purpose Hôtel de Ville is the heart of the city administration, and a place in which to entertain visiting dignitaries. Free exhibitions are held in the Salon d'Accueil (10am-6pm Mon-Fri). The rest of the building, accessible by weekly tours (book in advance), has parquet floors, marble statues and painted ceilings.

Maison Européenne de la Photographie

5-7 rue de Fourcy, 4th (01.44.78. 75.00, www.mep-fr.org). M° St-Paul. **Open** 11am-8pm Wed-Sun (last entry 7.30pm). **Admission** €6.50; free-€3.50 reductions. Map p102 B4 ❼

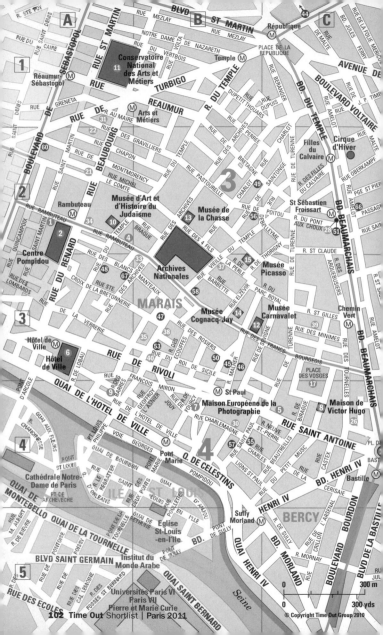

© Copyright Time Out Group 2010

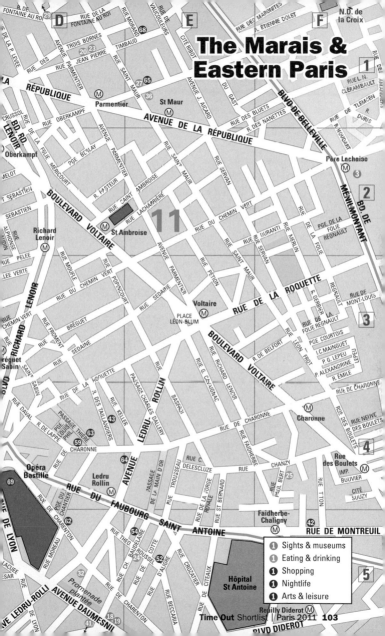

The Marais & Eastern Paris

	Sights & museums
	Eating & drinking
	Shopping
	Nightlife
	Arts & leisure

Probably the capital's best photography exhibition space, hosting retrospectives by Larry Clark and Martine Barrat, along with work by emerging photographers. The building, an airy mansion with a modern extension, contains a huge permanent collection.

Maison de Victor Hugo

Hôtel de Rohan-Guéménée, 6 pl des Vosges, 4th (01.42.72.10.16, www. musee-hugo.paris.fr). Mº Bastille or St-Paul. **Open** 10am-6pm Tue-Sun. **Admission** free. *Exhibitions* prices vary. **Map** p102 C4 ❽
Victor Hugo lived here from 1833 to 1848, and today the house is a museum devoted to the life and work of the great man. On display are his first editions, nearly 500 drawings and, more bizarrely, Hugo's home-made furniture.

Le Mémorial de la Shoah

17 rue Geoffroy-l'Asnier, 4th (01.42.77.44.72, www.memorialdela shoah.org). Mº Pont Marie or St-Paul. **Open** 10am-6pm Mon-Wed, Fri-Sun; 10am-10pm Thur. *Research centre* 10am-5.30pm Mon-Wed, Fri, Sun; 10am-7.30pm Thur. **Admission** free. **Map** p102 A4 ❾
Airport-style security checks mean queues, but don't let that put you off: the Mémorial du Martyr Juif Inconnu is an impressively presented and moving memorial to the Holocaust. Enter via the Wall of Names, where limestone slabs are engraved with the first and last names of each of the 76,000 Jews deported from France from 1942 to 1944 with, as an inscription reminds the visitor, the say-so of the Vichy government. The excoriation continues in the basement-level exhibition, which documents the plight of French and European Jews.

Musée d'Art et d'Histoire du Judaïsme

Hôtel de St-Aignan, 71 rue du Temple, 3rd (01.53.01.86.60, www.mahj.org). Mº Rambuteau. **Open** 11am-6pm Mon-Fri; 10am-6pm Sun. Closed Jewish hols. **Admission** €6.80; free-€4.50 reductions. **Map** p102 A2 ❿
This museum sprang from the collection of a private association formed in 1948 to safeguard Jewish heritage after the Holocaust. Displays illustrate ceremonies, rites and learning, and show how styles were adapted across the globe through examples of Jewish decorative arts. Photographic portraits of modern French Jews, each of whom tells his or her own story on the audio soundtrack, bring a contemporary edge. The Holocaust is marked by Boris Taslitzky's stark sketches from Buchenwald and Christian Boltanski's courtyard memorial to the Jews who lived in the building in 1939, 13 of whom died in the camps.
Event highlights Felix Nussbaum (22 Sept 2010-23 Jan 2011)

Musée des Arts et Métiers

60 rue Réaumur, 3rd (01.53.01.82.00, www.arts-et-metiers.net). Mº Arts et Métiers. **Open** 10am-6pm Tue, Wed, Fri-Sun; 10am-9.30pm Thur. **Admission** €6.50; free-€4.50 reductions. **Map** p102 A1 ⓫
Europe's oldest science museum is a fascinating, well laid out and vast collection of treasures. Here are beautiful astrolabes, celestial spheres, barometers, clocks, some of Pascal's calculating devices, the Lumière brothers' cinematograph, an enormous 1938 TV set, and still larger exhibits like Cugnot's 1770 'Fardier' (the first ever powered vehicle) and Clément Ader's steam-powered Avion 3. The visit concludes in the chapel, which contains old cars, a scale model of the Statue of Liberty and the monoplane in which Blériot crossed the Channel in 1909.

Musée Carnavalet

23 rue de Sévigné, 3rd (01.44.59. 58.58, www.carnavalet.paris.fr). Mº St-Paul. **Open** 10am-6pm Tue-Sun. **Admission** free. *Exhibitions* €7; free-€5.50 reductions. **Map** p102 B3 ⓬

Here, 140 rooms depict the history of Paris, from pre-Roman Gaul to the 20th century. Original 16th-century rooms house Renaissance collections, with portraits by Clouet and furniture and pictures relating to the Wars of Religion. The first floor covers the period up to 1789 and neighbouring Hôtel Le Peletier de St-Fargeau covers the period from 1789 onwards. Displays relating to 1789 detail that year's convoluted politics and bloodshed, with prints and memorabilia, including a chunk of the Bastille. There are items belonging to Napoleon, a cradle given by the city to Napoleon III, and a reconstruction of Proust's bedroom.

Event highlights Paris-Vuitton: Création en Capitale (13 Oct 2010-27 Feb 2011)

Musée de la Chasse et de la Nature

Hôtel Guénégaud, 62 rue des Archives, 3rd (01.53.01.92.40, www.chasse nature.org). M° *Rambuteau.* **Open** 11am-6pm Tue-Sun. **Admission** €6; free-€4.50 reductions. **Map** p102 B2 🔞
A two-year overhaul turned the three-floor hunting museum from a musty old-timer into something really rather special. The history of hunting and man's larger relationship with the natural world are examined in such things as a series of wooden cabinets devoted to the owl, wolf, boar and stag, each equipped with a bleached skull, small drawers you can open to reveal droppings and footprint casts, and a binocular eyepiece you can peer into for footage of the animal in the wild. A cleverly simple mirrored box contains a stuffed hen that is replicated into infinity on every side; and a stuffed fox is set curled up on a Louis XVI chair.

Musée Cognacq-Jay

Hôtel Donon, 8 rue Elzévir, 3rd (01.40.27.07.21, www.paris.fr/ musees). M° *St-Paul.* **Open** 10am-6pm Tue-Sun. **Admission** free. **Map** p102 B3 🔞

Computer culture

Digital arts download at the Gaîté Lyrique.

The biggest news on Paris's digital arts scene in 2010 is the creation of a major centre devoted specifically to this new medium. The **Théâtre de la Gaîté Lyrique** (3bis rue Papin, 3rd, www.gaite-lyrique.net) is set to reopen in December 2010 as a cultural complex for digital arts and contemporary music. Built in 1861-62, the theatre was originally managed by composer Jacques Offenbach, but it fell into decline. Long abandoned, it is finally being given new life with a redesign by architect Manuelle Gautrand.

The centrepiece of the new space is an auditorium with a seating capacity of over 300, which will be used for film projections, concerts, and a variety of performances. Other areas open to the public will include a theatre, café and two temporary exhibition spaces.

At the head of programming is Jérôme Delormas, who worked as co-director of Nuit Blanche. For Delormas, the aim of the new-look Gaîté Lyrique is to become one of the world leaders in digital arts by partnering with some of France's biggest contemporary art spaces, such as the Centre Pompidou and the Ferme du Buisson (www.laferme dubuisson.com). The centre also plans to collaborate with leading international organisations in the domain, such as ZKM in Karlsruhe and V2 in Rotterdam.

This museum houses a collection put together in the early 1900s by La Samaritaine founder Ernest Cognacq and his wife Marie-Louise Jay. They stuck mainly to 18th-century French works (Watteau, Fragonard, Boucher, Greuze and pastellist Quentin de la Tour), though some English artists (Reynolds, Romney, Lawrence) and Dutch and Flemish names (an early Rembrandt, Ruysdael, Rubens), plus Canalettos and Guardis, have managed to slip in. Pictures are displayed in panelled rooms with furniture, porcelain, tapestries and sculpture of the period.

Musée National Picasso

Hôtel Salé, 5 rue de Thorigny, 3rd (01.42.71.25.21, www.musee-picasso.fr). M° Chemin Vert or St-Paul. **Map** p102 B3 ⓮
The Musée Picasso is currently closed for restoration, and is due to reopen in 2012. Check the website for more details. In the meantime, the Centre Pompidou and Musée de l'Orangerie both contain Picasso collections.

Place de la Bastille

4th/11th/12th. M° Bastille. **Map** p102 C4 ⓰
Nothing remains of the prison that, on 14 July 1789, was stormed by revolutionary forces. Parts of the foundations can be seen in the métro. The Colonne de Juillet, topped by a gilded *génie* of Liberty, is a monument to Parisians who fell during the revolutions of July 1830 and 1848.

Place des Vosges

4th. M° St-Paul. **Map** p102 C4 ⓱
Paris's first planned square was commissioned in 1605 by Henri IV and inaugurated by his son Louis XIII in 1612. With harmonious red-brick and stone arcaded façades and pitched slate roofs, it differs from the later pomp of the Bourbons. Laid out symmetrically with carriageways through the taller Pavillon de la Reine on the north side and Pavillon du Roi on the south, the other

lots were sold off as concessions to royal officials and nobles. It was called place Royale prior to the Napoleonic Wars, when the Vosges was the first region of France to pay its war taxes. Mme de Sévigné, salon hostess and letter-writer, was born at no.1bis in 1626. At that time the garden hosted duels and trysts.

La Promenade Plantée

Av Daumesnil, 12th. M° Gare de Lyon or Ledru-Rollin. **Map** p103 D5 ⓲
The railway tracks atop the Viaduc des Arts were replaced in the late 1980s by a promenade planted with roses, shrubs and rosemary. It continues at ground level through the Jardin de Reuilly and the Jardin Charles Péguy on to the Bois de Vincennes.

Le Viaduc des Arts

15-121 av Daumesnil, 12th (www. viaduc-des-arts.com). M° Gare de Lyon or Ledru-Rollin. **Map** p103 D5 ⓳
Glass-fronted workshops in the arches beneath the Promenade Plantée provide showrooms for furniture and fashion designers, picture-frame gilders, tapestry restorers, porcelain decorators, and chandelier, violin and flute makers.

Eating & drinking

L'Alimentation Générale

64 rue Jean-Pierre-Timbaud, 11th (01.43.55.42.50, www.alimentation-generale.net). M° Parmentier. **Open** 5pm 2am Wed, Thur, Sun; 5pm-4am Fri, Sat. **Bar**. **Map** p103 D1 ⓴
The 'Grocery Store' is rue Jean-Pierre-Timbaud's answer to La Mercerie: it, too, is a big old space filled with junk. Cupboards of kitsch china and lampshades made from kitchen sponges are an inspired touch. The beer is equally well chosen – Flag, Sagres, Picon and Orval by the bottle – and the unusual €8 house cocktail involves basil and figs. DJs rock the joint: expect a €5 cover price for big names or bands. Oh yes – and it has the most brazen toilet walls this side of town.

L'Ambassade d'Auvergne

*22 rue du Grenier-St-Lazare, 3rd
(01.42.72.31.22, www.ambassade-auvergne.com). M° Arts et Métiers.*
Open noon-2pm, 7.30-10pm daily. **€€**.
Bistro. Map p102 A2 ㉑

This rustic *auberge* is a fitting embassy for the hearty fare of central France. An order of cured ham comes as two hefty, plate-filling slices, and the salad bowl is chock-full of green lentils cooked in goose fat, studded with bacon and shallots. The *rôti d'agneau* arrives as a pot of melting chunks of lamb in a rich, meaty sauce with a helping of tender white beans. Dishes arrive with the flagship *aligot*, the creamy, elastic mash-and-cheese concoction.

Andy Whaloo

69 rue des Gravilliers, 3rd (01.42.71.20.38). M° Arts et Métiers. **Open** 4pm-2am Tue-Sat. **Bar**. Map p102 A2 ㉒

Andy Whaloo, created by the people behind its neighbour 404 and London's Momo and Sketch, is Arabic for 'I have nothing'. Bijou? This place brings new meaning to the word. The formidably fashionable crowd fights for coveted 'seats' on upturned paint cans; it's a beautifully designed venue, crammed with Moroccan artefacts and a spice rack of colours. It's quiet early on, with a surge around 9pm.

Au P'tit Garage

63 rue Jean-Pierre-Timbaud, 11th (01.48.07.08.12). M° Parmentier.
Open 6pm-2am daily. **Bar**.
Map p103 D1 ㉓

This quite marvellous rock 'n' roll bar is the pick of the bunch on rue Jean-Pierre-Timbaud. Not that the owners have fitted it with Americana or waitresses on rollerskates; the L'il Garage is as basic as the real car-fit business a few doors down. Stuffing bursts out of the bar stools and salvaged chairs accompany wobbly tables of ill-matched colours. Regulars cluster around the twin decks at the bar, as music-savvy Frenchettes giggle and gossip at the back.

Le Baron Rouge

*1 rue Théophile-Roussel, 12th
(01.43.43.14.32). M° Ledru-Rollin.*
Open 10am-3pm, 5-10pm Tue-Thur; 10am-10pm Fri, Sat; 10am-3pm Sun.
Bar. Map p103 E5 ㉔

It sells wine, certainly – great barrels of the stuff are piled high and sold by the glass at very reasonable prices. But the Red Baron is not just a wine bar – more a local chat room, where regulars congregate to yak over their *vin*, along with a few draught beers and perhaps a snack of sausages or oysters. Despite its lack of seating (there are only four tables), it's a popular pre-dinner spot, so arrive early and don't expect much elbow room.

Le Bistrot Paul Bert

18 rue Paul-Bert, 11th (01.43.72.24.01). M° Charonne or Faidherbe Chaligny. **Open** noon-2pm, 7.30-11pm Tue-Thur; noon-2pm, 7.30-11.30pm Fri, Sat. Closed Aug. **€€**. **Bistro**.
Map p103 F4 ㉕

This heart-warming bistro gets it right almost down to the last crumb. A starter salad of *ris de veau* illustrates the point, with lightly browned veal sweetbreads perched on a bed of green beans and baby carrots with a sauce of sherry vinegar and deglazed cooking juices. A roast shoulder of suckling pig and a thick steak with a raft of golden, thick-cut *frites* look inviting indeed. Desserts are superb too, including what may well be the best *île flottante* in Paris. If you happen to be in the area at lunchtime, bear in mind that the prix fixe menu is remarkable value.

Bofinger

5-7 rue de la Bastille, 4th (01.42.72.87.82, www.bofingerparis.com). M° Bastille. **Open** noon-3pm, 6.30pm-1am daily. **€€**. **Brasserie**.
Map p102 C4 ㉖

Bofinger draws big crowds for its authentic art nouveau setting and its brasserie atmosphere. Downstairs is the prettiest place in which to eat, but

PARIS BY AREA

Andy Whaloo p107

the upstairs room is air-conditioned. An à la carte selection might start with plump, garlicky snails or a well-made langoustine terrine, followed by an intensely seasoned salmon tartare, a generous (if unremarkable) cod steak, or calf's liver accompanied by cooked melon. Alternatively, you could have the foolproof brasserie meal of oysters and fillet steak, washed down by the fine Gigondas at €35.50 a bottle.

Café Charbon

109 rue Oberkampf, 11th (01.43.57. 55.13, www.nouveaucasino.net). M° Ménilmontant or Parmentier. **Open** 9am-2am Mon, Tue, Sun; 9am-4am Wed-Sat. **Bar. Map** p103 E1 ㉗
The bar contained within this restored belle époque building sparked the Oberkampf nightlife boom. Its booths, mirrors and adventurous music policy put trendy locals at ease, capturing the essence of café culture spanning each end of the 20th century. After more than 15 years, the formula still works.

Cantine Merci

NEW *111 bd Beaumarchais, 3rd (01.42.77.78.92). M° St-Sébastien Froissart.* **Open** noon-3pm Mon-Sat. € **Café. Map** p102 C2 ㉓
The new fairtrade concept store Merci is all about feeling virtuous even as you indulge, and its basement canteen is a perfect example. Fresh and colourful salads, soup and risotto of the day, an organic salmon plate, and the *assiette merci* (perhaps chicken kefta with two salads) make up the brief, Rose Bakery-esque menu, complete with invigorating teas and juices.

Le Chateaubriand

129 av Parmentier, 11th (01.43.57. 45.95). M° Goncourt. **Open** noon-2pm, 8-11pm Tue-Fri; 8-11pm Sat. Closed 3wks Aug, 1wk Dec. €€€. **Bistro. Map** p103 D1 ㉙
Self-taught Basque chef Iñaki Aizpitarte runs this stylish bistro. Come at dinner to try the cooking at its most adventurous, as a much simpler (albeit cheaper) menu is served at lunch. Dishes have been deconstructed down to their very essence and put back together again. You'll understand if you try starters such as chunky steak tartare garnished with a quail's egg or asparagus with tahini foam and little splinters of sesame-seed brittle. The cooking's not always so cerebral – Aizpitarte's goat's cheese with stewed apple jam is brilliant.

Cru

NEW *7 rue Charlemagne, 4th (01.40.27. 81.84, www.restaurantcru.fr). M° St-Paul.* **Open** noon-3pm, 6.30pm-midnight Tue-Sun. €€. **Bistro. Map** p102 B4 ㉚
Opening a raw-food restaurant is a gamble, so the owners of Cru cheat here and there, offering root vegetable 'chips' and a few *plancha* dishes. Still, the menu has plenty for the crudivore, such as some unusual carpaccios (the veal with preserved lemon is particularly good) and intriguing 'red' and 'green' plates, variations on the tomato and cucumber.

Derrière

NEW *69 rue des Gravilliers, 3rd (01.44. 61.91.95). M° Arts et Métiers.* **Open** noon-3pm, 7.30-11pm Tue-Fri; 7.30-11pm Sat. €€. **Bistro. Map** p102 A1 ㉛
Mourad Mazouz, the man behind Momo and Sketch in London, has hit on another winning formula with this apartment-restaurant in the same street as his restaurant 404 and bar Andy Wahloo. The cluttered-chic look mixes contemporary fixtures and antique furniture. It attracts a young, hip crowd that appreciates the high-calorie comfort food, such as roast chicken with buttery mashed potatoes.

L'Encrier

55 rue Traversière, 12th (01.44.68. 08.16). M° Gare de Lyon or Ledru-Rollin. **Open** noon-2.15pm, 7.30-11pm Mon-Fri; 7.30-11pm Sat. Closed Aug & Christmas wk. €. **Bistro. Map** p103 D5 ㉜

Through the door and past the velvet curtain, you find yourself face to face with the kitchen – and a crowd of locals, many of whom seem to know the charming boss personally. Start with fried rabbit kidneys on a bed of salad dressed with raspberry vinegar, an original and wholly successful combination, and follow with goose *magret* with honey served with sautéed potatoes. To end, share a chocolate cake or try the popular profiteroles.

Le Gaigne

12 rue Pecquay, 4th (01.44.59.86.72, www.restaurantlegaigne.fr). M° Rambuteau. **Open** 12.15-2.30pm, 7.30-10.30pm Tue-Thur; 12.15-2.30pm, 7.30-11pm Fri, Sat. €€. **Bistro**. **Map** p102 B3 ③

It's a familiar story: young chef with haute cuisine credentials opens a small bistro in an out-of-the-way street. Here, the restaurant is even tinier than usual, with only 20 seats, and the cooking is unusually inventive. Chef Mickaël Gaignon worked with Pierre Gagnaire, and it shows in dishes such as *l'oeuf bio* – three open eggshells filled with creamed spinach, carrot and celeriac – or roast monkfish with broccoli purée and a redcurrant emulsion. The dining room is pleasantly modern.

Le Hangar

12 impasse Berthaud, 3rd (01.42.74. 55.44). M° Rambuteau. **Open** noon-2.30pm, 7.30-11pm Tue-Sat. Closed Aug. €. No credit cards. **Bistro**. **Map** p102 A2 ③

It's worth making the effort to find this bistro by the Centre Pompidou, with its terrace tucked away in a hidden alley and excellent cooking. A bowl of tapenade and toast is supplied to keep you going while choosing from the comprehensive *carte*. It yields, for starters, tasty and grease-free *rillettes de lapereau* (rabbit) alongside perfectly balanced pumpkin and chestnut soup. Main courses include pan-fried foie gras on a smooth potato purée made with olive oil.

Lizard Lounge

18 rue du Bourg-Tibourg, 4th (01.42. 72.81.34, www.cheapblonde.com). M° Hôtel de Ville. **Open** noon-2am daily. **Bar**. **Map** p102 B3 ③

An anglophone favourite deep in the Marais, this loud and lively joint provides lager in pints (€6), plus cocktails (€7) and a viewing platform for beer-goggled oglers. Bargain boozing (cocktails €5) kicks off at 5pm; from 8pm to 10pm there's another happy hour in the cellar bar; on Mondays it lasts all day.

La Mercerie

98 rue Oberkampf, 11th (01.56.98. 14.10). M° Parmentier. **Open** 5pm-2am daily. **Bar**. **Map** p103 E1 ③

The spacious Mercerie has bare walls (bare everything, in fact) and room for the usual Oberkampf shenanigans of death-wish drinking against a backdrop of loud, eclectic music. A DJ programme is lipsticked on the back bar mirror. Happy hour is from 7pm to 9pm, so you can cane the house vodkas and still have enough euros to finish the job. The back area, with its tea lights, provides intimacy.

La Perle

78 rue Vieille-du-Temple, 3rd (01.42.72.69.93). M° Chemin Vert or St-Paul. **Open** 6am-2am Mon-Fri; 8am-2am Sat, Sun. **Bar**. **Map** p102 B3 ③

The Pearl achieves a rare balance between all-day and late-night venue, and also has a good hetero/homo mix. It feels like a neighbourhood bar; labourers and screenwriters rub elbows with young dandies, keeping one eye on the mirror and an ear on the electro-rock.

Le Petit Fer à Cheval

30 rue Vieille-du-Temple, 4th (01.42.72.47.47, www.cafeine.com). M° St-Paul. **Open** 9am-2am daily. **Bar**. **Map** p102 B3 ③

Even a miniature Shetland pony would be pushed to squeeze his hoof into this *fer à cheval* (horseshoe) – this adorable little café has one of France's smallest bars. Tucked in behind the glassy façade is a friendly dining room lined with reclaimed métro benches; if you want scenery, the tables out front overlook the bustle of rue Vieille-du-Temple. In business for more than 100 years, the café enjoyed a retro makeover by Xavier Denamur in the 1990s, and today sports vintage film posters.

Le Petit Marché

9 rue de Béarn, 3rd (01.42.72.06.67). Mº Chemin Vert. **Open** noon-3pm, 7.30pm-midnight Mon-Fri; noon-4pm Sat, Sun. **€€**. **Bistro**. **Map** p102 C3 ㊴
Petit Marché's menu is short and modern with Asian touches. Raw tuna is flash-fried in sesame seeds and served with a Thai sauce, making for a refreshing starter; crispy-coated deep-fried king prawns have a similar oriental lightness. The main vegetarian risotto is rich in basil, coriander, cream and green beans. Pan-fried scallops with lime are precision-cooked and accompanied by a good purée and more beans. There's a short wine list.

Stolly's

16 rue Cloche-Perce, 4th (01.42.76. 06.76, www.cheapblonde.com). Mº Hôtel de Ville or St-Paul. **Open** 4.30pm-2am daily. **€€**. **Map** p102 B3 ㊵
This seen-it-all drinking den has been serving a mainly anglophone crowd for nights immemorial. The staff make the place what it is, and a summer terrace eases libation, as do the long happy hours; but don't expect anyone at Stolly's to faff about with food.

Le Train Bleu

Gare de Lyon, pl Louis-Armand, 12th (01.43.43.09.06, www.le-train-bleu.com). Mº Gare de Lyon. **Open** 11.30am-3pm, 7-11pm daily. **€€€**. **Brasserie**. **Map** p103 D5 ㊶
This listed dining room – with vintage frescoes and big oak benches – exudes a pleasant air of expectation. Don't expect cutting-edge cooking, but rather

fine renderings of French classics. Lobster served on walnut oil-dressed salad leaves is a generous, beautifully prepared starter. Mains of veal chop topped with a cap of cheese, and *sandre* (pike-perch) coupled with a 'risotto' of *crozettes* are also pleasant. A few reasonably priced wines would be a welcome addition.

Shopping

L'Autre Boulange

43 rue de Montreuil, 11th (01.43.72. 86.04). Mº Faidherbe Chaligny or Nation. **Open** 7.30am-1.30pm, 4-7.30pm Mon-Fri; 7.30am-1.30pm Sat. Closed Aug. **Map** p103 F5 ㊷
Michel Cousin bakes up to 23 types of organic loaf in his wood-fired oven – varieties include the *flutiot* (rye bread with raisins, walnuts and hazelnuts), the *sarment de Bourgogne* (sourdough and a little rye) and a spiced cornmeal bread.

Come On Eline

16-18 rue des Taillandiers, 11th (01.43.38.12.11). Mº Ledru-Rollin. **Open** *Sept-July* 11am-8.30pm Mon-Fri; 2-8pm Sun. *Aug* 2-8pm Mon-Fri. **Map** p103 D4 ㊸
The owners of this three-floor vintage wonderland have an eye for what's funky, from cowboy gear to 1960s debutantes frocks. The stock is in good condition, but prices are high.

Du Pain et des Idées

34 rue Yves Toudic, 10th (01.42.40.44.52, www.dupainetdes idees.com). Mº Jacques Bonsergent. **Open** 6.45am-8pm Mon-Fri. No credit cards. **Map** p102 C1 ㊹
Christophe Vasseur is a previous winner of the Gault-Millau prize for Best Bakery. Among his specialities are Le Rabelais – *pain brioché* with saffron, honey and nuts; and Le Pagnol aux Pommes, a bread studded with royal gala apple (with its skin on), raisins and orange flower water.

L'Eclaireur

*3ter rue des Rosiers, 4th (01.48.
87.10.22, www.leclaireur.com).
Mº St-Paul.* **Open** 11am-7pm Mon-
Sat. **Map** p102 B3 45

Housed in a dandified warehouse,
L'Eclaireur stocks designs by Comme
des Garçons, Martin Margiela and
Dries van Noten. Among its exclusive
finds, check out smocks by Finnish
designer Jasmin Santanen. A new space
in rue Boissy d'Anglas sells chic fashions for men and women.

L'Eclaireur Homme

*12 rue Malher, 4th (01.44.54.22.11,
www.leclaireur.com). Mº St-Paul.*
Open 11am-7pm Mon-Sat. **Map**
p102 B3 46

Amid the exposed ducts of this old
printworks you'll find items by Prada,
Comme des Garçons, Dries van Noten
and Martin Margiela. The star is
Italian Stone Island, whose radical
clothing features parkas with a steel
shell to counteract pollution.

Free 'P' Star

*8 rue Ste-Croix-de-la-Bretonnerie, 4th
(01.42.76.03.72, www.freepstar.com).
Mº St-Paul.* **Open** noon-11pm Mon-Sat;
2-10pm Sun. **Map** p102 B3 47

Late-night shopping is fun at this
Aladdin's cave of retro glitz, ex-army
wear and glad rags that has provided
fancy dress for many a Paris party.

I Love My Blender

*36 rue du Temple, 3rd (01.42.77.
50.32, www.ilovemyblender.fr).
Mº Hôtel de Ville.* **Open** 10am-7.30pm
Tue-Sat. **Map** p102 A3 48

Christophe Persouyre left a career in
advertising to share his passion for
English and American literature: all
the books he stocks were penned in
English, and here you can find their
mother-tongue and translated versions.

Julien, Caviste

*50 rue Charlot, 3rd (01.42.72.00.94).
Mº Filles du Calvaire.* **Open** 9am-

1.30pm, 3.30-7.30pm Tue-Sat; 10.30am-
1.30pm Sun. Closed 3rd wk Aug.
Map p102 B2 49

Julien promotes the small producers he
has discovered, and often holds wine
tastings on Saturdays.

K Jacques

*16 rue Pavée, 4th (01.40.27.03.57,
www.kjacques.fr). Mº St-Paul.* **Open**
10am-6.45pm Mon-Sat; 2-6.45pm Sun.
Map p102 B3 50

Set up in Saint-Tropez in 1933 by
Jacques Keklikian and his wife, the K
Jacques workshop started life stitching
together basic leather sandals for visitors to the Med resort. The Homère (or
Homer) was, and still is, the signature
piece – Picasso loved them, and over
the years they've counted the likes of
Colette and Brigitte Bardot among
their fans. Now the company offers a
range of around 60 styles.

Merci

NEW *111 bd Beaumarchais, 3rd
(01.42.77.00.33, www.merci-merci.com).
Mº St-Sébastien Froissart.* **Open** 10am-
7pm Mon-Sat. **Map** p102 C2 51

See box p113.

Moisan

*5 pl d'Aligre, 12th (01.43.45.46.60,
www.painmoisan.fr). Mº Ledru-Rollin.*
Open 7am-8pm Tue-Sat; 7am-2pm
Sun. No credit cards. **Map** p103 E5 52

Moisan's organic bread, *viennoiseries*
and rustic tarts are outstanding. At
this branch, situated by the market,
there's always a healthy queue.

Nodus

*22 rue Vieille-du-Temple, 4th
(01.42.77.07.96, www.nodus.fr).
Mº Hôtel de Ville or St-Paul.* **Open**
10.45am-2pm, 3-7.30pm Mon-Sat;
1-7.30pm Sun. **Map** p102 B3 53

Under the wooden beams of this cosy
men's shirt specialist are rows of
striped, checked and plain dress shirts,
stylish silk ties with subtle designs,
and silver-plated crystal cufflinks.

All in a good cause

Concept store and charity shop combined at Merci.

There's a buzz about the boulevard Beaumarchais. Here, at the eastern end of the Marais, Marie-France Cohen and her husband Bernard, owners of childrenswear brand Bonpoint, have opened **Merci** (see p112), Paris's latest shopping sensation housed in an elaborately reconfigured 19th-century fabric factory.

There are three ways to enter Merci, each one theatrical. The central entrance takes visitors through a quiet courtyard, home to the shop's emblem, a bright red Fiat Cinquecento; the side entrances lead shoppers through dark, quiet ante rooms – one a florist full of wild cow parsley and echinacea, the other a literary café with second-hand books from floor to ceiling like a snug reading room.

Inside the shop proper, there's a great mish-mash of merchandise. Three loft-like floors full of nooks and crannies heave with furniture, jewellery, stationery, fashion, household products, childrenswear and a haberdashery. The cross-selling doesn't stop at mixing what

you wear with what you eat with (or sew with) – Merci showcases the old with the new, the everyday with the fancy and the inexpensive with the pricey. So you'll find a vintage baseball jacket or Burberry mac next to contemporary designs from Stella or Les Prairies de Paris; a bodega beaker alongside a Philippe Starck goblet in Baccarat crystal; and enamel espresso cups on a vintage army campaign table. That's not all. In a move that takes retailer responsibility to a new level, Merci gives all its profits to charity, specifically to its own foundation that currently helps deprived children in Madagascar.

All this promise of inconspicuous consumption in a sumptuous setting makes Merci a bobo magnet. So whether the sight of an artfully scruffy but well-heeled customer waxing lyrical over a plastic ice bucket makes you think 'wonderful!' or something else beginning with 'w', what's for sure is that this most generous of general stores makes for great people watching too.

Première Pression Provence

NEW *3 rue Antoine Vollon, 12th (01.53.33.03.59, www.premiere-pression-provence.com). M° Ledru Rollin.* **Open** 11am-2.30pm, 3.30-7pm Tue-Fri; 10.30am-7pm Sat. **Map** p103 E5 **54**
Première Pression Provence is L'Occitane creator Olivier Baussan's latest project, where you are encouraged to taste spoonfuls of single-producer olive oil to educate your palate about the nuances of *vert*, *mûr* and *noir* (known as the '*fruités*') before buying.

Red Wheelbarrow

22 rue St-Paul, 4th (01.48.04.75.08, www.theredwheelbarrow.com). M° St Paul. **Open** 10am-6pm Mon; 10am-7pm Tue-Sat; 2-6pm Sun. **Map** p102 B4 **55**
Penelope Fletcher Le Masson and Abigail Altman run this friendly literary bookshop in the Marais, which also has an excellent children's section.

Shine

15 rue de Poitou, 3rd (01.48.05.80.10). M° Filles du Calvaire. **Open** 11am-7.30pm Mon-Sat; 2-7pm Sun. **Map** p102 B2 **56**
See By Chloe, Marc by Marc Jacobs and Acne Jeans, plus Repetto shoes and Véronique Branquino, are among the goodies in this glossy showcase.

Le Village St-Paul

Rue St-Paul, rue Charlemagne & quai des Célestins, 4th. M° St-Paul. **Open** 10am-7pm Mon-Sat. No credit cards. **Map** p102 B4 **57**
This colony of antiques sellers, housed in small, linking courtyards, is a source of retro furniture, kitchenware and wine gadgets.

Zadig & Voltaire

42 rue des Francs-Bourgeois, 3rd (01.44.54.00.60, www.zadig-et-voltaire.com). M° Hôtel de Ville or St-Paul. **Open** 10.30am-7.30pm Mon-Sat; 1.30-7.30pm Sun. **Map** p102 B3 **58**
Zadig & Voltaire's relaxed, urban collection is a winner. Popular separates include cotton tops, shirts and faded jeans; its collection of cashmere jumpers is superb.

Nightlife

Ateliers de Charonne

NEW *21 rue de Charonne, 11th (01.40.21.83.35, www.atelierscharonne.com). M° Charonne or Ledru-Rollin.* **Open** 7pm-1am Tue-Sat. **Admission** free. **Map** p103 D4 **59**
This spanking new jazz club is the place to see the rising stars of gypsy jazz (*jazz manouche*). If you want to grab a good spot near the front of the stage, reserve for dinner and the show.

Les Bains Douches

7 rue du Bourg-l'Abbé, 3rd (01.48.87.01.80, www.lesbainsdouches.net). M° Etienne Marcel. **Open** midnight-6am Wed-Sun (restaurant from 8pm). **Admission** €10-€20. **Map** p102 A2 **60**
Les Bains Douches lost its way in the 1990s, relying on its reputation to pull in tourists. This all changed recently, and now local star DJs like Busy P and international names such as Erol Alkan grace its decks once more.

Le Bataclan

50 bd Voltaire, 11th (01.43.14.00.30, www.le-bataclan.com). M° Oberkampf. **Open** times vary. **Map** p103 D2 **61**
Established in 1864, this highly distinctive venue is still standing after the odd facelift, and remains admirably discerning in its booking of rock, world, jazz and hip hop acts.

Le China

50 rue de Charenton, 12th (01.43.46.08.09, www.lechina.eu). M° Bastille or Ledru-Rollin. **Open** 6pm-2am Mon-Sat; noon-2am Sun. **Map** p103 D5 **62**
Le China has decor reminiscent of a 1930s Shanghai gentleman's club, an impressively long bar famed for its Singapore slings, and a reel of live

music in the basement. For a touch of glamour sink into a Chesterfield sofa and try the top-notch Cantonese food.

La Mécanique Ondulatoire

8 passage Thière, 11th (01.43.55.16.74, www.myspace.com/lamecanique). Mº Bastille or Ledru Rollin. **Open** 6pm-2am Mon-Sat. Concerts from 8pm Tue-Sat. **Admission** €4-€7. **Map** p103 D4 ❻❸
Cementing Bastille's status as Paris's prime hangout for rockers, this exciting venue has three levels and alternates eclectic DJs with live acts in the cellar, plus there's jazz on Tuesday nights.

Le Motel

8 passage Josset, 11th (01.58.30.88.52, www.myspace.com/lemotel). Mº Ledru Rollin. **Open** 6pm-1.45am Tue-Sun. Closed Aug. **Map** p103 E4 ❻❹
This most Anglophile of Paris bars, with Stone Roses and Smiths posters adorning the walls, manages to fit plenty of live bands, including some of the best local talent, on to its tiny stage.

Nouveau Casino

109 rue Oberkampf, 11th (01.43.57.57.40, www.nouveaucasino.net). Mº Parmentier. **Open** midnight-5am Wed-Sat. **Admission** €5 before 1am, €10 after. **Map** p103 E1 ❻❺
Nouveau Casino is a concert venue that also hosts some of the city's liveliest club nights. Local collectives, international names and record labels, such as Versatile, regularly host nights here; check the website for one-off parties.

Panic Room

NEW *101 rue Amelot, 11th (01.58.30.93.43). Mº St-Sebastien Froissart.* **Open** 6pm-2am Tue-Sat. Closed 2wks Aug. **Admission** free. **Map** p102 C2 ❻❻
This newcomer has quickly carved out a niche on the rock scene. The excellent Goldrush collective has live acts and DJs blasting the sound system in the basement, while upstairs friendly barmen serve affordable cocktails behind a concrete counter.

Arts & leisure

Les Bains du Marais

31-33 rue des Blancs-Manteaux, 4th (01.44.61.02.02, www.lesbainsdu marais.com). Mº St-Paul. **Open** Men 10am-11pm Thur; 10am-8pm Fri. Women 11am-8pm Mon; 10am-11pm Tue; 10am-7pm Wed. Mixed (swimwear required) 7-11pm Wed; 10am-8pm Sat; 10am-11pm Sun. Closed Aug. **Map** p102 A3 ❻❼
This hammam and spa mixes the modern and traditional (lounging beds and mint tea). Facials, waxing and essential oil massages (€70) are also available. The hammam is €35.

Maison des Métallos

94 rue Jean-Pierre Timbaud, 11th (01.48.05.88.27, www.maisondes metallos.org). Mº Parmentier or Couronnes. **Map** p103 E1 ❻❽
After serving over a century as a focal point for working-class activities, the Maison des Métallos reopened as a cutting-edge cultural showcase for contemporary artists. The venue offers up an ambitious multicultural programme of concerts, dance, film screenings, exhibitions, and popular debates.

Opéra National de Paris, Bastille

Pl de la Bastille, 12th (08.92.89.90.90, from abroad 01.71.25.24.23, www. operadeparis.fr). Mº Bastille. **Box office** (130 rue de Lyon, 12th) 10.30am-6.30pm Mon-Sat. By phone 9am-6pm Mon-Fri; 9am-1pm Sat. **Admission** €5-€196. **Map** p103 D4 ❻❾
The unfinished *salle modulable*, the unflattering acoustics and the miles of corridors combine to create an atmosphere more akin to an airport than an opera house, but the standard of performance is what matters and the Bastille looks set for some exciting evenings under director Nicolas Joel.
Event highlights Puccini's *Tosca* conducted by Renato Palumbo (20 Apr-18 May 2011).

Vedettes du Pont-Neuf

The Seine & Islands

The Seine

It's perhaps surprising that it took so long for the Seine to become a tourist magnet. For much of the 19th and 20th centuries, the Seine was barely given a second thought by anyone who wasn't working on it or driving along its quayside roads. But in 1994, UNESCO added 12 kilometres (7.5 miles) of Paris riverbank to its World Heritage register. Floating venues such as Batofar became super-trendy; and in the last ten years, it's been one new attraction after another.

It's at its best in summer. Port de Javel and Jardin Tino-Rossi become open-air dancehalls; and there's the jamboree of Paris-Plage, Mayor Delanoë's city beach that brings sand, palm trees, loungers and free entertainment to both sides of the Seine. Come on Sundays, and stretches of riverside roads will be closed for the benefit of cyclists and rollerskaters. And, of course, there's a wealth of boat tours on offer.

What's more, the river itself is cleaning up its act. The recent crackdown on pollution had a big symbolic payoff when, for the first time since records began, a sea trout was caught in the Seine on the western outskirts of the city.

Sights & museums

Vedettes du Pont-Neuf

Square du Vert-Galant, 1st (01.46.33.98.38, www.vedettesdu pontneuf.com). Mº Pont Neuf.
Tickets €12; free-€6 reductions.
Map p117 B1 ❶
The hour-long cruise takes in all the big sights, from the Eiffel Tower to Notre-Dame. You can sit inside just a foot or two above water level or outside on the top deck – where you may get drenched by pranksters throwing water from bridges as you pass underneath.

The Seine & Islands

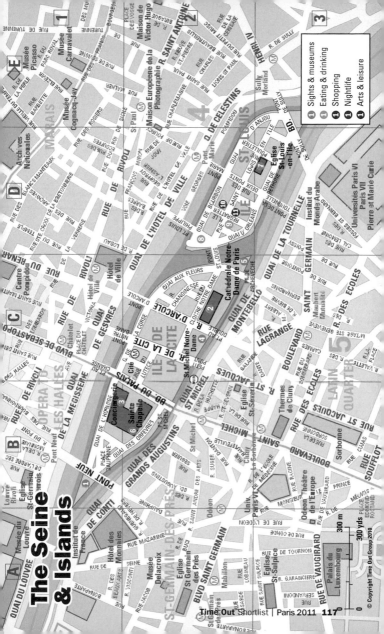

Map Key
- ● Sights & museums
- ● Eating & drinking
- ● Shopping
- ● Nightlife
- ● Arts & leisure

Areas and streets
MARAIS
ÎLE ST-LOUIS
ÎLE DE LA CITÉ
LES HALLES
OPÉRA
ST-GERMAIN-DES-PRÉS
LATIN QUARTER

Landmarks
Musée Picasso
Musée Carnavalet
Musée Cognacq-Jay
Archives Nationales
Maison Européenne de la Photographie
Maison de Victor Hugo
Église St-Paul
Centre Pompidou
Hôtel de Ville
Cathédrale Notre Dame de Paris
Église St-Louis-en-l'Île
Institut du Monde Arabe
Universités Paris VI Paris VII Pierre et Marie Curie
Conciergerie
Sainte Chapelle
Musée du Louvre
Église St-Germain l'Auxerrois
Institut de France
Hôtel des Monnaies
Musée Delacroix
Église St-Germain des Prés
Église St-Severin
Thermes de Cluny
Sorbonne
Odéon théâtre de l'Europe
St-Sulpice
Palais du Luxembourg

300 yds
300 m

© Copyright Time Out Group 2010

The bridges

From the honeyed arches of the oldest, the Pont Neuf, to the swooping lines of the newest, the Passerelle Simone-de-Beauvoir, the city's 37 bridges are among the best-known landmarks in the city, and enjoy some of its best views.

Over the years the city's *ponts* have been bombed, bashed by buses and boats, weather-beaten and even trampled to destruction: in 1634, the Pont St-Louis collapsed under the weight of a religious procession.

The 19th century was boom time for bridge-building: 21 were built in all, including the city's first steel, iron and suspension bridges. The Pont de la Concorde used up what was left of the Bastille after the storming of 1789; the romantic Pont des Arts was the capital's first solely pedestrian crossing (built in 1803 and rebuilt in the 1980s). The most glitteringly exuberant bridge is the Pont Alexandre III, with its bronze and glass, garlanding and gilded embellishments. More practical is the Pont de l'Alma, with its Zouave statue that has long been a flood monitor: when the statue's toes get wet, the state raises the flood alert and starts to close the quayside roads; when he's up to his ankles in Seine, it's no longer possible to navigate the river by boat. This offers some indication of how devastating the great 1910 flood was, when the plucky Zouave disappeared up to his neck – as did parts of central Paris.

The 20th century brought some spectacular additions. Pont Charles-de-Gaulle, for example, stretches like the wing of a huge aeroplane, and iron Viaduc d'Austerlitz (1905) is striking yet elegant as it cradles métro line 5. The city's newest crossing, the Passerelle Simone-de-Beauvoir, links the Bibliothèque Nationale to the Parc de Bercy.

Ile de la Cité

The Ile de la Cité is where Paris was born around 250 BC, when the Parisii, a tribe of Celtic Gauls, founded a settlement on this convenient bridging point of the Seine. Romans, Merovingians and Capetians followed, in what became a centre of political and religious power right into the Middle Ages: royal authority at one end, around the Capetian palace; the Church at the other, by **Notre-Dame**.

Perhaps the most charming spot on the island is the western tip, where Pont Neuf spans the Seine. Despite its name, it is in fact the oldest bridge in Paris. Its arches are lined with grimacing faces, said to be modelled on some of the courtiers of Henri III. Down the steps is leafy square du Vert-Galant. In the centre of the bridge is an equestrian statue of Henri IV; the original went up in 1635, was melted down to make cannons during the Revolution, and replaced in 1818.

Sights & museums

Cathédrale Notre-Dame de Paris

Pl du Parvis-Notre-Dame, 4th (01.42. 34.56.10, www.cathedraledeparis.com). M° Cité/RER St-Michel Notre-Dame. **Open** 8am-6.45pm Mon-Fri; 8am-7.15pm Sat, Sun. *Towers* Apr-Sept 10am-6.30pm daily (June, Aug until 11pm Sat, Sun). Oct-Mar 10am-5.30pm daily. **Admission** free. *Towers* €8; free-€5 reductions. **Map** p117 C2 ❷

Notre-Dame was constructed between 1163 and 1334, and the amount of time and money spent on it reflected the city's growing prestige. The west front remains a high point of Gothic art for the balanced proportions of its twin towers and rose window, and the three doorways with their rows of saints and sculpted tympanums: the *Last Judgement* (centre), *Life of the Virgin*

Cathédrale Notre-Dame de Paris p118

(left) and *Life of St Anne* (right). Inside, take a moment to admire the long nave with its solid foliate capitals and high altar with a marble *Pietà* by Coustou.

To truly appreciate the masonry, climb up the towers. The route runs up the north tower and down the south. Between the two you get a close-up view of the gallery of chimeras – the fantastic birds and hybrid beasts designed by Viollet-le-Duc along the balustrade. After a detour to see the Bourdon (the massive bell), a staircase leads to the top of the south tower.

La Conciergerie

2 bd du Palais, 1st (01.53.40.60.80).
Mº Cité/RER St-Michel Notre-Dame.
Open *Mar-Oct* 9.30am-6pm daily.
Nov-Feb 9am-5pm daily. **Admission**
€6.50; free-€4.50 reductions. *With*
Sainte-Chapelle €11; €7.50 reductions.
Map p117 B1 ❸

The Conciergerie looks every inch the forbidding medieval fortress. However, much of the façade was added in the 1850s, long after Marie-Antoinette, Danton and Robespierre had been imprisoned here. The visit takes you through the Salle des Gardes, the medieval kitchens with their four huge chimneys, and the Salle des Gens d'Armes, a vaulted Gothic hall built between 1301 and 1315. After the royals moved to the Louvre, the fortress became a prison under the watch of the Concierge. The wealthy had private cells with their own furniture, which they paid for; others had to make do with straw beds. A list of Revolutionary prisoners, including a hairdresser, shows that not all victims were nobles. In Marie-Antoinette's cell, the Chapelle des Girondins, are her crucifix, some portraits and a guillotine blade.

La Crypte Archéologique

Pl Jean-Paul II, 4th (01.55.42.50.10).
Mº Cité/RER St-Michel Notre-
Dame. **Open** 10am-6pm Tue-Sun.
Admission €4; free-€3 reductions.
Map p117 C2 ❹

Hidden under the forecourt in front of the cathedral is a large void that contains bits and pieces of Roman quaysides, ramparts and hypocausts, medieval cellars, shops and pavements, the foundations of the Eglise Ste-Geneviève-des-Ardens (the church where Geneviève's remains were stored during the Norman invasions), an 18th-century foundling hospital and a 19th-century sewer. It's not easy to work out which wall, column or staircase is which – but you do get a vivid sense of the layers of history piled one atop another during 16 centuries.

Mémorial des Martyrs de la Déportation

Sq de l'Ile de France, 4th (01.46.33.
87.56). Mº Cité/RER Châtelet or St-
Michel Notre-Dame. **Open** *Oct-Mar*
10am-noon, 2-5pm daily. *Apr-Sept*
10am-noon, 2-7pm daily. **Admission**
free. **Map** p117 C2 ❺

This tribute to the 200,000 Jews, Communists, homosexuals and *résistants* deported to concentration camps from France in World War II stands on the eastern tip of the island. A blind staircase descends to river level, where chambers are lined with tiny lights and the walls are inscribed with verse. A barred window looks on to the Seine.

Sainte-Chapelle

6 bd du Palais, 1st (01.53.40.60.80).
Mº Cité/RER St-Michel Notre-Dame.
Open *Mar-Oct* 9.30am-6pm daily.
Nov-Feb 9am-5pm daily. **Admission**
€8; free-€5 reductions. *With*
Conciergerie €10; €8 reductions.
Map p117 B2 ❻

Devout King Louis IX (St Louis, 1226-70) had a hobby of accumulating holy relics (and children: he fathered 11). In the 1240s he bought what was advertised as the Crown of Thorns, and ordered Pierre de Montreuil to design a shrine. The result was the exquisite Flamboyant Gothic Sainte-Chapelle. With 15m (49ft) windows, the upper level, intended for the royal family and the canons, appears to consist almost entirely of stained glass. The windows depict hundreds of scenes from the Old and New Testaments, culminating with the Apocalypse in the rose window.

Ile St-Louis

The Ile St-Louis is one of the most exclusive residential addresses in the city. Delightfully unspoiled, it has fine architecture, narrow streets and pretty views from the tree-lined quays, and still retains the air of a tranquil backwater, curiously removed from city life.

Rue St-Louis-en-l'Ile – lined with fine historic buildings that now house gift shops and gourmet food stores (many open on Sunday), quaint tearooms, stone-walled bars, restaurants and hotels – runs the length of the island. The grandiose Hôtel Lambert at no.2 was built by Le Vau in 1641 for Louis XIII's secretary, and has sumptuous interiors by Le Sueur, Perrier and Le Brun. At no.51 – Hôtel Chenizot – look out for the bearded faun adorning the florid doorway, which is flanked by stern dragons supporting the balcony.

At the western end there are great views of the buttresses of Notre-Dame from the terraces of the Brasserie de l'Ile St-Louis and the Flore en l'Ile café.

Sights & museums

Eglise St-Louis-en-l'Ile

19bis rue St-Louis-en-l'Ile, 4th (01.46.34.11.60, www.saintlouisenlile. com). M° Pont Marie. **Open** 9am-noon, 3-7pm Tue-Sun. **Map** p117 D3 ❼
The island's church was built between 1664 and 1765, following plans by Louis Le Vau and later completed by Gabriel Le Duc. The interior boasts Corinthian columns and a sunburst over the altar, and sometimes hosts classical music concerts.

Eating & drinking

Brasserie de l'Ile St-Louis

55 quai de Bourbon, 4th (01.43.54. 02.59). M° Pont Marie. **Open** noon-midnight Mon, Tue, Thur-Sun. Closed Aug. €. **Brasserie. Map** p117 D2 ❽
Happily, this old-fashioned brasserie soldiers on while exotic juice bars on the Ile St-Louis come and go. The terrace has one of the best summer views in Paris and is invariably packed. The dining room exudes shabby chic, though nothing here is gastronomically gripping: a well-dressed *frisée aux lardons*, perhaps, or a pan of warming tripe.

Mon Vieil Ami

69 rue St-Louis-en-l'Ile, 4th (01.40.46. 01.35, www.mon-vieil-ami.com). M° Pont Marie. **Open** noon-2.30pm, 7-11.30pm Wed-Sun. Closed 3wks Jan & 1st 3wks Aug. €€. **Bistro. Map** p117 D2 ❾
Antoine Westermann has created a true foodie destination here. Starters such as tartare of finely diced raw vegetables with sautéed baby squid on top impress with their deft seasoning. Typical of the mains is a casserole of roast duck with caramelised turnips and couscous.

Shopping

Arche de Noé

70 rue St-Louis-en-l'Ile, 4th (01.46.34. 61.60). M° Pont Marie. **Open** 10.30am-1pm, 2-7pm daily. **Map** p117 D2 ❿
'Noah's Ark' is a great place for Christmas shopping, with traditional wooden toys from eastern Europe, games, jigsaws and finger puppets.

L'Occitane

55 rue St-Louis-en-l'Ile, 4th (01.40.46. 81.71, www.loccitane.com). M° Pont Marie. **Open** 10.30am-7.30pm daily. **Map** p117 D2 ⓫
The many branches of this popular Provençal chain offer natural beauty products in neat packaging. Soap rules, along with essential oils and perfumes.

Eiffel Tower

The 7th & Western Paris

The seventh arrondissement is one large workshop, dotted with the machinery of state and diplomacy: this is the home of France's parliament, several ministries and a gaggle of foreign embassies, as well as the French army's training establishment and the headquarters of UNESCO. Visually speaking, much of the district is formal and aloof, albeit smart, and there are few attractions to draw the visitor – with the sizeable exceptions, naturally, of the Invalides, the Musée d'Orsay, the Rodin museum and a certain A-shaped assembly of 19th-century iron lattice beside the river.

Sights & museums

Les Egouts de Paris

Opposite 93 quai d'Orsay, by Pont de l'Alma, 7th (01.53.68.27.81). M° Alma Marceau/RER Pont de l'Alma. **Open** 11am-4pm (until 5pm May-Sept) Mon-Wed, Sat, Sun. Closed 3wks Jan. **Admission** €4.20; free-€3.50 reductions. No credit cards. **Map** p123 B1 ❶

For centuries the main source of drinking water in Paris was the Seine, which was also the main sewer. Construction of an underground sewerage system began at the time of Napoleon. Today the Egouts de Paris constitutes a smelly museum; each sewer in the 2,100km (1,305-mile) system is marked with a replica of the street sign above.

Eiffel Tower

Champ de Mars, 7th (01.44.11.23.23, www.tour-eiffel.fr). M° Bir-Hakeim/ RER Champ de Mars Tour Eiffel. **Open** *13 June-Aug 9am-12.45am daily. Sept-12 June 9.30am-11.45pm daily.* **Admission** *By stairs* (1st & 2nd levels, Sept-mid June 9.30am-6pm, mid June-Aug 9am-midnight) €4.50; free-€3.50 reductions. *By lift* (1st & 2nd levels) €8; free-€6.40 reductions; (3rd level) €13; free-€9.90 reductions. **Map** p123 A2 ❷

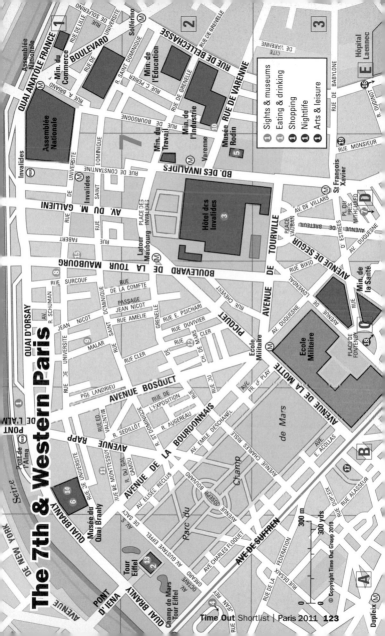

The 7th & Western Paris

Sights & museums
Eating & drinking
Shopping
Nightlife
Arts & leisure

Blind sight

Explore the history of braille at the Musée Valentin Haüy.

The **Musée Valentin Haüy** (see p126) is devoted to the history of braille, a story intimately connected with the French Enlightenment just before the Revolution. Valentin Haüy, whose statue you will see as you pass the gates of the Institut National des Jeunes Aveugles, was an 18th-century linguist and philanthropist. He established France's first school for the blind, and it was here that Louis Braille became a star pupil some 34 years later.

The one-room museum is hidden at the end of the nondescript corridors of the Valentin Haüy Association, which offers educational services to the blind. The door opens on to glass-fronted cases of exhibits with, in the centre, a huge braille globe. You can explore on your own with the aid of French, English or braille explanatory texts, or allow the curator, Noële Roy, to show you round. She will give a tour in English if preferred.

The first exhibit is a shocking print, depicting the fairground freak show that inspired Valentin Haüy to devote his life to educating not only the blind, but also the backward public who came to laugh at the likes of this blind orchestra forced to perform in dunce's hats. He wanted to prove that blind people had as great a capacity for learning and feeling as anyone else – in short, that they were human beings.

Next begins the tactile tour, with a chance to touch books printed by Haüy in embossed letters. After the Revolution, another philanthopist, Charles Barbier, tried to develop a universal writing system using raised dots, but it was difficult to read. Braille, the son of a harness-maker, arrived at the school as a ten-year-old in 1819, having been blind since the age of four after he accidentally stabbed himself in the eye with a stitching awl.

He spent his years at the school developing and perfecting his six-dot fingertip system. He was only 16 when he completed it, and went on to teach, write a treatise on arithmetic, and play the organ in two Paris churches. He died from tuberculosis at the age of 43. If it hadn't been for his childhood accident, this genius may never have had access to the education that led to his gift to humanity and his admission to the Pantheon.

No building better symbolises Paris than the Tour Eiffel. The radical cast-iron tower was built for the 1889 World Fair and the centenary of the 1789 Revolution by engineer Gustave Eiffel. Construction took more than two years and used some 18,000 pieces of metal and 2,500,000 rivets. Vintage double-decker lifts ply their way up and down; you can walk as far as the second level. There are souvenir shops, an exhibition space, café and even a post office on the first and second levels. At the top (third level), there's Eiffel's cosy salon and a viewing platform with panels pointing out what to see. Views can reach 65km (40 miles) on a good day.

Les Invalides & Musée de l'Armée

Esplanade des Invalides, 7th (08.10.11.33.99, www.invalides.org). M° La Tour-Maubourg or Les Invalides. **Open** *Apr-Sept* 10am-6pm daily. *Oct-Mar* 10am-5pm daily. Closed 1st Mon of mth. **Admission** *Musée de l'Armée & Eglise du Dôme* €8.50; free-€6.50 reductions. **Map** p123 D2 ❸
Topped by its gilded dome, the Hôtel des Invalides was (and in part still is) a hospital. Commissioned by Louis XIV for wounded soldiers, it once housed up to 6,000 invalids. The complex contains two churches – or, rather, a sort of double church: the Eglise St Louis was for the soldiers, the Eglise du Dôme for the king. An opening behind the altar connects the two.

The Invalides complex also houses the enormous Musée de l'Armée. The Antique Armour wing is packed full of armour and weapons that look as good as new. The Plans-Reliefs section is a collection of gorgeous 18th- and 19th-century scale models of French cities, used for military strategy. The World War I rooms are moving, with the conflict brought into focus by uniforms, paintings, a scale model of a trench on the western front and, most sobering of all, white plastercasts of the hideously mutilated faces of two soldiers. The

World War II wing takes in not just the Resistance, but also the Battle of Britain and the war in the Pacific (there's a replica of Little Boy, the bomb dropped on Hiroshima). Also included in the entry price is the Historial Charles de Gaulle.

Maison de la Culture du Japon

101bis quai Branly, 15th (01.44.37.95.01, www.mcjp.asso.fr). M° Bir-Hakeim/RER Champ de Mars Tour Eiffel. **Open** noon-7pm Tue, Wed, Fri, Sat; noon-8pm Thur. Closed Aug. **Admission** free. **Map** p123 A2 ❹
Constructed in 1996, this opalescent glass-fronted Japanese cultural centre screens films and puts on exhibitions and plays. It also contains a library, an authentic Japanese tea pavilion on the roof and a well-stocked shop.

Musée National Rodin

Hôtel Biron, 79 rue de Varenne, 7th (01.44.18.61.10, www.musee-rodin.fr). M° Varenne. **Open** *Apr-Sept* 9.30am-5.45pm Tue-Sun (gardens until 6.45pm). *Oct-Mar* 9.30am-4.45pm Tue-Sun (gardens until 5pm). **Admission** €6; free-€5 reductions. *Exhibitions* €7; €5 reductions. *Gardens* €1. **Map** p123 D2 ❺
The Rodin museum occupies the *hôtel particulier* where the sculptor lived in the final years of his life. The *Kiss*, the *Cathedral*, the *Walking Man*, portrait busts and early terracottas are exhibited indoors. Rodin's works are accompanied by pieces by his mistress and pupil, Camille Claudel. The walls are hung with paintings by Van Gogh, Monet, Renoir, Carrière and Rodin himself. Most visitors have greatest affection for the gardens: look out for the *Burghers of Calais*, the elaborate *Gates of Hell*, and the *Thinker*.

Musée du Quai Branly

37-55 quai Branly, 7th (01.56.61.70.00, www.quaibranly.fr). RER Pont de l'Alma. **Open** 11am-7pm Tue, Wed, Sun; 11am-9pm Thur-Sat. **Admission** €8.50; free-€6 reductions. **Map** p123 B1 ❻

Surrounded by trees on the banks of the Seine, this museum is a showcase for non-European cultures. Treasures include a tenth-century anthropomorphic Dogon statue from Mali, Aztec statues, Gabonese masks, Vietnamese costumes, Peruvian feather tunics and rare frescoes from Ethiopia.

Event highlights La Fabrique des Images (until 17 July 2011)

Musée Valentin Haüy

5 rue Duroc, 7th (01.44.49.27.27, www.avh.asso.fr). M° Duroc. **Open** 2.30-5pm Tue, Wed. **Admission** free. **Map** p123 D3 ❼
See box p124.

Eating & drinking

Le 144 Petrossian

18 bd de La Tour-Maubourg, 7th (01.44.11.32.32, www.petrossian.fr). M° La Tour Maubourg. **Open** noon-2.30pm, 7.30-10.30pm Tue-Sat. €€€. **Russian**. **Map** p123 C1 ❽
Senegalese-French chef Rougui Dia directs the kitchen of this famed caviar house. You'll find Russian specialities such as blinis, salmon and caviar from the Petrossian boutique downstairs, but Dia has added preparations and spices from all over the world in dishes such as lamb 'cooked for eleven hours' on a raisin-filled blini.

L'Ami Jean

27 rue Malar, 7th (01 47.05.86.89). M° Ecole Militaire. **Open** noon-2pm, 7pm-midnight Tue-Sat. Closed Aug. €€. **Bistro**. **Map** p123 C1 ❾
This long-running Basque address is an ongoing hit thanks to chef Stéphane Jégo. Excellent bread from baker Jean-Luc Poujauran is a perfect nibble, as are starters of sautéed baby squid on a bed of ratatouille. Tender veal shank comes de-boned with a side of baby onions and broad beans with tiny cubes of ham, and house-salted cod is soaked, sautéed and doused with an elegant vinaigrette.

L'Arpège

84 rue de Varenne, 7th (01.47.05. 09.06, www.alain-passard.com). M° Varenne. **Open** noon-2.30pm, 8-10.30pm Mon-Fri. €€€€. **Haute cuisine**. **Map** p123 E2 ❿
Assuming that you can swallow an exceptionally high bill – we're talking €42 for a potato starter – chances are you'll have a spectacular time at chef Alain Passard's Left Bank establishment. A main course of sautéed free-range chicken with a roasted shallot, an onion, potato *mousseline* and pan juices is the apotheosis of comfort food.

Au Bon Accueil

14 rue de Monttessuy, 7th (01.47.05. 46.11, www.aubonaccueilparis.com). M° Alma Marceau. **Open** noon-2.30pm, 7.30-10.30pm Mon-Fri. Closed 2wks Aug. €€. **Bistro**. **Map** p123 B1 ⓫
Jacques Lacipière runs Au Bon Accueil, and Naobuni Sasaki turns out the beautiful food. Perhaps most impressive is his elegant use of little-known fish such as grey mullet and meagre (*maigre*), rather than the usual endangered species. The €27 lunch menu might highlight such posh ingredients as *suprême de poulet noir du Cros de la Géline*, free-range chicken raised on a farm run by two former cabaret singers. But the biggest surprise comes with desserts, worthy of the finest pastry shops.

Le Café du Marché

38 rue Cler, 7th (01.47.05.51.27). M° Ecole Militaire. **Open** 7am-midnight Mon-Sat; 7am-5pm Sun. €. **Café**. **Map** p123 C2 ⓬
This well-loved address is frequented by trendy locals, shoppers hunting down a particular type of cheese and tourists who've managed to make it this far from the Eiffel Tower. Its *pichets* of decent house plonk go down a treat, and mention must be made of the food – such as the huge house salad served with lashings of foie gras and Parma ham.

La Pagode p128

Jules Verne

Pilier Sud, Eiffel Tower, 7th (01.45.55.61.44, www.lejulesverne-paris.com). M° Bir Hakeim or RER Tour Eiffel. **Open** 12.15-1.30pm, 7-9.30pm daily. €€€€. **Haute cuisine. Map** p123 A2 🔞

You have to have courage to take on an icon like the Eiffel Tower, but Alain Ducasse has done just that in taking over the Jules Verne, perched in its spectacular eyrie. He has transformed the cuisine and brought in his favourite designer, Patrick Jouin. But it's the food that counts, in the hands of Pascal Féraud, who updates French classics with dishes like lamb with artichokes, turbot with champagne zabaglione, and a fabulously airy ruby grapefruit soufflé. Reserve well ahead.

Les Ombres

27 quai Branly, 7th (01.47.53.68.00, www.lesombres-restaurant.com). M° Alma-Marceau. **Open** noon-2.30pm, 7-10.30pm daily. €€. **Bistro. Map** p123 B1 🔞

The full-on view of the Eiffel Tower at night would be reason enough to come to this restaurant on the top floor of the Musée du Quai Branly, but young chef Arnaud Busquet's food also demands that you take notice. His talent shows in dishes such as thin green asparagus curved into a nest with tiny *lardons* and topped with a breaded poached egg, ribbons of parmesan and meat *jus*.

Il Vino

13 bd de La Tour-Maubourg, 7th (01.44.11.72.00, www.ilvinobyenrico bernardo.com). M° La Tour-Maubourg. **Open** noon-2pm, 7pm-midnight daily. €€€€. **Italian. Map** p123 D1 🔞

Enrico Bernardo, winner of the World's Best Sommelier award, runs this restaurant where, for once, food plays second fiddle to wine. You are given nothing more than a wine list. Each of 15 wines by the glass is matched with a surprise dish, or the chef can build a meal around the bottle of your choice.

Best for a first visit is one of the blind tasting menus for €75, €100 or (why not?) €1,000. The impeccably prepared food shows a strong Italian influence.

Shopping

Fromagerie Quatrehomme

62 rue de Sèvres, 7th (01.47.34.33.45). M° Duroc or Vaneau. **Open** 8.45am-1pm, 4-7.45pm Tue-Thur; 8.45am-7.45pm Fri, Sat. **Map** p123 E3 🔞

Marie Quatrehomme runs this *fromagerie*. Justly famous for her comté fruité, beaufort and st-marcellin, she also sells specialities such as goat's cheese with pesto.

Marie-Anne Cantin

12 rue du Champ-de-Mars, 7th (01.45. 50.43.94, www.cantin.fr). M° Ecole Militaire or La Tour Maubourg. **Open** 2-7.30pm Mon; 8.30am-7.30pm Tue-Sat; 8.30am-1pm Sun. **Map** p123 B3 🔞

Cantin, a defender of unpasteurised cheese and supplier to posh Paris restaurants, offers aged *chèvres* and amazing morbier, mont d'or and comté.

Saxe-Breteuil

Av de Saxe, 7th. M° Ségur. **Open** 7am-2.30pm Thur; 7am-3pm Sat. **Map** p123 C3 🔞

Saxe-Breteuil has an unrivalled setting facing the Eiffel Tower, as well as the city's most chic produce. Look for farmer's goat's cheese, abundant oysters and a handful of small producers.

Arts & leisure

La Pagode

57bis rue de Babylone, 7th (01.45.55.48.48). M° St-François-Xavier. **Admission** €8.50; €7 Mon, Wed, students, under-21s. No credit cards. **Map** p123 D3 🔞

This glorious edifice is not, as local legend might have it, a block-by-block import, but a 19th-century replica of a pagoda. Renovated in the 1990s, this is one of the loveliest cinemas in the world.

Jardin du Luxembourg p130

St-Germain-des-Prés & Odéon

Like the Latin Quarter, St-Germain-des-Prés is another area that no longer quite lives up to its legend. In the middle third of the 20th century, the area was prime arts and intello territory, a place known as much for its high jinks as its lofty thinking: the haunt of Picasso, Giacometti, Camus, Prévert and, *bien sûr*, the Bonnie and Clyde of French philosophy, Jean-Paul Sartre and Simone de Beauvoir; the hotspot of the Paris jazz boom after World War II; and the heart of the Paris book trade. This is where the cliché of café terrace intellectualising was coined, but nowadays most of the patrons of the Flore and the Deux Magots are in the fashion business, and couturiers have largely replaced publishers. Never mind: it's a smart and attractive part of the city to wander around in, and also has some very good restaurants.

St-Germain-des-Prés grew up around the medieval abbey, the oldest church in Paris and site of an annual fair that drew merchants from across Europe. There are traces of its cloister and part of the abbot's palace behind the church on rue de l'Abbaye. Constructed in 1586 in red brick with stone facing, the palace prefigured the architecture of place des Vosges. Charming place de Furstemberg (once the palace stables) is home to the house and studio where the elderly Delacroix lived when painting the murals in St-Sulpice; it now houses the **Musée National Delacroix**. Wagner, Ingres and Colette all lived on nearby rue Jacob; its elegant 17th-century *hôtels particuliers* now contain specialist book, design and antiques shops and a few pleasant hotels. Further east, rue de Buci hosts a market and upmarket food shops.

Sights & museums

Ecole Nationale Supérieure des Beaux-Arts (Ensb-a)

14 rue Bonaparte, 6th (01.47.03.50.00, www.ensba.fr). M° St-Germain-des-Prés. **Open** *Courtyard* 9am-5pm Mon-Fri. *Exhibitions* 1-7pm Tue-Sun. **Admission** €4; €2 reductions. *Exhibitions* prices vary. **Map** p131 C1 **❶**

The city's most prestigious fine arts school resides in what remains of the 17th-century Couvent des Petits-Augustins, the 18th-century Hôtel de Chimay, some 19th-century additions and chunks of various French châteaux moved here after the Revolution (when the buildings briefly served as a museum of French monuments).

Eglise St-Germain-des-Prés

3 pl St-Germain-des-Prés, 6th (01.55.42. 81.33, www.eglise-sgp.org). M° St-Germain-des-Prés. **Open** 8am-7.45pm Mon-Sat; 9am-8pm Sun. **Map** p131 C2 **❷**

The oldest church in Paris. On the advice of Germain (later Bishop of Paris), Childebert, son of Clovis, had a basilica and monastery built here around 543. It was first dedicated to St Vincent, and came to be known as St-Germain-le-Doré because of its copper roof, then later as St-Germain-des-Prés ('of the fields'). During the Revolution the abbey was burned and a saltpetre refinery installed; the spire was added in a 19th-century restoration. Still, most of the present structure is 12th-century, and ornate carved capitals and the tower remain from the 11th. Tombs include those of Jean-Casimir, deposed King of Poland who became Abbot of St-Germain in 1669, and Scots nobleman William Douglas.

Eglise St-Sulpice

Pl St-Sulpice, 6th (01.42.34.59.98, www.paroisse-saint-sulpice-paris.org). M° St-Sulpice. **Open** 7.30am-7.30pm daily. **Map** p131 C3 **❸**

It took 120 years (starting in 1646) and six architects to finish St-Sulpice. The grandiose Italianate façade, with its two-tier colonnade, was designed by Jean-Baptiste Servandoni. He died in 1766 before the second tower was finished, leaving one tower five metres shorter than the other. The trio of murals by Delacroix in the first chapel – *Jacob's Fight with the Angel*, *Heliodorus Chased from the Temple* and *St Michael Killing the Dragon* – create a suitably sombre atmosphere.

Jardin & Palais du Luxembourg

Pl Auguste-Comte, pl Edmond-Rostand or rue de Vaugirard, 6th (01.44.54.19.49, www.senat.fr/visite). M° Odéon/RER Luxembourg. **Open** *Jardin* summer 7.30am-dusk daily; winter 8am-dusk daily. **Map** p131 C4 **❹**

The palace itself was built in the 1620s for Marie de Médicis, widow of Henri IV, by Salomon de Brosse on the site of the former mansion of the Duke of Luxembourg. Its Italianate style was intended to remind her of the Pitti Palace in her native Florence. The palace now houses the French parliament's upper house, the Sénat.

The mansion next door (Le Petit Luxembourg) is the residence of the Sénat's president. The gardens, though, are the real draw: part formal (terraces and gravel paths), part 'English garden' (lawns and mature trees), they are the quintessential Paris park. The garden is crowded with sculptures: a looming Cyclops, queens of France, a miniature Statue of Liberty, wild animals, busts of Flaubert and Baudelaire, and a monument to Delacroix. There are orchards and an apiary. The Musée National du Luxembourg hosts prestigious exhibitions. Most interesting, though, are the people: an international mixture of *flâneurs* and *dragueurs*, chess players and martial-arts practitioners, as well as children on ponies, in sandpits and playing with sailing boats on the pond.

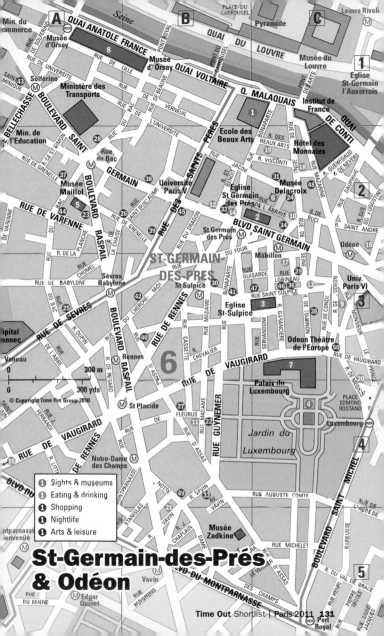

St-Germain-des-Prés & Odéon

Legend:
- Sights & museums
- Eating & drinking
- Shopping
- Nightlife
- Arts & leisure

© Copyright Time Out Group 2010

Work in progress

The Musée d'Orsay is having an overhaul.

In truth, 2010 is not a vintage year for Paris's museum scene. The Musée Picasso is closed until 2012 for major renovation work to upgrade facilities and increase exhibition space, and now the Musée d'Orsay's famed upper galleries are undergoing a serious brush-up too.

The **Musée d'Orsay** (*see p133*), originally a train station designed by Victor Laloux in 1900, houses a huge collection spanning the period between 1848 and 1914, and is normally home to a profusion of works by Delacroix, Corot, Manet, Renoir, Pissarro, Gauguin, Monet, Caillebotte, Cézanne, Van Gogh, Toulouse-Lautrec and others.

The end result of renovations in early 2011 will be a better display of artworks, larger exhibition areas and greater visitor pleasure, but in the meantime space is substantially reduced – the museum's website has a helpful guide to what remains on the walls.

Fortunately, though, this artistic cloud has a silver lining. Across the Seine, the Grand Palais (*see p35*) is staging the city's first big Monet show for 30 years, featuring hundreds of works on loan from the Musée d'Orsay, and a global tour of duty will see many of the museum's greatest works touch down at San Francisco's De Young Fine Arts Museum (25 Sept 2010-18 Jan 2011).

Musée Maillol

59-61 rue de Grenelle, 7th (01.42.22.59. 58, www.museemaillol.com). Mº Rue du Bac. **Open** 11am-6pm (last admission 5.15pm) Mon, Wed-Sun. **Admission** €8; free-€6 reductions. **Map** p131 A2 ❺

Dina Vierny was 15 when she met Aristide Maillol (1861-1944) and became his principal model for the next decade, idealised in such sculptures as *Spring, Air* and *Harmony.* In 1995 she opened this delightful museum, exhibiting Maillol's drawings, engravings, pastels, tapestry panels, ceramics and early Nabis-related paintings, as well as the sculptures and terracottas that epitomise his calm, modern classicism. The venue has works by Picasso, Rodin, Gauguin, Degas and Cézanne, a room of Matisse drawings, rare Surrealist documents and works by naïve artists. Vierny has also championed Kandinsky and Ilya Kabakov, whose *Communal Kitchen* installation recreates the atmosphere of Soviet domesticity. Monographic exhibitions are devoted to contemporary artists.

Musée National Delacroix

6 pl de Furstemberg, 6th (01.44.41. 86.50, www.musee-delacroix.fr). Mº St-Germain-des-Prés. **Open** *Sept-May* 9.30am-5pm Mon, Wed-Sun. *June-Aug* 9.30am-5.30pm Mon, Wed-Sun. **Admission** €5; free reductions. **Map** p131 C2 ❻

Eugène Delacroix moved to this apartment and studio in 1857 to be near the Eglise St-Sulpice, where he was painting murals. This collection includes small oil paintings, free pastel studies of skies, sketches and lithographs.

Musée National du Luxembourg

19 rue de Vaugirard, 6th (01.42.34. 25.95, www.museeduluxembourg.fr). Mº Cluny La Sorbonne or Odéon/RER Luxembourg. **Map** p131 C3 ❼

When it opened in 1750, this small museum was the first public gallery in France. Its stewardship by the national museums and French Senate brought imaginative touches and impressive coups. The museum is currently closed, but should reopen by early 2011. Check the website for more details

Musée d'Orsay

1 rue de la Légion-d'Honneur, 7th (01.40.49.48.14, recorded information 01 45,49.11.11, www.musee-orsay.fr). Mº Solférino/RER Musée d'Orsay. **Open** 9.30am-6pm Tue, Wed, Fri-Sun; 9.30am-9.45pm Thur. **Admission** €9.50; free-€7 reductions. **Map** p131 A1 **❽** See box p132.

Eating & drinking

Le Bar Dix

10 rue de l'Odéon, 6th (01.43.26.66.83, www.le10bar.com). Mº Odéon. **Open** 6pm-2am daily. No credit cards. **Bar**. **Map** p131 C3 **❾**
Generations of students have glugged back jugs of the celebrated home-made sangría (€3 a glass in happy hour) while squeezed into the cramped upper bar, tattily authentic with its Jacques Brel record sleeves, Yves Montand handbills and pre-war light fittings. Spelunkers and hopeless romantics negotiate the hazardous stone staircase to drink in the cellar bar, with its candlelight and old advertising murals. Can someone please come and slap a preservation order on the place?

Le Bar du Marché

75 rue de Seine, 6th (01.43.26.55.15). Mº Mabillon or Odéon. **Open** 8am-2am daily. **Bar**. **Map** p131 C2 **❿**
The market in question is the Cours des Halles, the bar a convivial corner café opening on to the pleasing bustle of St-Germain-des-Prés. Simple dishes like a ham omelette or a plate of herring in the €7 range, and Brouilly or muscadet at €4-€5 a glass, are proffered by beret-topped waiters. Locals easily outnumber tourists, confirming Rod Stewart's astute observation that Paris gives the impression that no one is ever working.

Bread & Roses

7 rue de Fleurus, 6th (01.42.22.06.06, www.breadandroses.fr). Mº St-Placide. **Open** 8am-8pm Mon-Sat. Closed Aug & 1wk Dec. €€. **Café**. **Map** p131 B4 **⓫**
Giant wedges of cheesecake sit alongside French pastries, and huge savoury puff-pastry tarts are perched on the counter. Attention to detail shows even in the taramasalata, which is matched with buckwheat-and-seaweed bread. Prices reflect the quality of the often organic ingredients.

Café de Flore

172 bd St-Germain, 6th (01.45 48, 55.26, www.cafe-de-flore.com). Mº St-Germain-des-Prés. **Open** 7.30am-1.30am daily. €€. **Café**. **Map** p131 B2 **⓬**
Bourgeois locals crowd the terrace tables at lunch, eating club sandwiches with knives and forks as anxious waiters frown at couples with pushchairs or single diners occupying tables for four. This historic café, former HQ of the Lost Generation intelligentsia, attracts tourists, and celebrities from time to time. But a *café crème* is €4.60, a Perrier €5 and the omelettes and *croques* are best eschewed in favour of the better dishes on the menu (€15-€25). There are play readings on Mondays and philosophy debates on the first Wednesday of the month, both at 8pm, in English.

Le Comptoir

Hôtel Le Relais Saint-Germain, 9 carrefour de l'Odéon, 6th (01.43.29. 12.05). Mº Odéon. **Open** noon-6pm, 8.30pm-midnight (last orders 9pm) Mon-Fri; noon-11pm Sat, Sun. Closed 3wks Aug. €. **Brasserie**. **Map** p131 C3 **⓭**
Yves Camdeborde runs the bijou 17th-century Hôtel Le Relais Saint-Germain, whose art deco dining room, modestly dubbed Le Comptoir, serves brasserie fare from noon to 6pm and on weekend nights, and a five-course prix fixe feast on weekday evenings. The single dinner sitting lets the chef take real pleasure in his work. On the daily menu, you might find dishes like rolled saddle

of lamb with vegetable-stuffed 'Basque ravioli'. The catch? The prix fixe dinner is booked up as much as six months in advance.

Les Deux Magots

6 pl St-Germain-des-Prés, 6th (01.45. 48.55.25, www.lesdeuxmagots.com). Mº St-Germain-des-Prés. **Open** 7.30am-1am daily. **€€**. **Café**. Map p131 B2 ⑭
If you stand outside Les Deux Magots, you have to be prepared to photograph tourists wanting proof of their encounter with French philosophy. The former haunt of Sartre and de Beauvoir now draws a less pensive crowd that can be all too *m'as-tu vu*, particularly at weekends. The hot chocolate is still good, though. Visit on a weekday afternoon when the editors return, manuscripts in hand, to the inside tables, leaving enough elbow room to engage in some serious discussion.

L'Epigramme

9 rue de l'Eperon, 6th (01.44.41.00.09). Mº Odéon. **Open** noon-2.30pm, 7-11.30pm Tue-Sat; noon-2pm Sun. **€**. **Bistro**. Map p131 C2 ⑮
L'Epigramme is a pleasantly bourgeois dining room with terracotta floor tiles, wood beams, a glassed-in kitchen and comfortable chairs. Like the decor, the food doesn't aim to innovate but sticks to tried and true classics with the occasional twist. Marinated mackerel in a mustardy dressing on toasted country bread gets things off to a promising start, but the chef's skill really comes through in main courses such as perfectly seared lamb with glazed root vegetables and intense *jus*. It's rare to find such a high standard of cooking at this price.

La Ferrandaise

8 rue de Vaugirard, 6th (01.43.26. 36.36, www.laferrandaise.com). Mº Odéon/RER Luxembourg. **Open** noon-2.30pm, 7-10.30pm Tue-Thur; noon-2.30pm, 7pm-midnight Fri; 7pm-midnight Sat. **€€**. **Bistro**. Map p131 A4 ⑯

This bistro has quickly established a faithful following. A platter of excellent ham, sausage and terrine arrives as you study the blackboard menu, and the bread is crisp-crusted, thickly sliced sourdough. Two specialities are the potato stuffed with escargots in a camembert sauce, and a wonderfully flavoured, slightly rosé slice of veal. Desserts might include intense chocolate with rum-soaked bananas.

J'Go

Rue Clément, 6th (01.43.26.19.02, www.lejgo.com). Mº Mabillon or Odéon. **Open** 11am-midnight daily. **€€**. **Wine bar**. Map p131 A4 ⑰
As its name suggests, J'Go (pronounced gigot) is all about lamb – well, meat of various kinds, actually: a buzzing wine bar by day, it becomes a *rôtisserie* at meal times, serving its speciality spit-roasted lamb from Quercy, black pig from Bigorre, and whole roasted chickens. The €36 set menu is well worth the splurge, offering a whole jar of pâté, a giant salad, and lamb with creamy stewed *haricots blancs*. If you'd rather stick to wine and tapas, sidle up to one of the wooden barrels, choose your poison (at €4 a glass all wines are good) and share a plate of charcuterie or foie gras *tartines* (€10).

La Palette

43 rue de Seine, 6th (01.43.26.68.15). Mº Odéon. **Open** 9am-2am Mon-Sat. Closed Aug. **€**. **Café**. Map p131 C2 ⑱
La Palette is the café-bar of choice for the Beaux-Arts students who study at the venerable institution around the corner, and young couples who steal kisses in the wonderfully preserved art-deco back room decorated with illustrations. Grab a spot on the leafy terrace if you can.

Le Restaurant

L'Hôtel, 13 rue des Beaux-Arts, 6th (01.44.41.99.01, www.l-hotel.com). Mº St-Germain-des-Prés. **Open** 12.30-2pm, 7.30-10pm Tue-Sat. **€€€**. **Haute cuisine**. Map p131 C2 ⑲

Café de Flore p133

L'Hôtel has the talented Philippe Bélisse in charge of the kitchen. You can choose from a short seasonal menu with such dishes as pan-fried tuna, John Dory or suckling pig. But for the same price you could also enjoy the marvellous four-course *menu dégustation* (€95) or, even better, the *menu surprise* (€115). Highlights of the spring menu were smoked Somme eel with horseradish and lime, and a main of roasted sea bass with shellfish, citrus and fennel.

Le Rostand

6 pl Edmond-Rostand, 6th (01.43.54. 61.58). RER Luxembourg. **Open** 8am-2am daily. **Bar**. Map p131 C3 ⑳
Le Rostand has a truly wonderful view of the Jardin du Luxembourg from its classy interior, decked out with oriental paintings, a mahogany bar and wall-length mirrors. Perfect for a civilised drink after a stroll round the gardens.

Le Timbre

3 rue Ste-Beuve, 6th (01.45.49.10.40, www.restaurantletimbre.com). M° Vavin. **Open** noon-2pm, 7.30-10.30pm Tue-Sat. Closed Aug & 1wk Dec. **€**. **Bistro**. Map p131 B4 ㉑
Chris Wright's restaurant, open kitchen included, might be the size of the average student garret, but this Mancunian aims high. Typical of his cooking is a plate of fresh asparagus elegantly cut in half lengthways and served with dabs of anise-spiked sauce and balsamic vinegar, and a little crumbled parmesan. Mains are also pure in presentation and flavour – a thick slab of pork, pan-fried, comes with petals of red onion.

Shopping

APC

38 rue Madame, 6th (01.42.22.12.77, www.apc.fr). M° St-Placide. **Open** 11am-7.30pm Mon-Sat. Map p131 B4 ㉒
The look is simple but stylish: think perfectly cut basics in muted tones. Hip without trying too hard, its jeans are a big hit.

L'Artisan Parfumeur

24 bd Raspail, 7th (01.42.22.23.32, www.artisanparfumeur.com). M° Rue du Bac. **Open** 10.30am-7.30pm Mon-Sat. Map p131 A2 ㉓
Among the scented candles, potpourri and charms, you'll find the best vanilla perfume that Paris can offer – Mûres et Musc, a bestseller for two decades.

Arty Dandy

NEW *1 rue de Furstemberg, 6th (01.43.54.00.36, www.artydandy.com). M° Mabillon.* **Open** 10am-7pm Mon-Sat. Map p131 C2 ㉔
Arty Dandy is a concept shop that embraces the surreal, the tongue-in-cheek and the poetic – an R.MUTT sticker to create your own Duchampian loo, and the 'Karl who?' bag (which KL himself has been carrying) are instant pleasers. More sublime offerings include Jaime Hayon's 'Lover' figurines.

Le Bon Marché

24 rue de Sèvres, 7th (01.44.39.80.00, www.bonmarche.fr). M° Sèvres Babylone. **Open** 10am-8pm Mon-Wed, Sat; 10am-9pm Thur, Fri. Map p131 A3 ㉕
Luxury boutiques take pride of place on the ground floor; escalators designed by Andrée Putman take you up to the fashion floor, which has an excellent selection of designer labels. Designer names also abound in Balthazar, the men's section. For top-notch nibbles, try the Grande Epicerie.

Bruno Frisoni

34 rue de Grenelle, 6th (01.42.84. 12.30, www.brunofrisoni.fr). M° Rue du Bac. **Open** 10.30am-7pm Tue-Sat. Map p131 B2 ㉖
Innovative Frisoni's shoes have a cinematic, pop edge: modern theatrics for the unconventional.

Christian Constant

37 rue d'Assas, 6th (01.53.63.15.15). M° Rennes or St-Placide. **Open** 9.30am-8.30pm Mon-Fri; 9am-8pm Sat, Sun. Map p131 B4 ㉗

A master chocolate-maker and *traiteur*, Constant scours the globe for ideas. His *ganaches* are subtly flavoured with verbena, jasmine or cardamom.

Deyrolle

46 rue du Bac, 7th (01.42.22.30.07, www.deyrolle.com). M° Rue du Bac. **Open** 10am-1pm, 2-7pm Mon; 10am-7pm Tue-Sat. **Map** p131 A2 ❷❽
See box right.

Gérard Mulot

76 rue de Seine, 6th (01.43.26.85.77, http://gerard-mulot.com). M° Odéon. **Open** 6.45am-8pm Mon, Tue, Thur-Sun. Closed Easter & Aug. **Map** p131 C3 ❷❾
Gérard Mulot rustles up stunning pastries. Try the *mabillon*: caramel mousse with apricot marmalade.

Hervé Chapelier

1bis rue du Vieux-Colombier, 6th (01.44.07.06.50, www.hervechapelier.fr). M° St-Germain-des-Prés or St-Sulpice. **Open** 10.15am-7pm Mon-Sat.
Map p131 B3 ❸⓿
Pick up a classic bicoloured bag. Prices range from a dinky purse at €22 to a weekend bag at €130.

Huilerie Artisanale Leblanc

6 rue Jacob, 6th (01.46.34.61.55, www.huile-leblanc.com). M° St-Germain-des-Prés. **Open** noon-7pm Tue-Fri; 10am-7pm Sat. Closed 2wks Aug. No credit cards. **Map** p131 C2 ❸❶
The Leblanc family started making walnut oil before branching out to press pure oils from hazelnuts, almonds, pine nuts, grilled peanuts and olives.

La Hune

170 bd St-Germain, 6th (01.45.48. 35.85). M° St-Germain-des-Prés. **Open** 10am-11.45pm Mon-Sat; 11am-7.45pm Sun. **Map** p131 B2 ❸❷
This Left Bank institution boasts a global selection of art and design books, and a truly magnificent collection of French literature and theory.

Animal attraction

Deyrolle's menagerie rises from the ashes.

In early 2008, a tragic fire swept through famous taxidermy shop **Deyrolle** (*see left*) and sent shockwaves across Paris. People watched in despair as the landmark store succumbed to the encroaching flames.

Opened in 1831 by Jean-Baptiste Deyrolle, a taxidermist and avid traveller, the shop had always been something of a curiosity. This haven of the exotic and eclectic was beloved of professional naturalists, amateur bug-hunters, and Surrealists such as Salvador Dalí and André Breton, who have all stood in awe at the bizarre menagerie of lions, giraffes, polar bears, butterflies and bugs of all shapes and sizes, all set in the confines of a 19th-century *hôtel particulier*.

In response to the fire, Parisians from all walks of life came together to save the shop. At the forefront was a group of 50 artists, led by Louis-Albert de Broglie, the owner of Deyrolle since 2001, who set about raising funds by creating an art collection inspired by the remains of the original Deyrolle collection, to be auctioned at Christie's.

The shop finally reopened in September 2009 and has amazingly lost little of its magic. It remains a great place to escape the city, buy a tiger for the living room, purchase a few creepy crawlies to scare friends and family, or simply to fire your children's imagination.

PARIS BY AREA

Le Bon Marché p136

Jean-Paul Hévin

3 rue Vavin, 6th (01.43.54.09.85, www.jphevin.com). M° Notre-Dame-des-Champs or Vavin. **Open** 10am-7.30pm Tue-Sat. Closed Aug. **Map** p131 B4 **33**
Hévin specialises in the beguiling combination of chocolate with potent cheese fillings, which loyal customers serve with wine as an aperitif.

Lefranc.ferrant

22 rue de l'Echaudé, 6th (01.44.07. 37.96, www.lefranc-ferrant.fr). M° St-Germain-des-Prés. **Open** 11am-7pm Tue-Sat and by appointment. **Map** p131 C2 **34**
Béatrice Ferrant and Mario Lefranc have a surreal approach to tailoring, as in a strapless yellow evening gown made like a pair of men's trousers – complete with flies. Prices are in the €1,000 range.

Marie-Hélène de Taillac

NEW *8 rue de Tournon, 6th (01.44.27. 07.07, www.mariehelenedetaillac.com). M° Mabillon.* **Open** 11am-7pm Mon-Sat. **Map** p131 C3 **35**
Marie-Hélène de Taillac is a fine jeweller, using diamonds and emeralds in simple settings. This combination of precious stones and modern styling has made her hugely popular with the fashion elite. They also adore her Left Bank shop – a Tom Dixon-designed space.

Marie Mercié

23 rue St-Sulpice, 6th (01.43.26.45.83). M° Odéon. **Open** 11am-7pm Mon-Sat. **Map** p131 C3 **36**
Mercié's creations make you wish you lived in an era when hats were de rigueur. Step out in one shaped like curved fingers (with shocking-pink nail varnish and pink diamond ring) or a beret like a face with red lips and turquoise eyes. Ready-to-wear starts at €30; *sur mesure* takes ten days.

Papillon pour Bonton

NEW *84 rue de Grenelle, 7th (01.42.84. 42.43). M° Rue du Bac.* **Open** 10am-7pm Mon-Sat. **Map** p131 A2 **37**

Bonton's new venture is all about nostalgia, with hand-knits, cashmere and alpaca, dinky stripes and Liberty prints. Pretty buttons accompany the fine finish that Bonton is famous for, and christening robes and pyjamas complete the collection, displayed in an old perfume shop amid flowery wallpaper and hunting trophies. Pure *Bagpuss*.

Patrick Roger

108 bd St-Germain, 6th (01.43.29. 38.42, www.patrickroger.com). M° Odéon. **Open** 10.30am-7.30pm Mon-Sat. **Map** p131 B2 **38**
Roger is shaking up the art of chocolate-making. Whereas other *chocolatiers* aim for gloss, Roger may create a brushed effect on hens so realistic you almost expect them to lay (chocolate) eggs.

Paul & Joe

64 rue des Sts-Pères, 7th (01.42.22. 47.01, www.paulandjoe.com). M° Rue du Bac or St-Germain-des-Prés. **Open** 10am-7pm Mon-Sat. **Map** p131 B2 **39**
Fashionistas have taken a shine to Sophie Albou's retro-styled creations. The latest collection dresses leggy young things in a range of winter shorts, colourful mini dresses and voluminous trousers, with their intellectual paramours in slouchy woollens, tailored jackets and chunky boots.

Peggy Huyn Kinh

9-11 rue Coëtlogon, 6th (01.42.84.83. 82, www.phk.fr). M° St-Sulpice. **Open** 11am-7pm Mon-Sat. **Map** p131 B3 **40**
Once creative director at Cartier, Peggy Huyn Kinh now makes bags of boar skin and python, plus silver jewellery.

Pierre Hermé

72 rue Bonaparte, 6th (01.43.54.47.77). M° Mabillon, St-Germain-des-Prés or St-Sulpice. **Open** 10am-7pm Tue-Fri, Sun; 10am-7.30pm Sat. Closed 1st 3wks Aug. **Map** p131 B3 **41**
Pastry superstar Hermé attracts connoisseurs from near and far with his seasonal collections.

PARIS BY AREA

Poilâne

*8 rue du Cherche-Midi, 6th (01.45.48.
42.59, www.poilane.com). M° Sèvres
Babylone or St-Sulpice.* **Open** 7.15am-
8.15pm Mon-Sat. **Map** p131 B3 ❷
Apollonia Poilâne runs the family
shop, where locals queue for fresh
country *miches*, flaky-crusted apple
tarts and shortbread biscuits.

Richart

*258 bd St-Germain, 7th (01.45.55.66.00,
www.richart.com). M° Solférino.* **Open**
10am-7pm Mon-Sat. **Map** p131 A1 ❸
Each chocolate *ganache* has an intricate design, packages look like jewel
boxes, and each purchase comes with
a tract on how best to savour the stuff.

Ryst Dupeyron

*79 rue du Bac, 7th (01.45.48.80.93,
www.dupeyron.com). M° Rue du Bac.*
Open 12.30-7.30pm Mon; 10.30am-
7.30pm Tue-Sat. Closed 2wks Aug.
Map p131 A2 ❹
The Dupeyrons have been selling
armagnac for four generations, and
still have bottles from 1868. Treasures
here include 200 fine Bordeaux wines.

Sonia Rykiel

*175 bd St-Germain, 6th (01.49.54.
60.60, www.soniarykiel.com). M° St-
Germain-des-Prés or Sèvres Babylone.*
Open 10.30am-7pm Mon-Sat. **Map**
p131 B2 ❺
The queen of St-Germain celebrated the
40th birthday of her flagship store with
a glamorous black and smoked glass
refit perfect for narcissists. Menswear is
located across the street, and two newer
boutiques stock the younger, more
affordable Sonia by Sonia Rykiel range.

Vanessa Bruno

*25 rue St-Sulpice, 6th (01.43.54.41.04,
www.vanessabruno.com). M° Odéon.*
Open 10.30am-7.30pm Mon-Sat.
Map p131 C3 ❻
Bruno's mercerised cotton tanks, flatter-
ing trousers and tops have a Zen-like
quality. She also makes great bags.

Yves Saint Laurent

*6 pl St-Sulpice, 6th (01.43.29.43.00,
www.ysl.com). M° St-Sulpice.* **Open**
11am-7pm Mon; 10.30am-7pm Tue-Sat.
Map p131 C3 ❼
The memory of the founding designer,
who died in 2008, lives on in this wonderfully elegant boutique, which was
splendidly refitted in red in the same
year. You'll find the menswear collection at no.12 (01.43.26.84.40).

Nightlife

Wagg

*62 rue Mazarine, 6th (01.55.42.22.01,
www.wagg.fr). M° Odéon.* **Open**
11.30pm-6am Fri, Sat; 3pm-midnight
Sun. **Admission** €12 Fri, Sat; €12
Sun (incl 1 drink). **Map** p131 C2 ❽
Wagg went through a period of attracting big name DJs, but has settled down
as home to a well-to-do Left Bank
crowd. Expect funk, house and disco.

Arts & leisure

Le Lucernaire

*53 rue Notre-Dame-des-Champs, 6th
(01.45.44.57.34, www.lucernaire.fr). M°
Notre-Dame-des-Champs or Vavin.* **Box
office** 10am-7pm daily. **Admission**
€10-€30. **Map** p131 B4 ❾
Three theatres, three cinemas, a restaurant and a bar make up this versatile
cultural centre. Molière and other classic playwrights get a good thrashing,
but so do up-and-coming authors.

Odéon, Théâtre
de L'Europe

*Pl de l'Odéon, 6th (01.44.85.40.00,
bookings 01.44.85.40.40, www.theatre-
odeon.fr). M° Odéon.* **Box office** 11am-
6.30pm Mon-Sat. **Admission** €6-€30.
Map p131 C2 ❺⓿
During 2010, both the main Odéon and
its sister theatre, Les Ateliers Berthier,
are showcasing politically engaging
plays about Europe as a whole.
Event highlights *Le Vrai Sang* by
Valère Novarina (5-30 Jan 2011)

Rue Mouffetard

The Latin Quarter & the 13th

The Latin Quarter

To many first-time visitors – especially those from the States – the Latin Quarter can be a big disappointment. Countless books have led them to believe that the area is somehow the quintessence of Paris, and they come with their heads stuffed with expat writers – Orwell, Hemingway, Henry Miller – only to find a touristy jam of bad restaurants and uninspiring shops. Granted, many of the narrow, crooked streets (like the Marais, the Latin Quarter was another part of Paris largely untouched by Haussmann) are charming, and there are some real architectural glories, especially ecclesiastical ones; but the crowds can make the experience of seeing them rather dispiriting.

The 'Latin' in the area's name probably derives from the fact that it has been the university quarter since medieval times, when Latin was the language of instruction. The district's long association with learning began in about 1100, when a number of renowned scholars, including Pierre Abélard, began to live and teach on Montagne Ste-Geneviève, independent of the established cathedral school of Notre-Dame. This loose association of scholars came to be referred to as a 'university'. The Paris schools attracted students from all over Europe and the 'colleges' multiplied, until the University of Paris was given official recognition with a charter from Pope Innocent III in 1215.

Sights & museums

Arènes de Lutèce
Rue Monge, rue de Navarre or rue des Arènes, 5th. M° Cardinal Lemoine or Place Monge. **Open** *Summer* 9am-

9.30pm daily. *Winter* 8am-5.30pm daily.
Admission free. **Map** p143 B4 ❶
This Roman arena, where wild beasts
and gladiators fought, could seat 10,000
people. It was still visible during the
reign of Philippe-Auguste in the 12th
century, then disappeared under rubble.
The site now attracts skateboarders,
footballers and boules players.

Eglise St-Etienne-du-Mont

*Pl Ste-Geneviève, 5th (01.43.54.
11.79). M° Cardinal Lemoine/RER
Luxembourg.* **Open** 10am-7pm
Tue-Sun. **Map** p143 B4 ❷
Geneviève, patron saint of Paris, is cred-
ited with having miraculously saved
the city from the ravages of Attila the
Hun in 451, and her shrine has been a
site of pilgrimage ever since. The present church was built in an amalgam of
Gothic and Renaissance styles between
1492 and 1626, and the interior is wonderfully tall and light, with soaring
columns and a classical balustrade. The
stunning Renaissance rood screen, with
its double spiral staircase and ornate
stone strapwork, is the only surviving
one in Paris. At the back of the church
(reached through the sacristy), the cat-
echism chapel constructed by Baltard
in the 1860s has a cycle of paintings
relating the saint's life story.

Eglise St-Séverin

*3 rue des Prêtres-St-Séverin, 5th
(01.42.34.93.50). M° Cluny La
Sorbonne or St-Michel.* **Open** 11am-
7.30pm daily. **Map** p143 A3 ❸
Built on the site of the chapel of the
hermit Séverin, itself set on a much
earlier Merovingian burial ground, this
lovely Flamboyant Gothic edifice
was long the parish church of the Left
Bank. The church dates from the 15th
century, though the doorway, carved
with foliage, was added in 1837 from
the demolished Eglise St-Pierre-aux-
Boeufs on Ile de la Cité. The double
ambulatory is famed for its forest of
'palm tree' vaulting, which meets at the

end in a unique spiral column that
inspired a series of paintings by Robert
Delaunay. The bell tower, a survivor
from one of the earlier churches on the
site, has the oldest bell in Paris (1412).

Eglise du Val-de-Grâce

*Pl Alphonse-Laveran, 5th (01.43.29.
12.31). RER Luxembourg or Port-Royal.*
Open noon-6pm Tue, Wed, Sat, Sun.
Admission €5; free-€2.50 reductions.
No credit cards. **Map** p143 A5 ❹
Anne of Austria, the wife of Louis XIII,
vowed to erect 'a magnificent temple'
if God blessed her with a son. She
got two. The resulting church and
surrounding Benedictine monastery –
these days a military hospital and the
Musée du Service de Santé des Armées
– were built by François Mansart and
Jacques Lemercier. This is the most
luxuriously baroque of the city's 17th-
century domed churches. In contrast,
the surrounding monastery offers the
perfect example of François Mansart's
classical restraint. Phone in advance if
you're after a guided visit.

Grande Galerie de l'Evolution

*36 rue Geoffroy-St-Hilaire, 2 rue
Bouffon or pl Valhubert, 5th
(01.40.79.56.01). M° Gare d'Austerlitz
or Jussieu.* **Open** *Grande Galerie* 10am-
6pm Mon, Wed-Sun. *Other galleries*
10am-5pm Mon, Wed-Fri; 10am-6pm
Sat, Sun. **Admission** *Grande Galerie*
€9; free-€7 reductions. *Other galleries*
(each) €7; free-€5 reductions. No credit
cards. **Map** p143 C5 ❺
One of the city's most child-friendly
attractions, this is guaranteed to bowl
adults over too. Located within the
Jardin des Plantes, this 19th-century
iron-framed, glass-roofed structure has
been modernised with lifts, galleries
and false floors, and filled with life-size
models of tentacle-waving squids,
open-mawed sharks, tigers hanging off
elephants and monkeys swarming
down from the ceiling. The centrepiece
is a procession of African wildlife

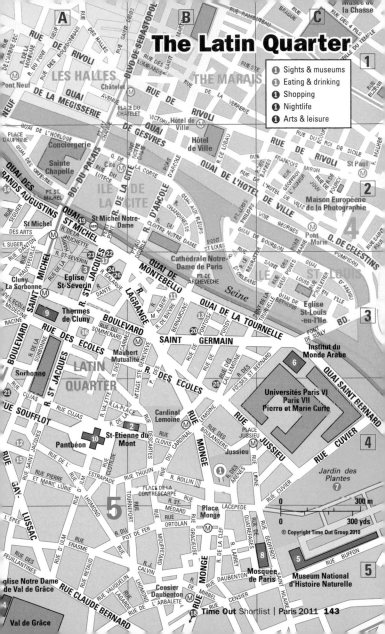

The Latin Quarter

A **B** **C**

❶ Sights & museums
❶ Eating & drinking
❶ Shopping
❶ Nightlife
❶ Arts & leisure

1

LES HALLES
RUE DE RIVOLI
QUAI DE LA MÉGISSERIE
Pont Neuf
Châtelet
AVENUE VICTORIA
PLACE DU CHÂTELET
THE MARAIS
RUE DE RIVOLI
St Paul
RUE DE RIVOLI
Musée de la Chasse

PLACE DAUPHINE
QUAI DE L'HORLOGE
Conciergerie
Sainte Chapelle
BD. DU PALAIS
QUAI DES GRANDS AUGUSTINS
Hôtel de Ville
Hôtel de Ville
QUAI DE L'HÔTEL DE VILLE

2

ÎLE DE LA CITÉ
RUE DE LA CITÉ
Maison Européene de la Photographie

St Michel
QUAI ST MICHEL
St Michel Notre-Dame
Cathédrale Notre-Dame de Paris
QUAI DE MONTEBELLO
Cluny La Sorbonne
Eglise St-Séverin
PT DE L'ARCHEVÊCHÉ
Seine
ÎLE ST-LOUIS
Eglise St-Louis-en-l'Île
Pont Marie
Q. DE CÉLESTINS

3

❾ Thermes de Cluny
BOULEVARD SAINT GERMAIN
QUAI DE LA TOURNELLE
Institut du Monde Arabe

RUE DES ECOLES
Sorbonne
LATIN QUARTER
Maubert Mutualité
R. DES ECOLES
❻
Universités Paris VI Paris VII Pierre et Marie Curie
QUAI SAINT BERNARD

4

RUE SOUFFLOT
❶❷
Panthéon
⑩
St-Etienne du Mont
Cardinal Lemoine
RUE MONGE
Jussieu
RUE JUSSIEU
PLACE JUSSIEU
RUE CUVIER
Jardin des Plantes
❼

5

PLACE DE LA CONTRESCARPE
Place Monge
Mosquée de Paris ❽
⑤
Museum National d'Histoire Naturelle
RUE BUFFON
Censier Daubenton
RUE CLAUDE BERNARD
Eglise Notre Dame de Val de Grâce
Val de Grâce
⑱

0 300 m
0 300 yds
© Copyright Time Out Group 2010

across the first floor that resembles the procession into Noah's Ark. Glass-sided lifts take you up through suspended birds to the second floor, which deals with man's impact on nature (crocodile into handbag). The third floor focuses on endangered species.

Institut du Monde Arabe

1 rue des Fossés-St-Bernard, 5th (01.40.51.38.38, www.imarabe.org). M° Jussieu. **Open** *Museum* 10am-6pm Tue-Sun. *Library* 1-8pm Tue-Sat. *Café* noon-6pm Tue-Sun. *Tours* 3pm Tue-Fri; 3pm & 4.30pm Sat, Sun. **Admission** *Roof terrace, library* free. *Museum* €5; free-€4 reductions. *Exhibitions* varies. *Tours* €8. **Map** p143 C3 ❻

A clever blend of high-tech and Arab influences, this Seine-side *grand projet* was constructed between 1980 and 1987 to a design by Jean Nouvel. Shuttered windows, inspired by the screens of Moorish palaces, act as camera apertures, contracting or expanding according to the amount of sunlight. A museum covering the history and archaeology of the Islamic Arab world occupies the upper floors: start at the seventh with Classical-era finds and work down via early Islamic dynasties to the present day. The Institut hosts several major, crowd-pleasing exhibitions throughout the year. What's more, there's an excellent Middle East bookshop on the ground floor and the views from the roof terrace (access is free) are fabulous.

Jardin des Plantes

36 rue Geoffroy-St-Hilaire, 2 rue Bouffon, pl Valhubert or 57 rue Cuvier, 5th. M° Gare d'Austerlitz, Jussieu or Place Monge. **Open** *Main garden* Winter 8am-dusk daily. Summer 7.30am-8pm daily. *Alpine garden* Apr-Sept 8am-5.30pm daily. Closed Oct-Mar. *Ménagerie* Apr-Sept 9am-5pm daily. **Admission** *Alpine Garden* free Mon-Fri; €1 Sat, Sun. *Jardin des Plantes* free. *Ménagerie* €8; free-€6 reductions. **Map** p143 C4 ❼

The Paris botanical garden – which contains more than 10,000 species and includes tropical greenhouses and rose, winter and Alpine gardens – is an enchanting place. Begun by Louis XIII's doctor as the royal medicinal plant garden in 1626, it opened to the public in 1640. The formal garden, which runs between two avenues of trees, is like something out of *Alice in Wonderland*. There's also a small zoo and the terrific Grande Galerie de l'Evolution. Ancient trees on view include a false acacia planted in 1636. A plaque on the old laboratory declares that this is where Henri Becquerel discovered radioactivity in 1896.

La Mosquée de Paris

2 pl du Puits-de-l'Ermite, 5th (01.45.35. 97.33, tearoom 01.43.31.38.20, baths 01.43.31.18.14, www.mosquee-de-paris.net). M° Monge. **Open** *Tours* 9am-noon, 2-6pm Mon-Thur, Sat, Sun (closed Muslim hols). *Tearoom* 10am-11.30pm daily. *Restaurant* noon-2.30pm, 7.30-10.30pm daily. *Baths (women)* 10am-9pm Mon, Wed, Sat; 2-9pm Fri; *(men)* 2-9pm Tue, Sun. **Admission** €3; free-€2 reductions. *Tearoom* free. *Baths* €15-€35. **Map** p143 C5 ❽

This vast Hispano-Moorish construct is the spiritual heart of France's Algerian-dominated Muslim population. In plan and function it divides into three sections: religious (grand patio, prayer room and minaret, all for worshippers and not curious tourists); scholarly (Islamic school and library); and, via rue Geoffroy-St-Hilaire, commercial (café and domed hammam). La Mosquée café is delightful – a courtyard shaded beneath green foliage and scented with the sweet smell of sheesha smoke.

Musée National du Moyen Age – Thermes de Cluny

6 pl Paul-Painlevé, 5th (01.53.73.78.00, www.musee-moyenage.fr). M° Cluny La Sorbonne. **Open** 9.15am-5.45pm Mon, Wed-Sun. **Admission** €8; free-€6 reductions. **Map** p143 A3 ❾

The national museum of medieval art is best known for the beautiful, allegorical *Lady and the Unicorn* tapestry cycle, but it also has important collections of medieval sculpture and enamels. The building itself, commonly known as Cluny, is also a rare example of 15th-century secular Gothic architecture, with its foliate Gothic doorways, hexagonal staircase jutting out of the façade and vaulted chapel. It was built from 1485 to 1498 – on top of a Gallo-Roman baths complex. The baths, built in characteristic Roman bands of stone and brick masonry, are the finest Roman remains in Paris. The vaulted *frigidarium* (cold bath), *tepidarium* (warm bath), *caldarium* (hot bath) and part of the hypocaust heating system are all still visible. A themed garden fronts the whole complex.

Le Panthéon

Pl du Panthéon, 5th (01.44.32.18.00). M° Cardinal Lemoine/RER Luxembourg. **Open** 10am-6pm (until 6.30pm summer) daily. **Admission** €8; free-€6 reductions. **Map** p143 A4 **⑩**
Soufflot's neo-classical megastructure was the architectural *grand projet* of its day, commissioned by a grateful Louis XV to thank Sainte Geneviève for his recovery from illness. But by the time it was ready in 1790, a lot had changed; during the Revolution, the Panthéon was rededicated as a 'temple of reason' and the resting place of the nation's great men. The austere barrel-vaulted crypt now houses Voltaire, Rousseau, Hugo and Zola. New heroes are installed but rarely: Pierre and Marie Curie's remains were transferred here in 1995; Alexandre Dumas in 2002. Mount the steep spiral stairs to the colonnade encircling the dome for superb views.

Eating & drinking

Atelier Maître Albert

1 rue Maître-Albert, 5th (01.56.81. 30.01, www.ateliermaitrealbert.com). M° Maubert Mutualité or St-Michel.

Open noon-2.30pm, 6.30-11.30pm Mon-Wed; noon-2.30pm, 6.30pm-1am Thur, Fri; 6.30pm-1am Sat; 6.30-11.30pm Sun. **€€**. **Bistro**. **Map** p143 B3 **⑪**
This Guy Savoy outpost in the fifth has slick decor by Jean-Michel Wilmotte. The indigo-painted, grey marble-floored dining room with open kitchen and rôtisseries on view is attractive but very noisy at night. The short menu lets you have a Savoy classic or two to start with, including oysters in seawater *gelée* or more inventive dishes such as the ballotine of chicken, foie gras and celery root in a chicken-liver sauce. Next up, perhaps, tuna served with tiny iron casseroles of dauphinois potatoes, and cauliflower in béchamel sauce.

Le Crocodile

6 rue Royer-Collard, 5th (01.43.54. 32.37, www.lecrocodile.fr). RER Luxembourg. **Open** 10pm-late Mon-Sat. Closed Aug. **Bar**. **Map** p143 A4 **⑫**
Ignore the apparently boarded-up windows at Le Crocodile; if you're here late, then it's open. Friendly young regulars line the sides of this small, narrow bar and try to decide what to drink – not easy, given the length of the cocktail list: at last count there were 312 varieties. The generous €6-per-cocktail happy hour (Monday to Thursday before midnight) will allow you to start with a champagne *accroche-coeur*, followed up with a Goldschläger (served with gold leaf) before moving on to one of the other 310.

Itinéraires

5 rue de Pontoise, 5th (01.46.33.60.11). M° Maubert Mutualité. **Open** noon-2pm, 8-11pm Tue-Fri; 8-11pm Sat. **€€**. **Bistro**. **Map** p143 B3 **⑬**
Chef Sylvain Sendra played to a full house every night at his little bistro Le Temps au Temps near the Bastille before moving to this larger space near Notre Dame. The sleek space brings together all the elements that make for a successful bistro today: a long *table d'hôte*, a bar for solo meals or quick

bites, and a reasonably priced, market-inspired menu. Not everything is a wild success, but it's hard to fault a chef who so often hits the mark, in dishes such as squid-ink risotto with clams, *botargo* (dried mullet roe) and tomato.

Lapérouse

51 quai des Grands-Augustins, 6th (01.56.79.24.31, www.laperouse.fr). M° St-Michel. **Open** noon-2.30pm, 7.30-10pm Mon-Fri; 7.30-10pm Sat. Closed 1wk Jan & Aug. €€€€. **Brasserie**. Map p143 A2 ⑭
Lapérouse was formerly a clandestine rendezvous for French politicians and their mistresses; the tiny private dining rooms upstairs used to lock from the inside. Chef Alain Hacquard does a reasonable take on classic French cooking: his beef fillet is smoked for a more complex flavour; a tender saddle of rabbit is cooked in a clay crust, flavoured with lavender and rosemary and served with ravioli of onions. The only snag is the cost, especially of the wine.

Le Pantalon

7 rue Royer-Collard, 5th (no phone). RER Luxembourg. **Open** 5.30pm-2am Mon-Sat. No credit cards. €. **Café**. Map p143 A4 ⑮
Le Pantalon is a local café that seems familiar yet is utterly surreal. It has the standard fixtures, including the old soaks at the bar – but the regulars and staff are enough to tip the balance into eccentricity. Friendly and funny French grown-ups and foreign students chat in a mishmash of languages; drinks are cheap enough to make you tipsy without the worry of a cash hangover.

Le Pré Verre

8 rue Thénard, 5th (01.43.54.59.47, www.lepreverre.com). M° Maubert Mutualité. **Open** noon-2pm, 7.30-10.30pm Tue-Sat. Closed 3wks Aug & 2wks Dec. €€. **Bistro**. Map p143 A3 ⑯
Philippe Delacourcelle knows how to handle spices like few other French chefs. Salt cod with cassia bark and

smoked potato purée is a classic: what the fish lacks in size it makes up for in rich, cinnamon-like flavour and crunchy texture, and smooth potato cooked in a smoker makes a startling accompaniment. Spices have a way of making desserts seem esoteric rather than decadent, but the roast figs with olives are an exception to the rule.

Ribouldingue

10 rue St-Julien-le-Pauvre, 5th (01.46.33.98.80). M° St-Michel. **Open** noon-2pm, 7-11pm Mon-Sat. €€. **Bistro**. Map p143 A3 ⑰
This bistro facing St-Julien-le-Pauvre church is the creation of Nadège Varigny, who spent ten years working with Yves Camdeborde before opening a restaurant inspired by the food of her childhood in Grenoble. It's full of people, including critics and chefs, who love simple, honest bistro fare, such as *daube de boeuf* or seared tuna on a bed of melting aubergine. If you have an appetite for offal, then you might want to opt for the gently sautéed brains with new potatoes or veal kidneys with a perfectly prepared potato gratin. For dessert, try the fresh ewe's cheese with bitter honey.

Shopping

Le Boulanger de Monge

123 rue Monge, 5th (01.43.37.54.20, www.leboulangerdemonge.com). M° Censier Daubenton. **Open** 7am-8.30pm Tue-Sun. Map p143 B5 ⑱
Dominique Saibron uses spices to give wonderful flavour to his organic sourdough *boule*. Every day about 2,000 bread-lovers visit this boutique, which also produces one of the city's best baguettes.

Bouquinistes

Along the quais, especially quai de Montebello & quai St-Michel, 5th. M° St-Michel. **Open** times vary from stall to stall, generally Tue-Sun. No credit cards. Map p143 A2 ⑲

Movie magic

Pathé is delving into its ample archives.

As if film buffs weren't already spoiled for choice in Paris, they'll have another reason to get excited in 2011. The Fondation Jérôme Seydoux-Pathé is opening a showcase centre for its collection of film memorabilia and artefacts.

Established in 1896, the Société Pathé Frères was one of the founding fathers of cinema, building its reputation on savvy technical innovations and the famed pre-film Pathé newsreels. Today, the company remains one of Europe's leading distributors, producers and cinema exhibitors, and the foundation's mission is to promote the history of cinema via the Pathé story. Its collection is composed of the company's archives for everything except film reels, and includes movie posters, props, cameras, and all sorts of projectionists' paraphernalia.

To house such a prestigious collection, Pathé commissioned Renzo Piano, architect of the Centre Pompidou, to design a new building on the site of a former cinema near place d'Italie. The only stipulation was that the building's old façade had to be conserved, as it was embellished with an elaborate sculpture by iconic artist Auguste Rodin. Piano's solution was to take visitors through the old entrance, across a short corridor, and into a brand new oval complex that will house the foundation's offices and collection. This five-storey building will be glass-fronted, with tinted panes used on certain floors to protect the archives. On the ground floor, a temporary exhibition space, including a small cinema, will host exhibitions. Visitors will be treated to original posters, props and stills from landmark movies such as Marcel Carné's post-war classic *Les Enfants du Paradis*, as well as recent crowd-pleasers such as *Bienvenue chez les Ch'tis*.

The centre will also exhibit Pathé studio cameras and film projectors through the ages. Outside, visitors will be able to admire the building's audacious architecture from a small garden.

The green, open-air boxes along the *quais* are one of the city's institutions. As well as the inevitable postcards and tourist tat, most sell a good selection of second-hand books – rummage through boxes packed with ancient paperbacks for something Existential.

Diptyque

34 bd St-Germain, 5th (01.43.26.77.44, www.diptyqueparis.com). M° Maubert Mutualité. **Open** *10am 7pm Mon-Sat.* **Map** p143 B3 ⑳
Diptyque's divinely scented candles are the quintessential gift from Paris. They come in 48 varieties and are probably the best you'll ever find.

Princesse Tam-Tam

52 bd St-Michel, 6th (01.40.51.72.99, www.princessetamtam.com). M° Cluny La Sorbonne. **Open** *1.30-7pm Mon; 10am-7pm Tue-Sat.* **Map** p143 A4 ㉑
This fun, inexpensive underwear and swimwear brand features lots of bright colours and sexily transparent gear.

Shakespeare & Company

37 rue de la Bûcherie, 5th (01.43.25.40.93, www.shakespeare andcompany.com). M° St-Michel. **Open** *10am-11pm Mon-Sat; 11am-11pm Sun.* **Map** p143 A3 ㉒
Unequivocally the best bookshop in Paris, the historic and ramshackle Shakespeare & Co is always packed to the rafters with expat and tourist book lovers. There is a large second-hand section, antiquarian books next door, and just about anything you could ask for new.

Nightlife

Caveau de la Huchette

5 rue de la Huchette, 5th (01.43.26. 65.05, www.caveaudelahuchette.fr). M° St-Michel. **Open** *Concerts 10.15pm-2.30am Mon-Wed, Sun; 10.15pm-6am Thur-Sat.* **Admission** €12 Mon-Thur, Sun; €14 Fri, Sat; €10 reductions. **Map** p143 A2 ㉓

This medieval cellar has been a mainstay for 60 years. The jazz shows are followed by early-hours performances in a swing, rock, soul or disco vein.

Caveau des Oubliettes

52 rue Galande, 5th (01.46.34. 23.09, www.caveaudesoubliettes.fr). M° St-Michel. **Open** *5pm-4am daily.* *Concerts* 10pm daily. **Admission** free. **Map** p143 A3 ㉔
Atmosphere abounds in this former dungeon, a tiny space complete with instruments of torture and underground passages. There are various jam sessions in the week, and on Sundays.

Paradis Latin

28 rue Cardinal Lemoine, 5th (01.43. 25.28.28, www.paradislatin.com). M° Cardinal Lemoine. **Dinner** 8pm. **Show** 9.30pm daily. **Admission** *9.30pm show* (incl champagne) €85. *Dinner & show* €123-€179. **Map** p143 B4 ㉕
This is the most authentic of the cabarets, not only because it's family-run (the men run the cabaret, the daughter does the costumes), but also because the clientele is mostly French, something which has a direct effect on the prices (this is the cheapest revue) and the cuisine, which tends to be high quality. Show-wise you can expect the usual fare: generous doses of glitter, live singing and cheesy *entr'acte* acts performed in a stunning belle époque room. There's also a twice-monthly matinée: lunch and show €95.

Arts & leisure

Studio Galande

42 rue Galande, 5th (01.43.54.72.71, www.studiogalande.fr). M° Cluny La Sorbonne or St-Michel. **Admission** €7.80; €6 Wed, students. No credit cards. **Map** p143 A3 ㉖
Some 20 different films are screened in subtitled versions at this venerable Latin Quarter venue every week: international arthouse fare, combined with the occasional instalment from the

Matrix series. On Friday and Saturday nights, dedicated fans of *The Rocky Horror Picture Show* turn up in drag, equipped with rice and water pistols.

The 13th

The construction in the mid-1990s of the **Bibliothèque Nationale de France** breathed life into the desolate area, now known as the ZAC Rive Gauche, between Gare d'Austerlitz and the Périphérique. The ambitious, long-term ZAC project includes a new university quarter, new housing projects and a tramway providing links to the suburbs. This is one of the city's fastest rising quarters.

Sights & museums

Bibliothèque Nationale de France François Mitterrand

10 quai François-Mauriac, 13th (01.53.79.59.59, www.bnf.fr). M° Bibliothèque François Mitterrand. **Open** 2-7pm Mon; 9am-7pm Tue-Sat; 1-7pm Sun. **Admission** *1 day* €3.30. *1 year* €35; €18 reductions. **Map** p151 E2 ㉗
Opened in 1996, the new national library was the last and costliest of Mitterrand's *grands projets*. Its architect, Dominique Perrault, was criticised for his curiously dated design. He also forgot to specify blinds to protect books from sunlight; they had to be added afterwards. The library houses over ten million volumes. Much of the library is open to the public: books, newspapers and periodicals are accessible to anyone over 18, and you can browse through photographic, film and sound archives in the audio-visual section.

Chapelle St-Louis-de-la-Salpêtrière

47 bd de l'Hôpital, 13th (01.42.16.04.24). M° Gare d'Austerlitz. **Open** 8.30am-6pm Mon-Fri, Sun; 11am-6pm Sat. **Admission** free. **Map** p151 C2 ㉘

This austerely beautiful chapel, designed by Bruand and completed in 1677, features an octagonal dome in the centre and eight naves in which the sick were separated from the insane, the destitute from the debauched. Around the chapel sprawls the vast Hôpital de la Pitié-Salpêtrière, which became a centre for research into insanity in the 1790s, when renowned doctor Philippe Pinel began to treat some of the inmates as sick rather than criminal; Charcot later pioneered neuropsychology here. Salpêtrière is one of the city's main teaching hospitals.

Manufacture Nationale des Gobelins

42 av des Gobelins, 13th (tours 01.44.08.53.49). M° Les Gobelins. **Open** *Tours* 2pm, 3pm Tue-Thur. **Admission** €10; free-€6 reductions. No credit cards. **Map** p151 B2 ㉙
The royal tapestry factory, founded by Colbert, is named after Jean Gobelin, a dyer who owned the site. Tapestries are still made here (mainly for French embassies), and visitors can watch weavers at work. The tour (in French) through the 1912 factory takes in the 18th-century chapel and the Beauvais workshops. Arrive 30 minutes before the tour starts.

Eating & drinking

L'Avant-Goût

26 rue Bobillot, 13th (01.53.80.24.00, www.lavantgout.com). M° Place d'Italie. **Open** noon-2pm, 7.45-10.45pm Tue-Sat. Closed 3wks Aug. **€**. **Bistro**. **Map** p151 B3 ㉚
Self-taught chef Christophe Beaufront has turned this nondescript street on the edge of the villagey Butte-aux-Cailles into a foodie destination. Typical of Beaufront's cooking is his *pot-au-feu de cochon aux épices*, a much-written-about dish that has been on his menu for years. It's good, if not earth-shaking; however, a starter of piquillo pepper stuffed with smoked haddock

The 13th

Sights & museums
Eating & drinking
Shopping
Nightlife
Arts & leisure

rillettes does illustrate his talent. Beaufront's food is available to take away at the *épicerie* across the street.

L'Ourcine
92 rue Broca, 13th (01.47.07.13.65). Mº Glacière or Les Gobelins. **Open** noon-2pm, 7-10.30pm Tue-Thur; noon-2.30pm, 7-11pm Fri, Sat. Closed 4wks July-Aug. €. **Bistro**. **Map** p151 B2 ③①
This restaurant near Gobelins is a wonderful bistro stop. Start with *pipérade*, succulent chorizo or a spread of sliced beef tongue with piquillo peppers; then try the sautéed baby squid with parsley, garlic and Espelette peppers, or the *piquillos* stuffed with puréed cod and potato. An appealing atmosphere is generated by a growing band of regulars.

Sputnik
14 rue de la Butte aux Cailles, 13th (01.45.65.19.82, www.sputnik.fr). Mº Place d'Italie. **Open** 2pm-2am Mon-Sat; 4pm-midnight Sun. **Café**. **Map** p151 B3 ③②
A hip young crowd gathers in this rock-oriented bar, which doubles as a sports bar during important football and rugby fixtures, and trebles as an internet café at other times. Ever-changing art exhibitions add interest to the walls, and live music once a month draws an indie crowd.

Nightlife

Batofar
Opposite 11 quai François-Mauriac, 13th (09.71.25.50.61, www.batofar. org). Mº Quai de la Gare. **Open** 11pm-6am Mon-Sat; 6am-noon 1st Sun of mth. **Admission** €5-€12. **Map** p151 E2 ③③
In recent years the Batofar has gone through a rapid succession of management teams. The current managers have helped revive the venue's tradition of playing cutting-edge music, including electro, dub step, techno and dancehall nights featuring international acts. It's also a destination for early morning clubbers determined to shun their beds.

Arts & leisure

MK2 Bibliothèque
128-162 av de France, 13th (08.92.69. 84.84, www.mk2.com). Mº Bibliothèque François Mitterrand or Quai de la Gare. **Admission** €10; €7 students and over-60s (except weekends); €5.90 under-18s; €19.80 monthly pass. **Map** p151 E2 ③④
The MK2 chain's flagship offers 14 screens, three restaurants, a bar open until 5am at weekends and two-person 'love seats'. A paragon of imaginative programming, MK2 is growing all the time; it has added ten more venues in town, including two situated along the Bassin de la Villette.

Musée National du Sport
93 av de France, 13th (01.45.83.15.80, www.museedusport.fr). Mº Bibliothèque François Mitterrand. **Open** 10am-6pm Tue-Fri; 2-6pm Sat. **Map** p151 E3 ③⑤
After years without a home, the Musée National du Sport has finally found a space for its permanent collection. The new museum traces the history of sport via a small selection of the 100,000 artefacts in its collection. Even if the thrust of the collection is French sports and heroes, many of the exhibits will be familiar to an international audience: a clutch of Olympic medals from the 1992 Winter Games in Albertville; an autographed ball used in France's triumphant 1998 World Cup victory; the *ballon d'or* won by Zinedine Zidane; and Alain Prost's protective bodysuit.

Piscine Josephine-Baker
Quai François-Mauriac, 13th (01.56. 61.96.50). Mº Quai de la Gare. **Open** 7-8.30am, 1-9pm Mon, Wed Fri; 1-11pm Tue, Thur; 11am-8pm Sat; 10am-8pm Sun. **Admission** €3; €1.70 reductions. **Map** p151 E2 ③⑥
Moored on the Seine, the Piscine Josephine-Baker complex boasts a 25m main pool (with sliding glass roof), a paddling pool and café, and a busy schedule of exercise classes.

Fondation Cartier pour l'Art Contemporain p154

Montparnasse

Yet another artists' quarter that has long since lost the character – and the characters – that made its name, Montparnasse is now conspicuously lacking in charm. Between the two world wars, it was the emblematic 'gay Paree' district of after-dark merriment and fruitful artistic exchange – and it was also remarkably cosmopolitan.

A great number of its most prominent figures were expats (including its best chronicler, the Hungarian photographer Brassaï), and the late-night bars and artists' studios formed a bubble of cordial international relations that was irreparably popped in 1939. The local atmosphere soured further with the completion of the much-loathed **Tour Montparnasse** in the early 1970s. Granted, it's rich territory for art museums – but with the exception of the **Fondation Cartier**, they're all about past glories.

The old Montparnasse station witnessed two events of historical significance. In 1898, a runaway train burst through its façade; and on 25 August 1944, the German forces surrendered Paris here. The station was rebuilt in the 1970s, a grey affair above which can be found the Jardin Atlantique, a modest oasis of granite paths, trees and bamboo spread over a roof, the Mémorial du Maréchal Leclerc and the Musée Jean Moulin.

Sights & museums

Les Catacombes
1 av Colonel Henri-Rol-Tanguy, 14th (01.43.22.47.63, www.catacombes-de-paris.fr). M°/RER Denfert Rochereau. **Open** 10am-5pm Tue-Sun. **Admission** €8; free-€6 reductions. **Map** p155 C3 ➊
This is the official entrance to the 3,000km (1,864-mile) tunnel network that runs under much of the city. With

public burial pits overflowing in the era of the Revolutionary Terror, the bones of six million people were transferred to the *catacombes*. The bones of Marat, Robespierre and their cronies are packed in with wall upon wall of their fellow citizens. A damp, cramped tunnel takes you through a series of galleries before you reach the ossuary, the entrance to which is announced by a sign engraved in the stone: 'Stop! This is the empire of death.' The tour lasts approximately 45 minutes and the temperature in the tunnels is 14°C.

Cimetière du Montparnasse

3 bd Edgar-Quinet, 14th (01.44.10. 86.50). M° Edgar Quinet or Raspail. **Open** *16 Mar-5 Nov* 8am-6pm Mon-Fri; 8.30am-6pm Sat; 9am-6pm Sun. *6 Nov-15 Mar* 8am-5.30pm Mon-Fri; 8.30am-5.30pm Sat; 9.30am-5.30pm Sun. **Admission** free. **Map** p155 B2 ❷

This huge cemetery was formed by commandeering three farms (you can still see the ruins of a windmill by rue Froidevaux) in 1824. As with much of the Left Bank, the boneyard has literary clout: Beckett, Baudelaire, Sartre, de Beauvoir, Maupassant, Ionesco and Tristan Tzara all rest here. There are also artists, including Brancusi, Henri Laurens, Frédéric Bartholdi (sculptor of the Statue of Liberty) and Man Ray. The celebrity roll-call continues with Serge Gainsbourg, André Citroën, Coluche and Jean Seberg.

Fondation Cartier pour l'Art Contemporain

261 bd Raspail, 14th (01.42.18.56.50, recorded information 01.42.18.56.51, www.fondation.cartier.fr). M° Denfert-Rochereau or Raspail. **Open** 11am-10pm Tue; 11am-8pm Wed-Sun. **Admission** €6.50; free-€4.50 reductions. **Map** p155 C2 ❸

Jean Nouvel's glass and steel building, an exhibition centre with Cartier's offices above, is as much a work of art as the installations inside. Shows by artists and photographers have wide-ranging themes. Live events around the shows are called Nuits Nomades.

Fondation Henri Cartier-Bresson

2 impasse Lebouis, 14th (01.56.80. 27.00, www.henricartierbresson.org). M° Gaîté. **Open** 1-6.30pm Tue, Thur, Fri, Sun; 1-8.30pm Wed; 11am-6.45pm Sat. Closed Aug & between exhibitions. **Admission** €6; €3 reductions. No credit cards. **Map** p155 A2 ❹

This two-floor gallery is dedicated to the work of acclaimed photographer Henri Cartier-Bresson. It consists of a tall, narrow *atelier* in a 1913 building, with a minutely catalogued archive, open to researchers, and a lounge on the fourth floor screening films. In the spirit of Cartier-Bresson, who assisted on three Jean Renoir films and drew and painted all his life (some drawings are also found on the fourth floor), the Fondation opens its doors to other disciplines with three annual shows. The convivial feel fosters relaxed discussion with staff and other visitors.

Musée Bourdelle

16-18 rue Antoine-Bourdelle, 15th (01.49.54.73.73, www.bourdelle. paris.fr). M° Falguière or Montparnasse Bienvenüe. **Open** 10am-6pm Tue-Sun. **Admission** free. *Exhibitions* prices vary. **Map** p155 A1 ❺

The sculptor Antoine Bourdelle (1861-1929), a pupil of Rodin, produced a number of monumental works, including the modernist relief friezes at the Théâtre des Champs-Elysées, inspired by Isadora Duncan and Nijinsky. Set around a small garden, the museum includes the artist's apartment and studios. A 1950s extension tracks the evolution of Bourdelle's equestrian monument to General Alvear in Buenos Aires, and his masterful *Hercules the Archer*. A new wing houses bronzes. **Event highlights** En Mai, Fais Ce Qu'il Te Plaît! (until 19 Sept 2010)

Musée du Montparnasse

*21 av du Maine, 15th (01.42.22.91.96,
www.museedumontparnasse.net).
Mº Montparnasse Bienvenüe.* **Open**
12.30-7pm Tue-Sun. **Admission** €5;
free-€4 reductions. No credit cards.
Map p155 A1 **6**

Set in one of the last surviving alleys
of studios, this was home to Marie
Vassilieff, whose own academy and
cheap canteen welcomed poor artists
Picasso, Cocteau and Matisse. Trotsky
and Lenin were also guests. Shows
focus on present-day artists and the
area's creative past.

Tour Montparnasse

*33 av du Maine, 15th (01.45.38.52.56,
www.tourmontparnasse56.com).
Mº Montparnasse Bienvenüe.* **Open**
Oct-Mar 9.30am-10.30pm daily.
Apr-Sept 9.30am-11.30pm daily.
Admission €10.50; free-€7.50
reductions. **Map** p155 A1 **7**

Built in 1974 on the site of the old station, this 209m (686ft) steel-and-glass
monolith is shorter than the Eiffel
Tower, but better placed for fabulous
views of the city – including, of course,
the Eiffel Tower itself. A lift whisks
you up in 38 seconds to the 56th floor,
where you'll find a display of aerial
scenes of Paris, an upgraded café-
lounge, a souvenir shop – and lots and
lots of sky.

Eating & drinking

La Cerisaie

*70 bd Edgar Quinet, 14th
(01.43.20.98.98). Mº Edgar Quinet
or Montparnasse.* **Open** noon-2pm,
7-10pm Mon-Fri. Closed Aug & 1wk
Dec. **€€**. **Bistro**. **Map** p155 A1 **8**

Nothing about La Cerisaie's unprepos-
sessing red façade hints at the talent
that lurks inside. With a simple starter
of white asparagus served with preserved lemon and drizzled with bright

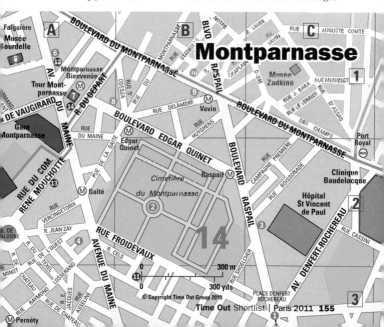

Cimetière du Montparnasse p154

green parsley oil, chef Cyril Lalanne proves his ability to select and prepare the finest produce. On the daily changing blackboard menu you might find *bourride de maquereau*, a thrifty take on the garlicky southern French fish stew, or *cochon noir de Bigorre*, an ancient breed of pig that puts ordinary pork to shame. *Baba à l'armagnac*, a variation on the usual rum cake, comes with great chantilly.

La Coupole

102 bd du Montparnasse, 14th (01.43.20.14.20, www.flobrasseries. com/coupoleparis). Mº Vavin. **Open** 8am-1am Mon-Fri; 8.30am-1am Sat, Sun. **€€. Brasserie. Map** p155 B1 **9**
La Coupole still glows with some of the old glamour. The people-watching remains superb, inside and out, and the long ranks of linen-covered tables, professional waiters, 32 art deco columns painted by different artists of the epoch, mosaic floor and sheer scale of the operation still make coming here an event. The set menu offers unremarkable steaks, foie gras, fish and autumn game stews, but the real treat is the shellfish, which is displayed along a massive counter. Take your pick from the *claires*, *spéciales* and *belons*, or go for a platter with crabs, oysters, prawns, periwinkles and clams.

Le Select

99 bd du Montparnasse, 6th (01.45.48.38.24). Mº Vavin. **Open** 7am-2am Mon-Thur, Sun; 7am-4am Fri, Sat. **€. Café. Map** p155 B1 **10**
For a decade between the wars, the junction of boulevards Raspail and du Montparnasse was where Man Ray, Cocteau and Lost Generation Americans hung out in the vast, glass-fronted cafés. Eight decades on, Le Select is the best of these inevitable tourist haunts. Sure, its pricey menu is big on historical detail and short on authenticity, but by and large it manages to hold on to its heyday with some dignity.

Shopping

Paris Accordéon

80 rue Daguerre, 14th (01.43.22. 13.48, www.parisaccordeon.com). Mº Denfert Rochereau or Gaîté. **Open** 9am-1pm, 2.30-7pm Tue-Fri; 9am-noon, 1-6pm Sat. **Map** p155 B3 **11**
Accordions galore, from squeezeboxes to beautiful tortoiseshell models, both second-hand and new.

Nightlife

Mix Club

24 rue de l'Arrivée, 15th (01.56.80.37.37, www.mixclub.fr). Mº Montparnasse Bienvenüe. **Open** 11pm-6am Wed-Sat; 5pm-1am Sun. **Admission** €12-€20. **Map** p155 A1 **12**
The Mix Club has one of the city's biggest dancefloors. Regular visitors include Erick Morillo's Subliminal and Ministry of Sound parties, and in-house events include David Guetta's 'Fuck Me I'm Famous' and 'Hipnotic', plus just about everyone else who's big in France – or anywhere else in the world.

Le Petit Journal Montparnasse

13 rue du Commandant-René-Mouchotte, 14th (01.43.21.56.70, www.petitjournal-montparnasse.com). Mº Gaîté or Montparnasse-Bienvenüe. **Open** 8pm-2am daily. *Concerts* 10pm Mon-Sat. **Admission** (incl 1 drink) €25; €15 reductions. **Map** p155 A2 **13**
Two-level jazz brasserie in the shadow of the Tour Montparnasse with Latin sounds, R&B and soul-gospel.

Red Light

34 rue du Départ, 15th (01.42.79. 94.53, www.enfer.fr). Mº Edgar Quinet or Montparnasse Bienvenüe. **Open** midnight-11am Fri, Sat. **Admission** (incl 1 drink) €20-€25. **Map** p155 A1 **14**
The former Enfer ('Hell') remains a trance, techno and house dynamo with local and global DJs spinning to a young, up-for-it, often gay crowd.

Château de Versailles p162

Worth the Trip

North

Basilique St-Denis

*1 rue de la Légion-d'Honneur, 93200
St-Denis (01.48.09.83.54). M° St-Denis
Basilique/tram 1.* **Open** *Apr-Sept* 10am-
6.15pm Mon-Sat; noon-6.15pm Sun.
Oct-Mar 10am-5.15pm Mon-Sat; noon-
5.15pm Sun. **Tours** 10.30am, 3pm
Mon-Sat; 12.15pm, 3pm Sun.
Admission €7; free-€4.50 reductions.
Legend has it that when St Denis was
beheaded, he picked up his noggin and
walked with it to Vicus Catulliacus (now
St-Denis) to be buried. The first church,
parts of which can be seen in the crypt,
was built over his tomb in around 475.
The present edifice was begun in the
1130s. It is considered to be the first
example of Gothic architecture. In the
13th century, mason Pierre de Montreuil
erected the spire and rebuilt the choir
nave and transept. St-Denis was the
burial place for all but three French
monarchs between 996 and the end of
the *ancien régime*, so the ambulatory is
a museum of French funerary sculpture.
It includes a fanciful Gothic tomb for
Dagobert, the austere effigy of Charles
V, and the Renaissance tomb of Louis
XII and his wife Anne de Bretagne. In
1792 these tombs were desecrated, and
the royal remains thrown into a pit.

Musée de l'Air
et de l'Espace

*Aéroport de Paris-Le Bourget, 93352
Le Bourget Cedex (01.49.92.71.62,
recorded information 01.49.92.70.00,
www.mae.org). M° Gare du Nord, then
bus 350/RER Le Bourget, then bus
152.* **Open** *Apr-Sept* 10am-6pm Tue-
Sun. *Oct-Mar* 10am-5pm Tue-Sun.
Admission free. *With Concorde &
Boeing 747* €6; free-€4 reductions.
The impressive air and space museum
is set in the former passenger terminal
at Le Bourget airport. The collection
begins with the pioneers, including
fragile-looking biplanes and the com-
mand cabin of a Zeppelin airship. On
the runway are Mirage fighters, a US

Thunderchief, and Ariane launchers 1 and 5. A hangar houses the prototype Concorde 001 and wartime survivors. A scale models gallery opened in 2008.

East

104

104 rue d'Aubervilliers, 19th (01.53.35. 50.00, www.104.fr). M° Riquet. **Open** 11am-9pm Tue-Thur, Sun; 11am-11pm Fri, Sat. **Admission** free. *Exhibitions* €5; €3 reductions.

It's more than a century since tourist-choked Montmartre was the centre of artistic activity in Paris. But now the north-east of Paris is again where the action is, in a previously neglected area of bleak railway goods yards and dilapidated social housing. 104, described as a 'space for artistic creation', occupies a vast 19th-century building on the rue d'Aubervilliers that used to house Paris's municipal undertakers. There aren't any constraints on the kind of work the resident artists do – 104 is open to 'all the arts' – but they're expected to show finished pieces in one of four annual 'festivals'. And they're also required to get involved in projects with the public.

La Cité des Sciences et de l'Industrie

La Villette, 30 av Corentin-Cariou, 19th (01.40.05.70.00, www.cite-sciences.fr). M° Porte de la Villette. **Open** 10am-6pm Tue-Sat; 10am-7pm Sun. **Admission** €8; free-€6 reductions.

This ultra-modern science museum pulls in five million visitors a year. Explora, the permanent show, occupies the upper two floors, whisking visitors through 30,000sq m (320,000sq ft) of space, life, matter and communication: scale models of satellites including the Ariane space shuttle, planes and robots, plus the chance to experience weightlessness, make for an exciting trip. In the Espace Images, try the delayed camera and other optical illusions, draw 3D images on a computer or lend your voice to the *Mona Lisa*. The hothouse garden investigates developments in agriculture and bio-technology. The Cité des Enfants runs workshops for younger children.

Disneyland Paris/ Walt Disney Studios Park

Marne-la-Vallée (08.25.30.60.30, from UK 0870 503 0303, www.disneyland paris.com). 32km E of Paris. RER A or TGV Marne-la-Vallée-Chessy. By car, A4 exit 14. **Open** *Disneyland Paris* Sept-mid July 10am-8pm Mon-Fri; 9am-8pm Sat, Sun. Mid July-Aug 9am-11pm daily. *Studios Park* Winter 10am-6pm Mon-Fri; 9am-6pm Sat, Sun. Summer 9am-7pm daily. **Admission** *1 park* €51; free-€43 reductions. *1-day hopper* (both parks) €62; free-€54 reductions.

Young ones will get a real kick out of Fantasyland, with its Alice maze, Sleeping Beauty's castle and teacup rides. Walt Disney Studios focuses on special effects and the tricks of the animation trade. Disney's newest adrenalin ride, the Twilight Zone Tower of Terror, sends daredevils plummeting down a 13-storey lift shaft.

South

Musée Fragonard

7 av du Général de Gaulle, 94704 Maisons-Alfort (01.43.96.71.72, http://musee.vet-alfort.fr). M° Ecole Vétérinaire de Maisons-Alfort. **Open** 2-6pm Wed, Thur; 1-6pm Sat, Sun. Closed Aug. **Admission** €7; free-€5 reductions.

In 18th-century French medical schools, study aids were produced in one of two ways. They were either painstakingly sculpted in coloured wax or made from the real things – organs, limbs, tangled vascular systems – dried or preserved in formaldehyde. Veterinary surgeon Honoré Fragonard (cousin of the famous rococo painter) was a master of the second method, and many of his most striking works are now on display here.

Homme à la mandibule is a flayed, grimacing man holding a jawbone in his right hand – an allusion to the story of Samson slaying the Philistines. *Tête humaine injectée* is a rather more sober human head whose blood vessels were injected with coloured wax, red for arteries and blue for veins. And, most grandiose of all, *Cavalier de l'apocalypse* is a flayed man on the back of a flayed galloping horse, inspired, according to the museum's notes, by a painting by Dürer.

Parc André Citroën

Rue Balard, rue St-Charles or quai Citroën, 15th. M° Balard or Javel. **Open** 8am-dusk Mon-Fri; 9am-dusk Sat, Sun, public hols.

This park is a fun, postmodern version of a French formal garden, designed by Gilles Clément and Alain Prévost. It comprises glasshouses, computerised fountains, waterfalls, a wilderness and themed gardens with different coloured plants and even sounds. Stepping stones and water jets make it a garden for pleasure as well as philosophy. The tethered Eutelsat helium balloon takes visitors up for panoramic views. If the weather looks unreliable, call 01.44.26.20.00 to check the programme.

West

Bois de Boulogne

16th. M° Les Sablons or Porte Dauphine. **Admission** free.

Covering 865 hectares, the Bois was once the Forêt de Rouvray hunting grounds. It was landscaped in the 1860s, when artificial grottoes and waterfalls were created around the Lac Inférieur. The Jardin de Bagatelle is famous for its roses, daffodils and water lilies. The Jardin d'Acclimatation is a children's amusement park, complete with miniature train, farm, rollercoaster and boat rides. The Bois also boasts two racecourses (Longchamp and Auteuil), sports clubs and stables, and restaurants.

Musée Marmottan – Claude Monet

2 rue Louis-Boilly, 16th (01.44.96.50.33, www.marmottan.com). **Open** 11am-6pm Mon, Wed-Sun (last entry 5.30pm); 11am-9pm Tue (last entry 8.30pm). **Admission** €9; free-€5 reductions.

This old hunting pavilion has become a famed holder of Impressionist art thanks to two bequests: the first by the daughter of the doctor of Manet, Monet, Pissarro, Sisley and Renoir; the second by Monet's son Michel. Its Monet collection, the largest in the world, numbers 165 works, plus sketchbooks, palette and photos. A special circular room was created for the stunning late water lily canvases; upstairs are works by Renoir, Manet, Gauguin, Caillebotte and Berthe Morisot, 15th-century primitives, a Sèvres clock and a collection of First Empire furniture.

Versailles

Centuries of makeovers have made Versailles the most sumptuously clad château in the world. Architect Louis Le Vau first embellished the original building – a hunting lodge built during Louis XIII's reign – after Louis XIV saw Vaux-le-Vicomte, the impressive residence of his finance minister, Nicolas Fouquet. The Sun King had the unlucky minister jailed, and stole not only his architect but also his painter, Charles Le Brun, and his landscaper, André Le Nôtre, who turned the boggy marshland into terraces, parterres, fountains and lush groves.

After Le Vau's death in 1670, Jules Hardouin-Mansart took over as principal architect, transforming Versailles into the château we know today. In 1682, Louis moved in, accompanied by his court; thereafter, he rarely set foot in Paris. In the 1770s, Louis XV commissioned Jacques-Ange Gabriel to add the

Suburban cycle

Pick up a Vélib' and pedal beyond Paris.

Despite ongoing problems with vandalism, Vélib' continues to flourish in Paris, and 2009 saw the municipal bike hire scheme move beyond the Périphérique. The Vélib' stations beyond the Périphérique offer a chance for adventurous visitors to explore new areas on two wheels, and the Bois de Boulogne and Bois de Vincennes are particularly well served. You can cycle through the former and exchange or deposit your bike at the stations bordering the wood in Neuilly and Boulogne-Billancourt. There is also a station in the centre of the park. West of here, stations at Puteaux allow for a Sunday whizz round the skyscrapers of La Défense, and from Suresnes you can even bike the five kilometres (three miles) west to Château de Malmaison and the Ile des Impressionistes at Rueil-Malmaison, famously depicted in Renoir's 1881 painting *Le Déjeuner des Canotiers*.

South of the Bois de Boulogne, station 21010 is close to the Musée National de Céramique and the beautiful Parc de Saint-Cloud. In the east, the Bois de Vincennes has several Vélib' stations in the wood itself, and you can stray further out to Nogent-sur-Marne and Joinville-le-Pont, where cycle paths run alongside the Marne river.

North of the Bois de Vincennes, the cafés and restaurants serving Montreuil's arty crowd are clustered around the place du Marché at Croix de Chavaux (stations 31007 and 31008), where you'll find a food market on Thursday and Sunday mornings and Friday afternoons – this is the perfect place to pick up some picnic supplies before heading down to the riverbank.

Remember that you need a chip and pin card to authorise the deposit and you need to check in your bike and take a new one every half hour to keep it free. An extra half hour costs €1, an extra hour €3, and it's €4 for every half hour thereafter. Maps of all the Vélib' stations can be downloaded from www.velib.paris.fr.

PARIS BY AREA

sumptuous Opéra Royal. The expense of building and running Versailles cost France dear. With the fall of the monarchy in 1792, most of the furniture was lost – but the château was saved from demolition after 1830 by Louis-Philippe.

The gardens are works of art in themselves, their ponds and statues once again embellished by a fully working fountain system. On summer weekends, the spectacular jets of water are set to music, a prelude to the occasional fireworks displays of the Fêtes de Nuit.

Château de Versailles

78000 Versailles (01.30.83.78.00, advance tickets 08.92.68.46.94, www. chateauversailles.fr). **Open** *Apr-Oct* 9am-6.30pm Tue-Sun. *Nov-Mar* 9am-5.30pm Tue-Sun. **Admission** €13.50; free-€10 reductions.

Versailles is a masterpiece – and it's almost always packed with visitors. Allow yourself a whole day to appreciate the sumptuous State Apartments and the Hall of Mirrors, the highlights of any visit and mainly accessible with a day ticket. The Grand Appartement, where Louis XIV held court, consists of six gilded salons (Venus, Mercury, Apollo and so on). No less luxurious, the Queen's Apartment includes her bedroom, where royal births took place in full view of the court. Hardouin-Mansart's showpiece, the Hall of Mirrors, where a united Germany was proclaimed in 1871 and the Treaty of Versailles was signed in 1919, is flooded with light from its 17 windows.

Domaine de Versailles

Gardens **Open** *Apr-Oct* 7am-dusk daily. *Nov-Mar* 8am-dusk daily. **Admission** *Winter* free (statues covered over). *Summer* €3; free-€1.50 reductions. *Grandes Eaux Musicales* (01.30.83.78.88). **Open** *Apr-Sept* Sat, Sun. **Admission** €8; free-€6 reductions. *Park* **Open** dawn-dusk daily. **Admission** free.

Sprawling across 8sq km (3sq miles), the gardens consist of formal parterres, ponds, elaborate statues – many commissioned by Colbert in 1674 – and a spectacular series of fountains, served by an ingenious hydraulic system only recently restored to working order. On weekend afternoons in the spring and autumn, the fountains are set to music for the Grandes Eaux Musicales.

Grand Trianon/Petit Trianon/Domaine de Marie-Antoinette

Open *Apr-Oct* noon-7pm daily. *Nov-Mar* noon-5.30pm daily. **Admission** *Summer* €10; €6 after 4pm; free under-18s. *Winter* €6; free under-18s.

In 1687, Hardouin-Mansart built the pink marble Grand Trianon in the north of the park, away from the protocol of the court. Here Louis XIV and his children's governess and secret second wife, Madame de Maintenon, could admire the intimate gardens from the colonnaded portico. It retains the Empire decor of Napoleon, who stayed here with his second Empress, Marie-Louise. The Petit Trianon, built for Louis XV's mistress Madame de Pompadour, is a wonderful example of neo-classicism. It later became part of the Domaine de Marie-Antoinette, an exclusive hideaway located beyond the canal in the wooded parkland. Given to Marie-Antoinette as a wedding gift by her husband Louis XVI in 1774, the domain also includes the chapel adjoining the Petit Trianon, plus a theatre, a neo-classical 'Temple d'Amour', and Marie-Antoinette's fairytale farm and dairy.

Getting there

By car

20km (12.5 miles) from Paris by the A13 or D10.

By train

For the station nearest the château, take the RER C5 (VICK or VERO trains) to Versailles-Rive Gauche.

Essentials

Hôtel Banke p172

Hotels

Paris's luxury palaces continue to offer the ultimate dream hotel experience: at the **Crillon**, the **Bristol**, the **George V**, the **Plaza Athénée** and the **Ritz** uniformed flunkeys whisk you through revolving doors to an otherworldly domain of tinkling china, thick carpets and concierges for whom your wish is their desire, for a generous tip. By the end of 2010 there should be even more competition in the luxury sector with the completion of a new Shangri-La, a Mandarin Oriental and the complete makeover of the Royal Monceau by Philippe Starck.

Better value for money can be found at Paris's increasingly luxurious boutique hotels, several of which opened in 2009. For several hundred euros less a night than a palace, you can be soothed by fine linen, marble baths and a dreamy pool and hammam at

Le Metropolitan, walk through silk taffeta curtains to your own terrace at **Le Petit Paris**, fall into a deep sleep at the pure white marvel that is the **Hôtel Gabriel**, and fraternise at the trendy cava bar of the Spanish-owned **Banke**. For those who like a bit more glitz, the sparkly **Opéra Diamond** and sexy **Sublim Eiffel** use fibre optics to create a starry galaxy.

Further down the scale, there is now a wide choice of moderately priced and even budget design hotels, especially in the trendy east and north-east of the city, such as the Starck-designed **Mama Shelter**, **Standard Design Hotel**, **Le Quartier Bastille** and **20 Prieuré**. But if Paris wouldn't be Paris for you without chintzy wallpaper, springy beds and a bathroom on the landing, never fear: faithful stalwarts the **Esmeralda** and **Henri IV** are still going strong.

Classification

We've divided the hotels by area, then listed them in four categories, according to the standard prices (not including seasonal offers or discounts) for one night in a double room with en suite shower/bath. For deluxe hotels (€€€€), you can expect to pay more than €350; for properties in the expensive bracket (€€€), €220-€350; for moderate properties (€€), allow €130-€219; while budget rooms (€) go for less than €130.

In the know

All hotels in France charge a room tax (*taxe de séjour*) of around €1 per person per night, although this is sometimes included in the rate.

Champs-Elysées & Western Paris

Four Seasons George V

31 av George V, 8th (01.49.52.70.00, www.fourseasons.com/paris). M° Alma Marceau or George V. €€€€.
There's no denying that the George V is serious about luxury: chandeliers, marble and tapestries, over-attentive staff, glorious flower arrangements, divine bathrooms, and ludicrously comfortable beds in some of the largest rooms in Paris. The Versailles-inspired spa area includes whirlpools, saunas and treatments; non-guests can reserve appointments. It's worth every euro.

Hôtel le Bristol

112 rue du Fbg-St-Honoré, 8th (01.53.43.43.00, www.hotel-bristol.com). M° Champs-Elysées Clémenceau. €€€€.
Set on the exclusive rue du Faubourg St-Honoré, near luxury boutiques such as Christian Lacroix, Azzaro, Salvatore Ferragamo, Givenchy and Dolce & Gabbana, the Bristol is a luxurious 'palace' hotel with a loyal following of

Best newcomers
- Hôtel Banke (see p172)
- Hôtel Gabriel (see p175)
- Le Petit Paris (see p181)

Best spa splurge
- Four Seasons George V (see p165)
- Hôtel Fouquet's Barrière (see p167)
- Le Meurice (see p171)

Best alfresco breakfast
- Hôtel de l'Abbaye Saint-Germain (see p179)
- Mama Shelter (see p173)

Best bars
- Hôtel Plaza Athénée (see p167)
- Kube Hotel (see p173)

Best for fashion week
- Le Bellechasse (see p176)
- L'Hôtel (see p179)
- Le Montalembert (see p177)

Best bathrooms
- Four Seasons George V (see p165)
- Renaissance Paris Arc de Triomphe (see p169)

Best bargain beds
- Grand Hôtel Jeanne d'Arc (see p175)
- Hôtel Chopin (see p169)
- Mama Shelter (see p173)
- St Christopher's Inn (see p173)

Chic sleeps
- L'Hôtel (see p179)
- Hôtel Amour (see p172)

Lap of luxury
- Hôtel le Bristol (see p165)
- Hôtel de Crillon (see p171)
- Hôtel Ritz (see p171)

ESSENTIALS

1-5 passage ruelle - Paris - 75018 - France
paris@kubehotel.com - www.kubehotel.com - t. +33 1 42 05 20 00

fashionistas and millionaires drawn by the location, impeccable service, larger than average rooms and a three Michelin-starred restaurant with Eric Fréchon at the helm. The Bristol's new seven-storey wing opened in late 2009, with 22 new rooms and four suites.

Hôtel Daniel
8 rue Frédéric-Bastiat, 8th (01.42.56. 17.00, www.hoteldanielparis.com). Mº Franklin D. Roosevelt or St Philippe-du-Roule. €€€€.
This romantic hideaway close to the Champs-Elysées is decorated in chinoiserie and a palette of rich colours, with 26 rooms (free Wi-Fi) cosily appointed in *toile de Jouy* and an intricately hand-painted restaurant that feels like a courtyard. At about €50 a head, the gastronomic restaurant Le Lounge, run by chef Denis Fetisson, is a good deal for this neighbourhood.

Hôtel Fouquet's Barrière
46 av George V, 8th (01.40.69. 60.00, www.fouquets-barriere.com). Mº George V. €€€€.
This grandiose five-star is built around the fin-de-siècle brasserie Le Fouquet's. Five buildings form the hotel complex, with 107 rooms (including 40 suites), upmarket restaurant Le Diane, the Sparis spa, indoor pool and a rooftop terrace for hire. Jacques Garcia, of Hôtel Costes and Westin fame, was responsible for the interior design, which retains the Empire style of the exterior while incorporating luxurious touches inside – flat-screen TVs and mist-free mirrors in the marble bathrooms. And, of course, it's unbeatable for location – right at the junction of avenue George V and the Champs-Elysées.

Hôtel Plaza Athénée
25 av Montaigne, 8th (01.53.67. 66.65, www.plaza-athenee-paris.com). Mº Alma Marceau. €€€€.
This palace is ideally placed for power shopping at Chanel, Louis Vuitton, Dior and other avenue Montaigne boutiques.

Material girls and boys will enjoy the high-tech room amenities, such as remote-controlled air con, internet and video-game access on the TV via infrared keyboard, and mini hi-fi. Make time for a drink in the Bar du Plaza, a cocktail bunny's most *outré* fantasy.

Hôtel Square
3 rue de Boulainvilliers, 16th (01.44. 14.91.90, www.hotelsquare.com). Mº Passy/RER Avenue du Pdt Kennedy. €€€€.
Located in the upmarket 16th, this courageously modern hotel has a dramatic yet welcoming interior, and attentive service that comes from having to look after only 22 rooms. They're decorated in amber, brick or slate colours, with exotic woods, quality fabrics and bathrooms seemingly cut from one huge chunk of Carrara marble. View exhibitions in the atrium gallery or mingle with media types at the hip Zebra Square restaurant and DJ bar.

Jays Paris
6 rue Copernic, 16th (01.47.04.16.16, www.jays-paris.com). Mº Kléber or Victor Hugo. €€€€.
Jays is a luxurious *boutique-apart* hotel that trades on a clever blend of antique furniture, modern design and high-tech equipment. The marble staircase, lit entirely by natural light filtered through the glass atrium overhead, gives an instant feeling of grandeur, and leads to five suites, each with a fully equipped kitchenette and free Wi-Fi. A cosy salon is available to welcome in-house guests and their visitors.

Le Metropolitan
NEW *10 pl de Mexico, 16th (01.56.90.40.04, www.radisson blu.com). Mº Trocadero.* €€€.
This new 40-room offering from Radisson Blu is supremely sleek. The discreet entrance is only a few metres wide, but once inside the triangular structure opens out into surprising volumes, with a monumental art deco-

ESSENTIALS

Sleep well

Chill out at Paris's first detox hotel.

Hôtel Gabriel (see p175) is a shrine to quality kip and healthy living, offering up a chilled respite for everyone from the terminally jetlagged to weekend clubbers.

To test it out, we checked in after a heavy weekend of partying. On a hot day, the air-conditioned, pure white room seemed rather clinical, but at night the 'Glowing Room' came alive with dancing silhouettes on the cupboards and illuminated cubbyholes stocked with health-food snacks. The TV may be neatly hidden behind mirrored glass, but the room is not short on techno wizardry: there's a chrome mini-bar that unfolds from inside its white knobless cupboard; an iPod station for which you can borrow an iPod pre-programmed with anything from Goldfrapp to Shirley Bassey; free Wi-Fi, of course; and the *sine qua non* of sleep aids, the NightCove device, conceived by a sleep professor and designer Jean-Philippe Nuel.

This white box is easily programmed to emit sounds and light that stimulate melatonin: choose between sleep, nap or wake-up programmes such as the sound of rain or tropical birdsong. When you do manage to wake up, there's a cold room-service menu including lobster salad delivered fresh from specialist boutique hotel caterers; a minimalist bathroom with Korres products made from natural ingredients in Greece; and a scrumptious breakfast of organic yoghurt, chocolate muesli and mini croissants.

If you're still feeling rundown, then take yourself downstairs for a detox massage courtesy of Franco-Japanese masseuse Mitchiko and her colleagues – potent enough to make the next glass of wine course through your veins in an alarming way. A partner gym, suggested jogging routes and green taxis complete the healthy vibe.

style fireplace, and cream leather and black granite reminiscent of New York in the 1930s. The first floor contains a swank insiders' cocktail bar, but the biggest surprise of all is the breathtaking view of the Eiffel Tower from the front façade, best enjoyed through the huge oval window while lying on the four-poster bed of the sixth floor suite. All rooms exude *luxe, calme et volonté* with solid oak floors, linen curtains and baths or showers carved from black or cream marble. And below ground is a sublime swimming pool and hammam reserved for guests.

Opéra Diamond

NEW *4 rue de la Pépinière, 8th (01.44.70.02.00, www.paris-hotel-diamond.com). M° St-Lazare.* €€.
This sparkling newcomer lives up to its name with a night-sky decor made up of black granite resin punctuated with crystals and LEDs. The 30 rooms are equally splendid, with Swarovski crystal touches to the furniture, black bathrooms and satin curtains that close to become a photomontage of a female nude crossed with architectural imagery. The Executive rooms have iPod stations, Nespresso machines, and speakers in the bathrooms. A courtyard with a fountain adds to the appeal.

Renaissance Paris Arc de Triomphe

NEW *39 av de Wagram, 17th (01.55.37.55.37, www.marriott.com). M° Ternes.* €€€.
You can't miss it. This six-storey undulating glass façade on avenue de Wagram is like no other part of the neighbourhood. All rooms are stylishly done out in pale greys, charcoals and dark wood, with Eames-style furniture. Nice high-tech touches include an iPod dock on the bedside radio and a large flat-screen TV with Wi-Fi keyboard. Bathrooms are a glory of polished metal, tasteful tiles and gleaming glass. The Makassar restaurant serves delicate and delicious Franco-Asian fusion food.

Le Sezz

6 av Frémiet, 16th (01.56.75.26.26, www.hotelsezz.com). M° Passy. €€€.
Le Sezz has 27 sleek, luxurious rooms and suites. The understated decor represents a refreshingly modern take on luxury, with black parquet flooring, rough-hewn stone walls and bathrooms partitioned off with sweeping glass façades. The bar and public areas are equally sleek and chic. Free Wi-Fi.

Opéra to Les Halles

Hôtel Brighton

218 rue de Rivoli, 1st (01.47.03.61.61, www.esprit-de-france.com). M° Tuileries. €€.
With several of the bedrooms looking out over the Tuileries gardens, the Brighton is great value, so ask for a room with a view. Recently restored, it has a classical atmosphere, from the high ceilings in the rooms to the faux-marble and mosaic decor downstairs.

Hôtel Chopin

10 bd Montmartre or 46 passage Jouffroy, 9th (01.47.70.58.10, www.hotel-chopin.com). M° Grands Boulevards. €.
Handsomely set in a historic, glass-roofed arcade next door to the Grévin musuem, the Chopin's original 1846 façade adds to its old-fashioned appeal. The 36 rooms are quiet and functional, done out in salmon and green or blue.

Hôtel Concorde St-Lazare

108 rue St-Lazare, 8th (01.40.08.44.44, www.concordestlazare-paris.com). M° St-Lazare. €€€.
Guests here are cocooned in sound-proofed luxury. The 19th-century Eiffel-inspired lobby with jewel-encrusted pink granite columns is a historic landmark: the high ceilings, walls and sculptures look much as they have for over a century. Rooms are spacious, with double entrance doors and exclusive Annick Goutal toiletries; the belle époque brasserie, Café Terminus,

ESSENTIALS

and sexy Golden Black Bar were designed by Sonia Rykiel. Guests have access to a nearby fitness centre and there's free Wi-Fi.

Hôtel de Crillon
10 pl de la Concorde, 8th (01.44.71. 15.00, www.crillon.com). M° Concorde. €€€€.
The Crillon lives up to its *palais* reputation with decor strong on marble, mirrors and gold leaf. If you have euros to spare, opt for the Presidential Suite (the only one with a view over the American Embassy). The Winter Garden tearoom is a must.

Hôtel Madeleine Opéra
12 rue Greffulhe, 8th (01.47.42.26.26, www.hotel-madeleine-opera.com). M° Havre-Caumartin or Madeleine. €.
This bargain hotel is located just north of the Eglise de la Madeleine, in the heart of the city's theatre and *grands magasins* districts. Its sunny lobby sits behind a 200-year-old façade that was once a shopfront. The 23 rooms are perhaps a touch basic, but still nice enough, and breakfast is brought to your room every morning.

Hôtel Ritz
15 pl Vendôme, 1st (01.43.16.30.30, www.ritzparis.com). M° Concorde or Opéra. €€€€.
Chic hasn't lost its cool at the grande dame of Paris hotels, where each of the 162 bedrooms, from the romantic Frédéric Chopin to the glitzy Impérial, ooze sumptuousness. But then what else can one expect from a hotel that has proffered hospitality to the likes of Coco Chanel, the Duke of Windsor, Proust, and Dodi and Di? There are plenty of corners to strike a pose or quench a thirst, from Hemingway's cigar bar to the poolside hangout.

Hôtel Westminster
13 rue de la Paix, 2nd (01.42.61.57.46, www.warwickwestminsteropera.com). M° Opéra/RER Auber. €€€€.

This luxury hotel near place Vendôme has more than a touch of British warmth about it, no doubt owing to the influence of its favourite 19th-century guest, the Duke of Westminster (after whom the hotel was named; the current Duke reportedly still stays here). The hotel fitness centre has an enviable top-floor location, with a beautiful tiled steam room and views over the city, and the cosy bar features deep leather chairs, a fireplace and live jazz at weekends.

InterContinental Paris Le Grand
2 rue Scribe, 9th (01.40.07.32.32, www.paris.intercontinental.com). M° Opéra. €€€€.
This 1862 hotel is the chain's European flagship – but, given its sheer size, perhaps 'mother ship' would be more appropriate: this landmark establishment occupies the entire block (three wings, almost 500 rooms) next to the opera house; some 80 of the honey-coloured rooms overlook the Palais Garnier. The space under the vast *verrière* is one of the best oases in town, and the hotel's restaurant and elegant coffeehouse, the Café de la Paix, poached its chef, Laurent Delarbre, from the Ritz. For a truly relaxing daytime break, head to the I-Spa for one of its seawater treatments.

Le Meurice
228 rue de Rivoli, 1st (01.44.58.10.10, www.lemeurice.com). M° Tuileries. €€€€.
With its extravagant Louis XVI decor, intricate mosaic tiled floors and clever, modish restyling by Philippe Starck, Le Meurice is looking grander than ever. All 160 rooms (kitted out with iPod-ready radio alarms) are done up in distinct historical styles; the Belle Etoile suite on the seventh floor provides stunning 360-degree panoramic views of Paris from its terrace. You can relax in the Winter Garden to the strains of jazz performances; for

Hôtel Westminster p171

some more intensive intervention, head over to the lavish spa complex with treatments by Valmont.

Montmartre & Pigalle

Hôtel Amour
8 rue Navarin, 9th (01.48.78.31.80, www.hotelamour.com). M° St-Georges. €€.
This boutique hotel is a real hit with the in crowd. Each of the 20 rooms (with free Wi-Fi) is unique, decorated on the theme of love or eroticism by a coterie of contemporary artists and designers such as Marc Newson, M&M, Stak, Pierre Le Tan and Sophie Calle. Seven of the rooms contain artists' installations, and two others have their own private bar and a large terrace on which to hold your own party. The late-night brasserie has a coveted outdoor garden.

Hôtel Banke
NEW *20 rue La Fayette, 9th (01.55.33.22.22, www.derbyhotels.com). M° Le Peletier.* €€€.
So called because the Haussmann-era building it occupies used to be a bank, the latest four-star addition to the Derby Hotels chain opened in 2009. It may well have the most eye-popping

lobby in the city, a huge two-storey space done in outrageous belle époque style, all crimson, black pillars and gold leaf beneath a whopping glass roof. After such opulence, the rooms are perhaps something of a let-down; but they are stylish and comfortably equipped. The mezzanine bar partakes of the lobby's *luxe*, and the Josefin restaurant serves nouvelle Med cuisine.

Hôtel Particulier Montmartre
23 av Junot, 18th (01.53.41.81.40, www.hotel-particulier-montmartre.com). M° Lamarck Caulaincourt. €€€€.
Visitors lucky (and wealthy) enough to manage to book a suite at the Hôtel Particulier Montmartre will find themselves in one of the city's hidden gems. Nestled in a quiet passage off rue Lepic, this sumptuous *Directoire*-style house is dedicated to art, with each of the five luxurious suites personalised by an avant-garde artist. Free Wi-Fi.

Hôtel Royal Fromentin
11 rue Fromentin, 9th (01.48.74.85.93, www.hotelroyalfromentin.com). M° Blanche or Pigalle. €€.
Wood panelling, art deco windows and a vintage glass lift echo the hotel's

ESSENTIALS

origins as a 1930s cabaret hall; its theatrical feel attracted Blondie and Nirvana. Many of its 47 rooms have views of Sacré-Coeur. Rooms have been renovated in French style, with bright fabrics and an old-fashioned feel, and offer free Wi-Fi.

Kube Hotel

1-5 passage Ruelle, 18th (01.42.05. 20.00, www.kubehotel.com). M° La Chapelle. €€€.

The younger sister of the Murano Urban Resort, Kube is a more hip and affordable design hotel. Like the Murano, it sits behind an unremarkable façade in an unlikely neighbourhood, the ethnically diverse Goutte d'Or. The Ice Kube bar serves vodka in glasses that, like the bar itself, are carved from ice. Also on the menu are 'apérifood' and 'snackubes' by Pierre Auge. Access to the 41 rooms is by fingerprint identification technology and there's free Wi-Fi access.

North-east Paris

Hôtel Garden Saint-Martin

35 rue Yves Toudic, 10th (01.42. 40.17.72, www.hotelgardensaint martin-paris.com). M° Jacques Bonsergent. €.

The shops, cafés and bars along the Canal St-Martin draw visitors to this hotel, where creature comforts are guaranteed at an excellent rate. No prizes will be won for the ordinary decor, but there is a very pleasant patio garden, and the staff are helpful.

Mama Shelter

109 rue de Bagnolet, 20th (01.43.48. 49.49, www.mamashelter.com). M° Alexandre Dumas, Maraîchers or Porte de Bagnolet. €.

Philippe Starck's latest design commission is set a stone's throw east of Père Lachaise, and its decor appeals to the young-at-heart with Batman and Incredible Hulk light fittings, dark walls, polished wood and splashes of bright fabrics. Every room comes with an iMac computer, TV, free internet access and a CD and DVD player; and when hunger strikes, there's a brasserie with a romantic terrace. If you're sure of your dates, book online and take advantage of the saver's rate.

St Christopher's Inn

159 rue de Crimée, 19th (01.40.34.34.40, www.st-christophers. co.uk/paris-hostels). M° Crimée, Jaurès, Laumière or Stalingrad. €.

If you don't mind bunking up with others, you could try this Paris branch of the English youth hostel chain housed in a former boat hangar on the ever-gentrifying Canal de l'Ourcq. The decor in the bedrooms has a sailor's cabin feel, with round, colourful mirrors, bubble-pattern wallpaper and 1950s-inspired cabin furniture. The hostel really comes into its own in its bar, Belushi's, where the usual backpack brigade are joined by Parisians bent on taking advantage of the canalside setting, satellite sports, lunchtime brasserie and some of the cheapest drinks in the capital.

The Marais & Eastern Paris

Le 20 Prieuré Hôtel

20 rue du Grand Prieuré, 11th (01.47.00.74.14, www.hotel20 prieure.com). M° République. €.

In a road where budget sleeps are fast metamorphosing into hip hotels, this young, funky and affordable place benefits from particularly welcoming staff. Each room features a huge blow-up of a Paris landmark covering the entire wall behind the bed, giving you the illusion that you are sleeping halfway up the Eiffel Tower, or on Bir-Hakeim bridge as the métro speeds by. Bathrooms are mundane in comparison, but things brighten up again in the light-flooded breakfast room, with pop art portraits and a reworked 1970s look.

ESSENTIALS

RENTALS IN PARIS

QUALITY APARTMENTS IN EXCELLENT CENTRAL LOCATIONS IN THE HEART OF PARIS

MY PARIS VISIT APARTMENTS ARE CAREFULLY SELECTED FOR THEIR MIX OF PARISIAN CHARM, CONTEMPORARY COMFORT AND STYLE AND GOOD VALUE FOR MONEY

MANAGED APARTMENTS WITH PROFESSIONAL BILINGUAL WELCOME SERVICE

NO AGENCY FEES - SAVINGS UP TO 25%

PARIS VISIT SERVICES: 56, RUE DE L'ARBRE SEC 75001 PARIS
Tel: +33 (0) 1 42 96 17 84

Email: direct@parisvisitservices.com

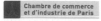

www.myparisvisit.com

Grand Hôtel Jeanne d'Arc

3 rue de Jarente, 4th (01.48.87.62.11, www.hoteljeannedarc.com). M° Chemin Vert. €.

The Jeanne d'Arc's strong point is its lovely location on a quiet road close to pretty place du Marché-Ste-Catherine. Recent refurbishment has made the reception area striking. Rooms are simple but comfortable.

Hôtel Bourg Tibourg

19 rue du Bourg-Tibourg, 4th (01.42.78.47.39, www.hotel bourgtibourg.com). M° Hôtel de Ville. €€€.

The Bourg Tibourg has the same owners as Hôtel Costes and the same interior decorator – but don't expect this jewel box of a boutique hotel to look like a miniature replica. Aside from its enviable location in the heart of the Marais and its fashion-pack fans, here it's all about Jacques Garcia's neo Gothic-cum-Byzantine decor – impressive and imaginative. Exotic, scented candles, mosaic-tiled bathrooms and luxurious fabrics in rich colours create the perfect escape from the outside world. There's no restaurant or lounge – posing is done in the neighbourhood bars. Free Wi-Fi.

Hôtel de la Bretonnerie

22 rue Ste-Croix-de-la-Bretonnerie, 4th (01.48.87.77.63, www.bretonnerie. com). M° Hôtel de Ville. €€.

With its combination of wrought ironwork, exposed stone and wooden beams, the labyrinth of corridors and passages in this 17th-century *hôtel particulier* are full of atmosphere. Tapestries, rich colours and the occasional four-poster bed give the 29 suites and bedrooms individuality. Location is convenient too. Free Wi-Fi.

Hôtel Gabriel

NEW *25 rue du Grand Prieuré, 11th (01.47.00.13.38, www.gabrielparis marais.com). M° République. €€.*

See box p168.

Hôtel du Petit Moulin

29-31 rue de Poitou, 3rd (01.42.74. 10.10, www.hoteldupetitmoulin.com). M° St-Sébastien Froissart. €€.

Within striking distance of the hip shops situated on and around rue Charlot, this listed, turn-of-the-century façade masks what was once the oldest *boulangerie* in Paris, lovingly restored as a boutique hotel by Nadia Murano and Denis Nourry. The couple recruited no lesser figure than fashion designer Christian Lacroix for the decor, and the result is a riot of colour, trompe l'oeil effects and a savvy mix of old and new. Each of its 17 exquisitely appointed rooms is unique, and the walls in rooms 202, 204 and 205 feature swirling, extravagant drawings and scribbles taken from Lacroix's sketchbook. Free parking.

Hôtel St-Merry

78 rue de la Verrerie, 4th (01.42.78. 14.15, www.hotelmarais.com). M° Châtelet or Hôtel de Ville. €€.

The Gothic decor of this former presbytery attached to the Eglise St-Merry is ideal for a Dracula set, with wooden beams, stone walls and plenty of iron; behind the door of room nine, an imposing flying buttress straddles the carved antique bed. There are 11 rooms in all, spread over five floors. On the downside, the historic building has no lift, and only the suite has a TV.

Murano Urban Resort

13 bd du Temple, 3rd (01.42.71.20.00, www.muranoresort.com). M° Filles du Calvaire or Oberkampf. €€€€.

Behind this unremarkable façade is a super cool and supremely luxurious hotel, popular with the fashion set for its slick lounge-style design, excellent restaurant and high-tech flourishes – including coloured light co-ordinators that enable you to change the mood of your room at the touch of a button. The handsome bar has a mind-boggling 140 varieties of vodka to sample, which can bring the op art fabrics in the lift

Hôtel de l'Abbaye Saint-Germain p179

to life and make the fingerprint access to the hotel's 43 rooms and nine suites (two of which feature private pools) a late-night godsend. Free Wi-Fi.

Le Quartier Bastille, Le Faubourg

9 rue de Reuilly, 12th (01.43.70. 04.04, www.lequartierhotelbf.com). Mº Faidherbe Chaligny or Reuilly-Diderot. €€.
Within walking distance of Bastille and the hip 11th arrondissement, the Quartier Bastille (a branch of Franck Altruie's chain of budget design hotels) flashes funky, neo-1970s furniture and just the right amount of colour. Rooms are minimalist but very comfortable.

The Seine & Islands

Hôtel des Deux-Iles

59 rue St-Louis-en-l'Ile, 4th (01.43.26. 13.35, www.deuxiles-paris-hotel.com). Mº Pont Marie. €€.
This peaceful 17th-century townhouse offers 17 soundproofed, air-conditioned rooms kitted out in toned-down stripes, *toile de Jouy* fabrics and neo colonial-style furniture. Its star features are a tiny courtyard off the lobby and a vaulted stone breakfast area. All the rooms and bathrooms were freshened up in 2007 (fortunately saving the blue earthenware tiles on the bathroom walls). There's free Wi-Fi too.

Hôtel du Jeu de Paume

54 rue St-Louis-en-l'Ile, 4th (01.43.26.14.18, www.jeudepaume hotel.com). Mº Pont Marie. €€€.
With a discreet courtyard entrance, 17th-century beams, private garden and a unique timbered breakfast room that was once a real tennis court built under Louis XIII, this is a charming and romantic hotel. These days it is filled with an attractive array of modern and classical art, and has a coveted billiards table. A dramatic glass lift and catwalks lead to the rooms and two self-catering apartments, which are simple and tasteful, the walls hung with Pierre Frey fabric.

The 7th & Western Paris

Le Bellechasse

8 rue de Bellechasse, 7th (01.45.50. 22.31, www.lebellechasse.com). Mº Assemblée Nationale or Solférino/ RER Musée d'Orsay. €€€€.

ESSENTIALS

A former *hôtel particulier*, the Bellechasse fell into the hands of Christian Lacroix, already responsible for the makeover of the Hôtel du Petit Moulin. It reopened in 2007, duly transformed into a trendy boutique hotel. Only a few steps away from the Musée d'Orsay, it offers 34 splendid – though small – rooms, in seven decorative styles. Book early, as the Bellechasse remains *the* hotel of the moment.

Hôtel Duc de Saint-Simon

14 rue de St-Simon, 7th (01.44.39. 20.20, www.hotelducdesaintsimon.com). Mº Rue du Bac. €€€.
A lovely courtyard leads the way into this popular hotel on the edge of St-Germain-des-Prés. Of the 34 bedrooms, four have terraces over a closed-off, leafy garden. It's perfect for lovers, though if you can do without a four-poster bed there are more spacious rooms than the Honeymoon Suite.

Hôtel Eiffel Rive Gauche

6 rue du Gros-Caillou, 7th (01.45.51.51.51, www.hotel-eiffel.com). Mº Ecole Militaire. €.
The Provençal decor and warm welcome make this a nice retreat. All 29 rooms feature Empire-style bedheads and modern bathrooms. Outside, there's a tiny, tiled courtyard with a bridge. If this is fully booked, try sister hotel Eiffel Villa Garibaldi (48 bd Garibaldi, 15th, 01.56.58.56.58).

Hôtel Lenox

9 rue de l'Université, 7th (01.42.96. 10.95, www.lenoxsaintgermain.com). Mº St-Germain-des-Prés. €€.
Its location may be in the seventh arrondissement, but this venerable literary and artistic haunt is unmistakably part of St-Germain-des-Prés. The art deco-style Lenox Club Bar, open to the public, features comfortable leather club chairs and jazz instruments on the walls. Bedrooms, which are reached by an astonishing glass lift, have traditional decor and city views.

Le Montalembert

3 rue Montalembert, 7th (01.45.49. 68.68, www.montalembert.com). Mº Rue du Bac. €€€.
Grace Leo-Andrieu's impeccable boutique hotel is a benchmark of quality and service. It has everything that *mode* maniacs could want: bathrooms stuffed with Molton Brown toiletries, a set of digital scales and plenty of mirrors with which to keep an eye on their figure. Decorated in pale lilac, cinnamon and olive tones, the entire hotel has Wi-Fi access, and each room is equipped with a flat-screen TV. Clattery two-person stairwell lifts are a nice nod to old-fashioned ways.

Sublim Eiffel

94 bd Garibaldi, 15th (01.40.65.95.95, www.sublimeiffel.com). Mº Sèvres-Lecourbe. €€.
Some Barry White on your iPod is essential for this luuurve hotel not far from the Eiffel Tower. Carpets printed with paving stones and manhole covers lead to the rooms, where everything has been put in place for steamy nights. It's all to do with the lighting effects, which include a starry Eiffel Tower or street-scene lights above the bed and sparkling LEDs in the showers, filtered by coloured glass doors. All guests get the use of the mini-gym and hammam, and there is a massage room too. The bar adds a bit of jazz.

St-Germain-des-Prés & Odéon

Artus Hotel

34 rue de Buci, 6th (01.43.29.07.20, www.artushotel.com). Mº Mabillon. €€.
The recently renovated Artus Hotel is the ideal spot for a classic taste of Paris – you couldn't be any closer to the heart of the Left Bank action if you tried. Inside the look is chic boutique, with 27 individually designed rooms and suites, ranging from cosy to capacious. Staff are eager to help and full of local tips.

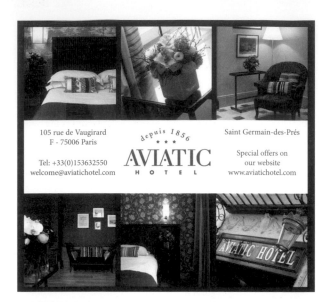

Le Clos Médicis

*56 rue Monsieur-le-Prince, 6th
(01.43.29.10.80, www.closmedicis.com).
Mº Odéon/RER Luxembourg.* €€.
Designed more like a stylish, private
townhouse than a hotel, Le Clos
Médicis is located by the Luxembourg
gardens. The hotel's decor is refreshingly modern, with rooms done out
with taffeta curtains and chenille bed-
covers, and antique floor tiles in the
bathrooms. The cosy lounge has a
working fireplace.

Grand Hôtel de l'Univers

*6 rue Grégoire-de-Tours, 6th
(01.43.29.37.00, www.hotel-paris-
univers.com). Mº Odéon.* €€.
Making the most of its 15th-century
origins, this hotel features exposed
wooden beams, high ceilings, antique
furnishings and toile-covered walls.
Manuel Canovas fabrics lend a posh
touch, but there are also useful services
such as a laptop for hire. The same team
runs the Hôtel St Germain des Prés (36
rue Bonaparte, 6th, 01.43.26.00.19).

L'Hôtel

*13 rue des Beaux-Arts, 6th
(01.44.41.99.00, www.l-hotel.com). Mº
Mabillon or St-Germain-des-Prés.* €€€.
Guests at the sumptuously decorated
L'Hôtel are more likely to be models
and film stars than the starving writers
who frequented it during Oscar Wilde's
last days (the playwright died in a room
on the ground floor in November 1900).
Under Jacques Garcia's restoration,
each room has a theme: Mistinguett's
chambre retains its art deco mirror bed,
and Wilde's tribute room is appropri-
ately clad in green peacock murals. In
the basement is a small pool, which is
wonderfully private – only two people
are allowed down here at a time.

Hôtel de l'Abbaye
Saint-Germain

*10 rue Cassette, 6th (01.45.44.38.11,
www.hotelabbayeparis.com). Mº Rennes
or St-Sulpice.* €€€.

A monumental entrance opens the way
through a courtyard into this tranquil
hotel, originally part of a convent. Wood
panelling, well-stuffed sofas and an open
fireplace in the drawing room make for
a relaxed atmosphere, but, best of all,
there's a surprisingly large garden
where breakfast is served in the warmer
months. The 43 rooms and duplex apartment are tasteful and luxurious.

Hôtel du Globe

*15 rue des Quatre-Vents, 6th
(01.43.26.35.50, www.hotel-du-
globe.fr). Mº Odéon.* €€.
The Hôtel du Globe has managed to
retain much of its 17th-century character – and very pleasant it is too.
Gothic wrought-iron doors open into
the florid corridors, and an unex-
plained suit of armour supervises
guests from the tiny salon. The rooms
with baths are somewhat larger than
those with showers, and if you're an
early booker you might even get the
room with the four-poster bed.

Hôtel des Saints-Pères

*65 rue des Sts-Peres, 6th (01.45.44.
50.00, www.espritfrance.com).
Mº St-Germain-des-Prés.* €€.
Built in 1658 by one of Louis XIV's
architects, this hotel has an enviable
location near St-Germain-des-Prés'
boutiques. It boasts a charming garden
and a sophisticated, if small, bar. The
most coveted room is no.100, with its
fine 17th-century ceiling by painters
from the Versailles School; it also has
an open bathroom, so you can gaze at
scenes from the myth of Leda and the
Swan while you scrub.

Relais Saint-Germain

*9 carrefour de l'Odéon, 6th
(01.43.29.12.05, www.hotel-paris-relais-
saint-germain.com). Mº Odéon.* €€€.
The rustic, wood-beamed ceilings
remain intact at the Relais Saint-
Germain, a 17th-century hotel bought
and renovated by acclaimed chef Yves
Camdeborde (originator of the

ESSENTIALS

Le Bellechasse p176

bistronomique dining trend) and his wife Claudine. Each of the 22 rooms has a different take on eclectic Provençal charm, and the marble bathrooms are huge by Paris standards. Guests get first dibs on highly sought-after seats in the 15-table Le Comptoir restaurant next door.

The Latin Quarter & the 13th

Familia Hôtel
11 rue des Ecoles, 5th (01.43.54.55.27, www.hotel-paris-familia.com). M° Cardinal Lemoine or Jussieu. €.
This old-fashioned Latin Quarter hotel has balconies hung with tumbling plants and walls draped with replica French tapestries. Owner Eric Gaucheron extends a warm welcome, and the 30 rooms have personalised touches such as sepia murals, cherry-wood furniture and stone walls. The Gaucherons also own the Minerve next door – book in advance for both.

Five Hôtel
3 rue Flatters, 5th (01.43.31.74.21, www.thefivehotel.com). M° Les Gobelins or Port Royal. €€€.

The rooms in this stunning boutique hotel may be small, but they're all exquisitely designed, with Chinese lacquer and velvety fabrics. Fibre optics built into the walls create the illusion of sleeping under a starry sky, and you can choose from four fragrances to subtly perfume your room. Guests staying in the suite have access to a private garden with a jacuzzi.

Hôtel les Degrés de Notre-Dame
10 rue des Grands-Degrés, 5th (01.55.42.88.88, www.lesdegreshotel. com). M° Maubert-Mutualité or St-Michel. €€.
On a tiny street across the river from Notre-Dame, this vintage hotel is an absolute gem. Its ten rooms are full of character, with original paintings, antique furniture and exposed wooden beams (nos.47 and 501 have views of the cathedral). It has an adorable restaurant and, a few streets away, two studio apartments that the owner rents to preferred customers only.

Hôtel la Demeure
51 bd St-Marcel, 13th (01.43.37.81.25, www.hotel-paris-lademeure.com). M° Les Gobelins. €€.

This comfortable, modern hotel on the edge of the Latin Quarter has 43 air-conditioned rooms with internet access, plus suites with sliding doors to separate sleeping and living space. The wrap-around balconies of the corner rooms offer lovely views of the city, and bathrooms feature luxurious tubs or shower heads with elaborate massage possibilities.

Hôtel du Panthéon

19 pl du Panthéon, 5th (01.43.54. 32.95, www.hoteldupantheon.com). M° Cluny La Sorbonne or Maubert Mutualité/RER Luxembourg. €€.
The 36 rooms of this elegant hotel are beautifully decorated with classic French *toile de Jouy* fabrics, antique furniture and painted woodwork. Some enjoy impressive views of the Panthéon; others squint out on to a hardly less romantic courtyard, complete with chestnut tree.

Hôtel Résidence Henri IV

50 rue des Bernardins, 5th (01.44.41. 31.81, www.residencehenri4.com). M° Cardinal Lemoine. €€.
This belle époque-style hotel has a mere eight rooms and five apartments, so guests are assured of the staff's full attention. Peacefully situated next to leafy square Paul-Langevin, it's just minutes away from Notre-Dame. The four-person apartments come with a mini-kitchen featuring a hob, fridge and microwave. Free Wi-Fi available.

Hôtel de la Sorbonne

6 rue Victor-Cousin, 5th (01.43.54. 58.08, www.hotelsorbonne.com). M° Cluny La Sorbonne/RER Luxembourg. €€.
It's out with the old at this charming, freshly renovated hotel, whose new look is very much a modern take on art nouveau, with bold wallpapers, floral prints, lush fabrics and quotes from French literature woven into the carpets. Rooms are all equipped with iMac computers.

Le Petit Paris

NEW *214 rue St-Jacques, 5th (01.53. 10.29.29, www.hotelpetitparis.com). M° Maubert Mutualité/RER Luxembourg.* €€€.
This brand new Latin Quarter venture is a dynamic exercise in taste and colour. The 20 rooms, designed by Sybille de Margerie, are arranged by era, running from the puce and purple of the medieval rooms to the wildly decadent orange, yellow and pink of the swinging '60s rooms, replete with specially commissioned sensual photographs of Paris monuments. Luxury abounds with finest silks, velvets and taffetas. Some of the rooms have small terraces, and those with baths have a TV you can watch while soaking. An honesty bar in the lounge and jukebox encourage conviviality.

Montparnasse

Hôtel Aviatic

105 rue de Vaugirard, 6th (01.53.63. 25.50, www.aviatic.fr). M° Duroc, Montparnasse Bienvenüe or St-Placide. €€.
This historic hotel has masses of character, from the Empire-style lounge and garden atrium to the bistro-style breakfast room and marble floor in the lobby. New decoration throughout, in beautiful steely greys, warm reds, elegant, striped velvets and *toile de Jouy* fabrics, lends an impressive touch of glamour, and the service is excellent.

Hôtel Istria Saint-Germain

29 rue Campagne-Première, 14th (01.43.20.91.82, www.hotel-istria-paris.com). M° Raspail. €€.
Behind this unassuming façade is the place where the artistic royalty of Montparnasse's heyday – the likes of Man Ray, Marcel Duchamp and Louis Aragon – once lived. The Istria Saint-Germain has been modernised since then, but it still has plenty of charm, with 26 bright, simply furnished rooms.

ESSENTIALS

Getting Around

Airports

Roissy-Charles-de-Gaulle

01.70.36.39.50, www.adp.fr. 30km (19 miles) north-east of Paris.
For most international flights. The two main terminals are some way apart; check which one you need for your flight back. The terminals are linked by the CDGVAL free driverless train. The **RER B** line (08.92.69.32.46, www.transilien.com) is the quickest way to central Paris (40mins to Gare du Nord; 45mins to RER Châtelet-Les Halles; €8.50 single). RER trains run every 10-15mins, 4.58am-11.58pm daily.

Air France buses (08.92.35.08.20, www.cars-airfrance.com; €15 single, €24 return) leave every 15mins, 5.45am-11pm daily, from both terminals, and stop at Porte Maillot and place Charles-de-Gaulle (35-50min trip). Buses also run to Gare Montparnasse and Gare de Lyon (€16.50 single, €27 return) every 30mins (45-60min trip), 7am-9pm daily; a bus between Roissy and Orly (€19) runs every 30mins, 5.55am-10.30pm daily from Roissy.

RATP Roissybus (08.92.69.32.46, www.ratp.fr; €9.10) runs every 15-20mins, 5.45am-11pm daily, between the airport and the corner of rue Scribe/rue Auber (at least 45mins); buy your tickets on the bus.

Paris Airports Service is a 24-hour door-to-door minibus service between airports and hotels, seven days a week. Roissy prices go from €26 for one to €12.40 each person for eight people, 6am-8pm (minimum €41, 4-6am, 8-10pm); you can reserve a place on 01.55.98.10.80, www.paris airportservice.com. A **taxi** into central Paris from Roissy-Charles-de-Gaulle airport should take 30-60mins and cost €30-€50, plus €1 per luggage item.

Orly

01.70.36.39.50, www.adp.fr. About 18km (11 miles) south of Paris.
Orly-Sud terminal is mainly international and Orly-Ouest is mainly domestic.

Air France buses (08.92.35.08.20, www.cars-airfrance.com; €11.50 single, €18.50 return) leave both terminals every 30mins, 6.15am-11.15pm daily, and stop at Invalides and Montparnasse (30-45mins).

The **RATP Orlybus** (08.92.69.32.46, www.ratp.fr) runs to Denfert-Rochereau every 15mins, 6am-11.50pm Mon-Fri, 6am-12.50am Sat, Sun (30mins); buy tickets (€6.40) on the bus. High-speed **Orlyval** shuttle trains (www.orlyval.fr) run every 4-7mins (6am-11pm daily) to RER B station Antony (€9.85 to Châtelet-les-Halles); allow about 35mins for central Paris.

Orly prices for the Paris Airports Service (*see left*) are €25 for one and €5-€12 per passenger depending on the number. A **taxi** takes 20-40mins and costs €16-€26.

Paris Beauvais

08.92.68.20.66, www.aeroport beauvais.com. 70km (43 miles) north of Paris.
Budget hub. **Buses** (€13) to/from Porte Maillot leave 15-30mins after each arrival and 3hrs 15mins before each departure. Tickets from Arrivals or buy tickets on the bus.

Arriving by car

Options for crossing the Channel with a car include: **Eurotunnel** (0844 353 535, www.eurotunnel.com); **Brittany Ferries** (0871 244 0744, www.brittanyferries.com), **P&O Ferries** (0871 664 5645,

ESSENTIALS

www.poferries.com) and
SeaFrance (0845 458 0666,
www.seafrance.com).

Arriving by coach

International coaches arrive at
**Gare Routière Internationale
Paris-Galliéni** at Porte de
Bagnolet, 20th. For tickets
(in English) call Eurolines on
08.92.89.90.91 or (UK) 01582 404
511, or visit www.eurolines.fr.

Arriving by rail

Eurostar from London St Pancras
International (01233 617 575,
www.eurostar.com) to Paris Gare
du Nord (08.92.35.35.39) takes
2hrs 15mins direct. You must
check in at least 30mins before
departure. Fares start at £69 for
a return ticket.

Cycles can be taken as hand
luggage if they are dismantled
and carried in a bike bag. You
can also check them in at the
Eurodispatch depot at St Pancras
(Esprit Parcel Service, 08705 850
850) or Sernam depot at Gare du
Nord (01.55.31.58.40). Check-in
must be done 24hrs ahead; a
Eurostar ticket must be shown.
The service costs £20/€25.

Maps

Free maps of the métro, bus and
RER systems are available at
airports and métro stations.

Public transport

RATP (08.92.69.32.46, www.ratp.fr)
runs the bus, métro and suburban
tram routes, as well as lines A and B
of the RER express railway, which
connects with the métro inside Paris.
State rail **SNCF** (08.92.35.35.35,
www.sncf.com) runs RER lines C,
D and E for the suburbs.

Fares & tickets

Paris and its suburbs are divided
into six travel zones, with 1 and 2
covering the city centre. RATP
tickets and passes are valid on the
métro, bus and RER. Tickets and
carnets can be bought at métro
stations, tourist offices and
tobacconists; single tickets can be
bought on buses. Retain your ticket
in case of spot checks; you'll also
need it to exit from RER stations.

A ticket is €1.60, a carnet of ten
€11.60. A Mobilis day pass is €5.90
for zones 1 and 2 and €16.70 for
zones 1-6 (not including airports).

Métro & RER

The Paris **métro** is the fastest way
of getting around. Trains run daily
5.30am-12.40am Mon-Thur, 5.30am-
1.30am Fri-Sun. Numbered lines
have their direction named after
the last stop. Follow the orange
Correspondance signs to change
lines. The five **RER** lines run
5.30am-1am daily across Paris
and into commuterland. Métro
tickets are valid for RER journeys
within zones 1 and 2.

Buses

Buses run 6.30am-8.30pm, with
some routes continuing until
12.30am, Mon-Sat; limited services
operate on selected lines Sun and
public holidays. You can use a
métro ticket, a ticket bought from
the driver (€1.70) or a travel pass.
Tickets should be punched in the
machine next to the driver; passes
should be shown to the driver.

Night buses

The 47 **Noctilien** lines run from
place du Châtelet to the suburbs
(hourly 12.30am-5.30am Mon-Thur;
half-hourly 1am-5.35am Fri, Sat);

ESSENTIALS

look out for the Noctilien logo or the N in front of the route number. A ticket costs €1.60 (€1.70 from the driver); travel passes are valid.

River transport

Batobus

08.25.05.01.01, www.batobus.com. Nov, Feb-mid Mar 10.30am-4.30pm; mid Mar-May, Sept, Oct 10am-7pm; June-Aug 10am-9.30pm. One-day pass €12 (€6, €8 reductions).
River buses stop every 15-25mins at the Eiffel Tower, Musée d'Orsay, St-Germain-des-Prés (quai Malaquais), Notre-Dame, Jardin des Plantes, Hôtel de Ville, the Louvre, Champs-Elysées (Pont Alexandre III). Tickets are available from Batobus stops, RATP and tourist offices.

Rail travel

Versailles and Disneyland Paris are served by the RER. Most locations out of the city are served by the SNCF railway; the TGV high-speed train is steadily being extended to all the main regions. Tickets can be bought at any SNCF station, SNCF shops and travel agents. If you reserve online or by phone, you can pay and pick up your tickets from the station or have them sent to your home. SNCF automatic machines (*billeterie automatique*) only work with French credit/debit cards. Buy tickets in advance to secure the cheaper fare. Before you board any train, stamp your ticket in the orange *composteur* machines on the platforms, or you might have to pay a hefty fine.

SNCF

08.92.35.35.35, www.sncf.com.
Open 7am-10pm daily.
The line can also be reached (inside France) by dialling 3635 and saying '*billet*' at the prompt.

Taxis

Taxis are hard to find at rush hour or early in the morning. Ranks are indicated with a blue sign. A white light on a taxi's roof means it's free; an orange one means it's busy. You also pay for the time it takes your radioed taxi to arrive. Payment by credit card – mention this when you make the booking – is usually €15 minimum.

Airportaxis
01.41.50.42.50, www.taxiparisien.fr.
Alpha
01.45.85.85.85, www.alphataxis.fr.
G7
01.47.39.47.39, www.taxis-g7.fr.
Taxis Bleus
08.91.70.10.10, www.taxis-bleus.com.

Driving

If you're planning to bring your car to France, you must bring its registration and insurance documents with you.

Traffic information for Ile-de-France
08.26.02.20.22, www.securiteroutiere.gouv.fr.

Breakdown services

The AA and RAC do not have reciprocal arrangements with an equivalent organisation in France, so it's advisable to take out additional breakdown insurance cover, for example with Europ Assistance (UK: 0870 737 5720, www.europ-assistance.co.uk). If you don't have insurance, you can use its service (08.10.00.50.50), but it will charge you the full cost. Other 24-hour breakdown services in Paris include: AB Auto (01.45.58.49.58) and Dan Dépann Auto (08.00.25.10.00).

ESSENTIALS

Parking

There are still a few free on-street parking areas in Paris, but they're often full. If you park illegally, your car may be clamped or towed away. Don't park in zones marked for deliveries (*livraisons*) or taxis. *Horodateurs*, pay-and-display machines, take a special card (*carte de stationnement* at €10 or €30, from tobacconists). Parking is often free at weekends, after 7pm and in August. Underground car parks cost around €2.50 per hour. Some have lower rates after 6pm. See www.parkingsdeparis.com.

Vehicle removal

If your car is impounded, contact the nearest police station. There are eight car pounds (*préfourrières*) in Paris; to find out where your car might be, contact 01.53.73.53.73, 08.91.01.22.22 or www.prefecture-police-paris.interieur.gouv.fr.

Car hire

To hire a car you must be 25 or over and have held a licence for at least a year. Some agencies accept drivers aged 21-24, but a day fee of €20-€25 is usual. Take your licence and passport. Bargain firms may have a high charge for damage: read the small print before signing.

Ada
08.25.16.91.69, www.ada.fr.
Avis
08.20.05.05.05, www.avis.fr.
Budget
08.25.00.35.64, www.budget.fr.
EasyCar
01.70.61.85.52, www.easycar.com.
Europcar
08.25.35.83.58, www.europcar.fr.
Hertz
01.55.31.93.21, www.hertz.fr.
Rent-a-Car
08.91.70.02.00, www.rentacar.fr.

Cycling

In 2007, the mayor launched a municipal bike hire scheme – Vélib (www.vclib.paris.fr). There are now over 20,000 bicycles available 24 hours a day, at nearly 1,500 'stations' across the city. Just swipe your travel card to release the bikes from their stands. The *mairie* actively promotes cycling in the city and the Vélib scheme is complemented by the 400km (250 miles) of bike lanes snaking their way around Paris.

A free *Paris a Vélo* map can be picked up at any *mairie* or from bike shops. Cycle lanes (*pistes cyclables*) run mostly N–S and E–W. N–S routes include rue de Rennes, av d'Italie, bd Sébastopol and av Marceau. E–W routes take in the rue de Rivoli, bd St-Germain, bd St-Jacques and av Daumesnil. You could be fined (€22) if you don't use them, which is a bit rich considering the lanes are often blocked by delivery vans. Cyclists are also entitled to use certain bus lanes (especially the new ones set off by a strip of kerb stones).

Cycle hire

Note that bike insurance may not cover theft: check before you sign.

Freescoot
63 quai de la Tournelle, 5th (01.44.07.06.72, www.freescoot.fr). M° Maubert Mutualité or St Michel. **Open** 9am-1pm, 2-9pm daily; closed Sun Oct-mid Apr.
Bicycles and scooters for hire.

Left Bank Scooters
(06.82.70.13.82, www.leftbank scooters.com).
This company hires out vintage-style Vespas (from €70 per day), with delivery and collection from your apartment or hotel. Tours available.

Resources A-Z

For information on travelling to France from within the European Union, including details of visa regulations and healthcare provision, see the EU's travel website: http://europa.eu/travel.

Accident & emergency

In a medical emergency, you should call Sapeurs-Pompiers, who have trained paramedics.

Ambulance (SAMU)	**15**
Police	**17**
Fire (Sapeurs-Pompiers)	**18**
Emergency	
(from a mobile phone)	**112**

Credit card loss

Call one of these 24hr services.

American Express *01.47.77.70.00*
Diners Club *08.20.82.05.36*
MasterCard *01.45.67.84.84*
Visa *08.92.70.57.05*

Customs

Non-EU residents can claim a tax refund or *détaxe* (around 12%) on VAT if they spend over €175 in one purchase and if they live outside the EU for more than six months in the year. At the shop ask for a *bordereau de vente à l'exportation*.

Dental emergencies

Look in the *Pages Jaunes* (www. pagesjaunes.fr) under *Dentistes*. For emergencies contact:

Hôpital de la Pitié-Salpêtrière
47-83 bd de l'Hôpital, 13th (01.42. 16.00.00). M° Gare d'Austerlitz.
Open 24hrs.

SOS Dentaire
87 bd Port-Royal, 13th (01.43.36.36.00). M° Les Gobelins/RER Port-Royal.
Open by phone 9am-midnight.

Disabled

General information (in French) is available on the Secrétaire d'Etat aux Personnes Handicapées website: www.handicap.gouv.fr.

Electricity

France uses the standard 220-240V, 50-cycle AC system. Visitors with 240V British appliances need an adapter (*adaptateur*). US 110V appliances need an adapter and a transformer (*transformateur*).

Embassies & consulates

Australian Embassy
4 rue Jean-Rey, 15th (01.40.59.33.00, www.france.embassy.gov.au). M° Bir-Hakeim. **Open** *Consular services* 9.15am-noon, 2-4.30pm Mon-Fri. *Visas* 10am-noon Mon-Fri.
British Embassy
35 rue du Fbg-St-Honoré, 8th (01.44. 51.31.00, www.ukinfrance.fco.gov.uk). M° Concorde. Consular services 18bis rue d'Anjou, 8th. M° Concorde. **Open** 9.30am-12.30pm, 2.30-4.30pm Mon-Fri. *Visas 16 rue d'Anjou, 8th (01.44.51. 31.01).* **Open** 9.30am-noon (by phone), 2.30-4.30pm Mon-Fri.
British citizens wanting consular services (such as new passports) should ignore the queue at 16 rue d'Anjou and walk in at no.18bis.
Canadian Embassy
35 av Montaigne, 8th (01.44.43. 29.00, www.amb-canada.fr). M° Franklin D Roosevelt. Consular

services (01.44.43.29.02). **Open**
9am-noon Mon-Fri. Visas 37 av
Montaigne, 8th (01.44.43.29.16).
Open 8.30-11am Mon-Fri.

Irish Embassy
12 av Foch, 16th. Consulate 4 rue
Rude, 16th (01.44.17.67.00,
www.embassyofireland.fr). M° Charles
de Gaulle Etoile. **Open** Consular/visas
9.30am-noon Mon-Fri. By phone
9.30am-1pm, 2.30-5.30pm Mon-Fri.

New Zealand Embassy
7ter rue Léonard-de-Vinci, 16th
(01.45.01.43.43, www.nzembassy.
com/france). M° Victor Hugo. **Open**
Sept-June 9am-1pm, 2-5.30pm Mon-
Thur; 9am-1pm, 2-4pm Fri. July,
Aug 9am-1pm, 2-4.30pm Mon-Thur;
9am-2pm Fri. Visas 9am-12.30pm
Mon-Fri.
Visas for travel to New Zealand can
be applied for on the website www.
immigration.govt.nz.

South African Embassy
59 quai d'Orsay, 7th (01.53.59.23.23,
www.afriquesud.net). M° Invalides.
Open 8.30am-5.15pm Mon-Fri.
Consulate/visas 8.30am-noon Mon-Fri.

US Embassy
2 av Gabriel, 8th (01.43.12.22.22,
http://france.usembassy.gov). M°
Concorde. Consulate and visas 4 av
Gabriel, 8th (08.10.26.46.26). M°
Concorde. **Open** Consular services
9am-12.30pm, 1-3pm Mon-Fri. Visas
08.92.23.84.72.

Internet

Milk
31 bd de Sébastopol, 1st (01.40.13.
06.51, www.milklub.com), M° Châtelet
or Rambuteau/RER Châtelet Les Halles.
Open 24hrs daily.

Opening hours

Standard opening hours for shops
are generally 9am/10am-7pm/8pm
Mon-Sat. Some close on Mondays,
some for lunch (usually 12.30-2pm)
and some in August.

Pharmacies

All pharmacies sport a green neon
cross. If closed, a pharmacy will
have a sign indicating the nearest
one open. Staff can provide basic
medical services like disinfecting
and bandaging wounds (for a small
fee) and will indicate the nearest
doctor on duty. The following are
all open late:

Matignon
2 rue Jean-Mermoz, 8th (01.43.59.
86.55). M° Franklin D Roosevelt.
Open 8.30am-2am daily.

Pharmacie des Champs-Elysées
84 av des Champs-Elysées, 8th
(01.45.62.02.41). M° George V.
Open 24hrs daily.

**Pharmacie Européenne
de la Place de Clichy**
6 pl de Clichy, 9th (01.48.74.65.18).
M° Place de Clichy. **Open** 24hrs daily.

Pharmacie des Halles
10 bd de Sébastopol, 4th (01.42.72.
03.23). M° Châtelet. **Open** 9am-
midnight Mon-Sat; 9am-10pm Sun.

Police

The French equivalent of 999/911
is **17** (**112** from a mobile), but
don't expect a speedy response. If
you're assaulted or robbed, report
the incident as soon as possible.
Make a statement (procès verbal)
at the point d'accueil closest to
the crime. To find it, contact the
Préfecture Centrale (08.91.01.22.22)
or go to www.prefecture.police.
paris.interieur.gouv.fr. You'll
need to obtain a statement for
insurance purposes.

Post

Post offices (bureaux de poste)
are open 8am-7pm Mon-Fri; 8am-
noon Sat, apart from the 24hr one
listed below. All are listed in the
phone book: under Administration

ESSENTIALS

des PTT in the *Pages Jaunes*;
under *Poste* in the *Pages Blanches*.
Most post offices have machines
that weigh your letter, print out
a stamp and give change, saving
you from queuing. You can also
buy stamps at a tobacconist.

Main Post Office
52 rue du Louvre, 1st (36.31).
M° Les Halles or Louvre Rivoli.
Open 24hrs daily.

Smoking

Smoking is prohibited in all
enclosed public spaces. Hotels
can still offer smoking rooms.

Telephones

All French phone numbers have
ten digits. Paris and Ile-de-France
numbers begin with 01; the rest of
France is divided into four zones,
02 to 05. Mobile phone numbers
start with 06. Numbers beginning
with 08 can only be reached from
inside France. The France country
code is 33; leave off the first 0 at
the start of the ten-digit number.
Most public phones use *télécartes*
(phonecards). These are sold at
post offices and tobacconists, and
they cost €7.50 for 50 units or
€15 for 120 units.

Time

France is one hour ahead of GMT
and uses the 24hr system (for
example, 18h means 6pm).

Tipping

A service charge of ten to 15%
is legally included in your bill at
all restaurants, cafés and bars.
However, it's polite to round up
the final amount for drinks, or to
leave a cash tip of €1-€2 or more
for a meal, depending on service.

Tourist information

Espace du Tourisme
d'Ile de France
Carrousel du Louvre, 99 rue de Rivoli,
1st (www.nouveau-paris-ile-de-
france.com). M° Pyramides.
Open 8.30am-7pm Mon-Fri.
For Paris and the Ile-de-France.
Maison de la France
20 av de l'Opéra, 1st (01.42.96.
70.00, www.franceguide.com). M°
Opéra. **Open** 10am-6pm Mon-Fri;
10am-5pm Sat.
Office de Tourisme et des
Congrès de Paris
25 rue des Pyramides (08.92.68.30.00,
www.parisinfo.com). M° Pyramides.
Open 9am-7pm daily.
Info on Paris and the suburbs; tickets.
Other locations *Anvers, 72 bd*
Rochechouart, 9th. Gare de Lyon,
20 bd Diderot, 12th. Gare du Nord,
18 rue de Dunkerque, 10th. Gare de
l'Est, Place du 11 Novembre 1918,
10th. Montmartre, 21 pl du Tertre,
18th. Porte de Versailles, 1 place de
la Porte de Versailles, 15th.

Visas

European Union nationals do not
need a visa to enter France, nor
do US, Canadian, Australian, New
Zealand or South African citizens
for stays of up to three months.
Nationals of other countries should
enquire at the nearest French
Consulate before leaving home.
If you are travelling to France
from one of the countries included
in the Schengen agreement (most
of the EU, but not Britain or
Ireland), the visa from that
country should be sufficient.

What's on

Two publications compete for
consumers of listings information:
L'Officiel des Spectacles (€0.35)
and *Pariscope* (€0.40).